Workshop on Events and Stories in the News 2017

Held at ACL 2017

Vancouver, Canada
4 August 2017

ISBN: 978-1-5108-4577-0

EventStory 2017

Events and Stories in the News

Proceedings of the Workshop

August 4, 2017
Vancouver, Canada

Events, one of the most basic ontological constructs of human perception, pose fascinating challenges for natural language processing (NLP). A small but growing number of researchers are investigating various facets of that problem.

This volume contains the proceedings of the First Workshop on Events and Stories in the News. This workshop is the result of the combination of the EVENTS workshops (held four times in conjunction with NAACL 2013—2016) and the Computing News Storylines workshops (held twice, in conjunction with ACL 2015 and EMNLP 2016). As researchers continue investigating event detection, event identity and coreference, and causal, topical, temporal, and spatial relations between events, we as organisers saw a strong connection between the two workshop series and decided to join forces in this new workshop.

We received 20 submissions to this workshop, from which 13 were accepted for presentation. The accepted submissions display the links between events and stories, as well as show the breadth of the field; ranging from domains such as digital humanities and security to creating ontologies and corpora for events and storylines all the way to approaches and experiments to extract this information from text.

In addition to regular presentations and a poster session, the workshop will also contain a keynote by James F. Allen (University of Rochester) and a hands-on annotation session. Through the annotation task, we will work towards common definitions for core concepts such as events and storylines and add to common resources for annotating and evaluating events and storylines in an NLP setting.

We thank the members of the Program Committee for their timely reviews and the authors for their contributions. We are also grateful to NewsEdge Inc. for sponsoring travel grants to PhD students to attend the workshop.

Organizers:

Tommaso Caselli, Vrije Universiteit Amsterdam (NL)
Ben Miller, Georgia State University (U.S.A)
Marieke van Erp, Vrije Universiteit Amsterdam (NL)
Piek Vossen, Vrije Universiteit Amsterdam (NL)
Martha Palmer, Linguistics, UCB 295 Hellems, University of Colorado (U.S.A)
Eduard Hovy, Language Technologies Institute, Carnegie Mellon University (U.S.A)
Teruko Mitamura, Language Technologies Institute, Carnegie Mellon University (U.S.A)
David Caswell, Reynolds Journalism Institute, University of Missouri (U.S.A)

Programme Committee:

Sabine Bergler, Computer Science, Columbia University (Canada)
Alexandra Balahur, European Commission Joint Research Centre, Ispra (Italy)
John Beieler, Johns Hopkins University (USA)
Ann Bies, Linguistic Data Consortium (USA)
Nate Chambers, US Naval Academy (USA)
Leon Derczynski, University of Sheffield (UK)
Benjamin van Durme, Johns Hopkins University (USA)
Jacob Eisenstein, Computational Linguistics Lab, Georgia Tech (USA)
Mark Finlayson, Florida International University (USA)
Robert Frederking, Carnegie Mellon University (USA)
Erik van der Goot, European Commission Joint Research Centre, Ispra (Italy)
Ruihong Huang, Texas A&M University (USA)
Martijn Kleppe, Koninklijke Bibliotheek, Den Haag (The Netherlands)
Bernardo Magnini, Fondazione Bruno Kessler (Italy)
Roser Morante, Vrije Universiteit Amsterdam (The Netherlands)
Vivi Nastase, Heidelberg University (Germany)
Tim O'Gorman, University of Colorado (USA)
Alexis Palmer, University of North Texas (USA)
Silvia Pareti, Google Inc. (Switzerland)
Octavian Popescu, IBM Watson Research Center (USA)
Georg Rehm, DFKI (Germany)
German Rigau, Universidad del Pais Vasco (Spain)
Ellen Riloff, University of Utah (USA)
Tomohide Shibata, Kyoto University (Japan)
Ian Soboroff, NIST (USA)
Anneke Sools, University of Twente (The Netherlands)
Xavier Tannier, LIMSI-CNRS (France)
Naushad UzZaman, Nuance Communications (USA)
Ivan Titov, University of Edinburgh (UK)
Sara Tonelli, Fondazione Bruno Kessler (Italy)
Lucy Vanderwende, Microsoft (USA)
Marc Verhagen, Brandeis University (USA)
Laure Vieu, CNRS (France)
Travis Wolfe, John Hopkins University (USA)
Luke Zettlemoyer, University of Washington (USA)

Table of Contents

Workshop Program

Friday, August 4, 2017

09:00–10:30   Session 1:

09:00–09:05   *Welcome and Opening Remarks*

09:05–10:05   *A theory of events unifying semantic parsing and reasoning*
James F. Allen, University of Rocherster

10:05–10:30   *newsLens: building and visualizing long-ranging news stories*
Philippe Laban and Marti Hearst

10:30–11:00   *Coffee Break*

11:00–12:30   Session 2:

11:00–12:30   *Annotation Exercise*

12:30–14:00   *Lunch*

14:00–16:00   Session 3:

14:00–14:05   *Detecting Changes in Twitter Streams using Temporal Clusters of Hashtags*
Yunli Wang and Cyril Goutte

14:05–14:10   *Event Detection Using Frame-Semantic Parser*
Evangelia Spiliopoulou, Eduard Hovy and Teruko Mitamura

14:10–14:15   *Improving Shared Argument Identification in Japanese Event Knowledge Acquisition*
Yin Jou Huang and Sadao Kurohashi

14:15–14:20   *Tracing armed conflicts with diachronic word embedding models*
Andrey Kutuzov, Erik Velldal and Lilja Øvrelid

14:20–14:25   *The Circumstantial Event Ontology (CEO)*
Roxane Segers, Tommaso Caselli and Piek Vossen

14:25–14:30   *Event Detection and Semantic Storytelling: Generating a Travelogue from a large Collection of Personal Letters*
Georg Rehm, Julian Moreno Schneider, peter bourgonje, Ankit Srivastava, Jan Nehring, Armin Berger, Luca König, Sören Räuchle and Jens Gerth

14:30–14:35   *Inference of Fine-Grained Event Causality from Blogs and Films*
Zhichao Hu, Elahe Rahimtoroghi and Marilyn Walker

14:35–14:40   *On the Creation of a Security-Related Event Corpus*
Martin Atkinson, Jakub Piskorski, Hristo Tanev and Vanni Zavarella

14:40–14:45   *Inducing Event Types and Roles in Reverse: Using Function to Discover Theme*
Natalie Ahn

14:45–16:00   ***Poster session***

15:30–16:00   ***Coffee Break***

newsLens: building and visualizing long-ranging news stories

Philippe Laban
UC Berkeley
`phillab@berkeley.edu`

Marti Hearst
UC Berkeley
`hearst@berkeley.edu`

Abstract

We propose a method to aggregate and organize a large, multi-source dataset of news articles into a collection of major stories, and automatically name and visualize these stories in a working system. The approach is able to run online, as new articles are added, processing 4 million news articles from 20 news sources, and extracting 80000 major stories, some of which span several years. The visual interface consists of lanes of timelines, each annotated with information that is deemed important for the story, including extracted quotations. The working system allows a user to search and navigate 8 years of story information.

1 Introduction

Complex news events unfold over months, and the sequence of events over time can be thought of as forming *stories*. Our objective is to generate, from publicly available news articles, story outlines and visualizations that help readers digest and navigate complex, long-lasting stories across a large number of news articles. We attempt this construction of stories by building a dataset with multiple news sources, exploiting the overlap in coverage by different sources. Our contributions include:

1. A method for creating a dataset of articles from multiple sources across a decade from scratch,

2. A topic detection method that handles interruption in topics,

3. A novel way to name stories, and

4. A method for clustering, rating, and displaying quotations associated with the stories.

The demo is available at
`newslens.berkeley.edu/`

The remainder of the paper is organized as follows. Section 2 presents current related research work. The aggregation of the dataset and the creation of the timelines is explained in Section 3. Section 4 presents the interface with the created timelines, as well as the extraction process for the information shown. Finally Section 5 concludes the paper and presents future work directions.

2 Related Work

Related work includes prior methods for generating stories from topics, for visualizing stories, and for summarizing news.

Topic Detection and Tracking refers to techniques to automatically process a streamable dataset of text into related groups called topics. In the context of news, the topics detected and tracked are commonly called stories.

Swan and Allan (2000) use the Topic Detection and Tracking (TDT) and TDT2 datasets, consisting of 50,000 news articles to produce 146 stories, called clusters. The clustering process is done using named entities and noun phrases, as opposed to unigrams. They report an inability to merge clusters if there are large gaps in time with no articles, and their algorithm does not group documents in an online fashion.

Pouliquen et al. (2008) build a large dataset of news articles, named the Europe Media Monitor (EMM). Their topic detection creates local clusters in each language. The monolingual stories are then linked across languages to form global stories. A reported drawback is the clustering cannot handle merging and splitting between disparate topics and cannot mend gaps between stories that last more than 8 days.

Ahmed et al. (2011) propose an online infer-

Proceedings of the Events and Stories in the News Workshop, pages 1–9,
Vancouver, Canada, August 4, 2017. ©2017 Association for Computational Linguistics

ence model named Storylines that clusters articles into storylines which are assigned to broader topics. Emphasis is put on scalability with a goal of processing one article per second.

Poghosyan and Ifrim (2016) leverage keywords in social media to generate storylines, and Vossen et al. (2015) propose to use news timelines to build storylines, structured index of events in the timeline, and event relationships.

Visualizing news stories focuses on building a user interface to present a given story to help the user digest a complex story. Using the EMM dataset, Krstajić et al. (2013) propose a visual analytics system to represent relationships between news stories and their evolution over time. Each story element is represented as a tile in a vertical list. Over time (x-axis), the placement of story elements is adjusted on the vertical axis according to the level of activity in the story.

Shahaf et al. (2012) propose a "Metro map" view for a given story. Article headlines are selected in the story corpus to maximize coverage of pieces of information. The selected items are put in different "lines" of the metro maps, showing how the story developed. Only headline information is accessible on the produced metro map.

Tannier and Vernier (2016) build timelines for journalistic use. Based on a user query, documents are retrieved and dates are extracted from sentences. A timeline is built where peaks represents important dates, and key dates are annotated with representative article headlines and an image from the article when available.

3 The newsLens pipeline

In order to build news stories over long time spans based on a variety of news sources, there are two main challenges: an organizational challenge of collecting news articles, and an algorithmic and computational challenge of building the stories. We describe our solutions to both problems.

We first describe how we use the Internet Archive to recover a dataset of news articles. Given an article dataset, we propose a lightweight pipeline to process articles into topics in a streamable fashion, so that timelines can be updated as new articles are added. The pipeline we propose has the following stages: extracting keywords from articles, creating *topics*: local groups of articles in time, solidifying the local topic clusters into *stories*: long-ranging sets of articles that

Table 1: Number of articles collected by source

Source name	# articles
reuters.com	1.2 million
allafrica.com	1 million
foxnews.com	475000
washingtonpost.com	440000
telegraph.co.uk	390000
france24.com	250000
nytimes.com	230000
cnn.com	140000
theguardian.com	51000
Other sources	166000

share a common theme, and automatically naming the stories. We then present timing measurements for each step of the pipeline.

3.1 Collecting news articles

For each article in our dataset, we require some information, from which we can build the features needed for our processing. The minimum information required is: the publication date, the url, the headline, and the content of the article. Most common news sources build their news websites with specific patterns, to make their articles easier to index. For instance, CNN.com, France24.com and NYTimes.com article urls match the following regular expressions, respectively:

http://cnn.com/yyyy/mm/dd/*
http://france24.com/en/yyyymmdd*
http://nytimes.com/yyyy/mm/dd/*

We collected 20 such patterns from globally recognized English-language news sources, and collected all news articles matching these patterns through the Internet Archive's advanced search interface. We start our collection on January 1st 2010 and collect until the present time. The publication date is extracted from the url pattern, and we access the news article's webpage to extract the headline and content.

A somewhat unexpected complication we faced was the process of deduplicating some articles. Some news agencies publish up to 7 different versions of a news article, each with a very minor change (for instance, to the headline, or by adding or removing a single sentence to the content). Because we use counts of articles to measure importance and create stories, it is important to remove duplicate articles. We apply a simple but effective method:

1. For a given source, group articles into small ranges of time (e.g. 1 week),

2. Compute bag of word vectors for each article,

3. Transform the bag of words for each group into a tf-idf matrix,

4. If two articles are above a certain cosine similarity, they are assumed to be duplicates,

5. Retain only the most recent article, as it may have corrected information.

Roughly 10% of articles across all sources are deleted in the deduplication process. After deduplication, our dataset contains 4 million news articles in English, or an average of 1,500 articles per day. The detail of number of articles per source is given in Table 1. A study of how article duplicates are created and the types of modifications that news sources create would be interesting.

3.2 Generating the topics

3.2.1 Extracting article keywords

We use a standard method to extract keywords from an article's content. Given a set of articles with no keywords, we represent each document as a bag of words vector. We apply a tf-idf transform on the bag of words corpus and select a word w_i in document d_j as a keyword for the document if the tf-idf score $S(w_i, d_j) > T$, where T is manually set. If we are trying to extract keywords for a large dataset, we process the articles in batches of a fixed size and randomize the order in which we take the articles. Each article is processed a single time. The keywords are lemmatized and lowercased. Although simple, this approach is effective: for the France24 news article with headline:

> Battle to retake Mosul from Islamic State group has begun, says Iraqi

the keywords obtained are:

> shiite, force, abadi, militia, mosul, iraq

3.2.2 Local topic graph

There is not one clear definition of when two articles are about the same "story" in news. Our goal is to cluster articles into local groups we call topics, which are then merged over time into stories. We define two articles to be in the same topic if they share several keywords, and are published in a close range of time.

We propose to group articles into common local topics by building a graph of articles. The algorithm for building the graph is:

1. For each article a_i over a small range of N days, prepare keyword set kw_i

2. Articles (a_i, a_j) are assigned an edge between them if $\|kw_i \cap kw_j\| \geq T_2$, where T_2 is a manually set threshold.

An example graph obtained over a range of 6 days is shown in Figure 1. The graph obtained is not connected and has several components. One can think at first that each component represents a story, however, it is possible for different densely connected topics to erroneously connect over a few edges. This can be seen on Figure 1, where two large components: the Ferguson and Hong Kong protests are loosely connected by a single edge. To avoid the problem of merging topics due to erroneous edges, we use a community detection algorithm, whose role is to find correct assignment of the nodes into communities that maximize a quality function on the communities obtained. We use a standard community detection algorithm, the Louvain method (Blondel et al., 2008), which is both lightweight and efficient at finding the correct clusters. It can be seen in Figure 1 that the Louvain method correctly assigns the two protests to different communities.

3.2.3 From topics to stories

So far we have presented a method to group articles into topics that are local in time. However, it is not computationally tractable to process the graph for a large number of days, given that we have a total of $N \simeq 3000$ days to process. Apart from the computational complexity, we would like a streamable method where adding new articles updates already existing stories and creates new ones, while avoiding recomputing all stories from scratch. The method we propose to merge topics into long-ranging stories is two-fold: a sliding window to enlarge the topics, and a topic matching process for stories that might be interrupted in time.

The first step is to run the local topic assignment in chronological order using a sliding window. For instance, if we choose $N = 5$ for the number of days in a local graph, and 50% for the window overlap, the topic assignment is first run for days 1 to 6, and then run for days 3 to 8, etc.

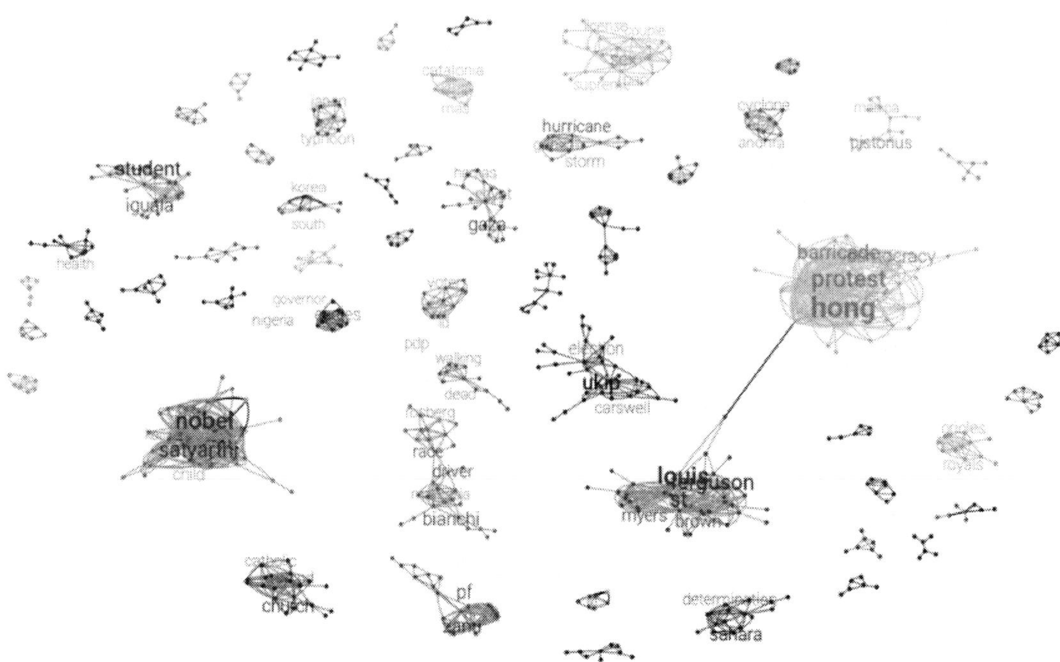

Figure 1: Local topic graph from June 10th 2014 to June 16th 2014. Nodes on the graph are news articles, edges are placed according to our method. Color of the node represents the topic assigned by community detection. Even though the Ferguson and Hong Kong protests form a single connected component, they get assigned to different communities. Keywords are placed on the display for convenience of the reader.

This sequence of overlapping graph clustering creates interesting dynamics. Linking, splitting, and merging are three phenomena we believe are important for story generation from topics.

Linking consists of assigning a topic from a preceding graph to a topic in the current graph: given a cluster in the current graph, if a majority of nodes in the cluster have previously been assigned another topic (in a previous graph, because of the sliding window), no new topic is created, and the cluster is assigned to the old topic, enabling topics to span more than N days. Linking happens for instance on the story about the French elections, that lasted more than 5 days: the articles from the first 5 days formed a topic, and as later articles appear, they are linked into this topic that already exists. The story experiences no interruption greater than 5 days (the span of the window) from January 15th to May 10th 2017, and linking combines all articles in a single topic.

Splitting occurs when one topic is later on divided into 2 distinct topics: it can happen that a topic's start, a few initial articles are clustered together, and then diverge into clusters that are detected as separate by the community detection. In this case, the smallest cluster gets assigned to a new topic. An example of splitting: the shooting of Jo Cox (Brexit story), and the Orlando Shooting occurred within a few days of each other. The first articles covering each topic were at first assigned in the same topic, due to enough common keywords (shooting, death, killing, etc). However as each story grew with new articles, the topics became more distinct, at which point the topics were split.

Merging is similar to linking: if a current cluster found contains articles that have already been assigned to two distinct old topics, both topics are merged. An example of merging: the "Olympics in Rio" and the topic related to "Athletes worried about the Zika virus" were at first separated, but as the Athletes arrived in Rio, the stories were merged. This does not occur as often as linking and splitting.

A story is what emerges when many local topics are linked or merged. With linking, we see how local topics can be connected into stories with an unbounded time span. As long as a topic has new articles appearing continuously, all articles are linked to the same topic, and the story grows.

The assumption that a story must be uninterrupted is constraining, as some stories can have arbitrarily large gaps in time. Consider the "MH317 Malaysia Airline plane crash" story shown in Figure 4, where new evidence was found a few months after the crash, and then again years after the crash happened. The second step for creating stories is to merge topics into a common story if they do not overlap in time but are similar enough in keyword distribution. We build a vector $v(t_i)$ for topic t_i which contains the counts of keywords in all articles of topic t_i. When a new topic t_j is created, its similarity to old topics is computed using a cosine similarity:

$$sim(t_i, t_j) = \frac{v(t_i) \cdot v(t_j)}{\|v(t_i)\|\|v(t_j)\|}$$

If the similarity is above a threshold T_3, and the two topics do not overlap in time significantly, the topics are merged. The final topics obtained after these two steps represent the stories we will display in our interface. The choice of T_2 and T_3 affect the precision and recall of the algorithm. Increasing T_2 reduces the number of edges on the graph, reducing the number of articles placed in topics. In our implementation, we choose high thresholds ($T_2 = 4$, $T_3 = 0.8$), which limits the number of errors (high precision). The drawback is that only 10% of articles of the overall dataset get assigned to topics. When setting $T_2 = 3$, the number of articles in topics raises to 20%, but we expect more incorrect topics to be created.

3.2.4 Naming stories

Finding a good name to represent the story that can encompass several thousands of articles is challenging. We propose a simple system based on observations of what makes a good title for a topic. Here are examples of good titles we want to be able to pick: *"North Korea nuclear tests"*, *"Ukraine crisis"*, *"Ebola outbreak"*, *"Brexit vote"*, *"Paris attacks"*. The features these names have in common are:

1. A story name is a noun phrase,

2. It contains a proper noun (entity),

3. It contains a common noun or word, and

4. One of the words is abstract (test, crisis, outbreak, ...).

For each headline in our story, we extract all maximal noun phrases and assign a score to each. For example, in the headline below (from telegraph.co.uk), noun phrases are underlined:

<u>Pakistan</u> frees <u>Taliban prisoners</u> to help <u>Afghan peace process</u>

Notice that noun phrases such as "peace process" and "prisoners" are not proposed as they are enclosed in a larger (maximal) noun phrase. The highest scoring noun phrase is chosen as the name of the story. Here are the features used to score a noun phrase p:

1. $f_1(p) = 1$ if there is a proper noun else 0

2. $f_2(p) = 1$ if there is a common noun else 0

3. $f_3(p) = log_{10}(count(p))$, where $count(p)$ is the number of occurrences of phrase p in all headlines of the story

4. $f_4(p) = \sum_{w \in p} f(w)$, w are the words in p, $f(w)$ is the frequency of w in the titles

5. $f_5(p) = \max_{w \in p} abstractness(w)$, where $abstractness(w)$ is a word abstractness measure (Kato et al., 2008)

6. $f_6(p) = length(p)$, number of words in p

The final score is then computed as a linear combination of the features:

$$score(p) = \sum_{i=1}^{6} \lambda_i f_i(p)$$

We choose the λ_i manually, and $p_{final} = arg\,max_p score(p)$. The five titles presented above are results for some of the major stories available in the system.

3.3 Processing Times

The processing speed determines the system's capacity, if it is to run in real-time. Table 2 presents the speed per unit for each stage of the pipeline, as well as the total time spent when processing 20 sources, with 4 million articles over 7 years.

4 Visualizing stories with lanes

We have now presented a method to retrieve 4 million news articles and organize them into more than 80000 stories. Many of these stories have hundreds or thousands of articles. We are posed

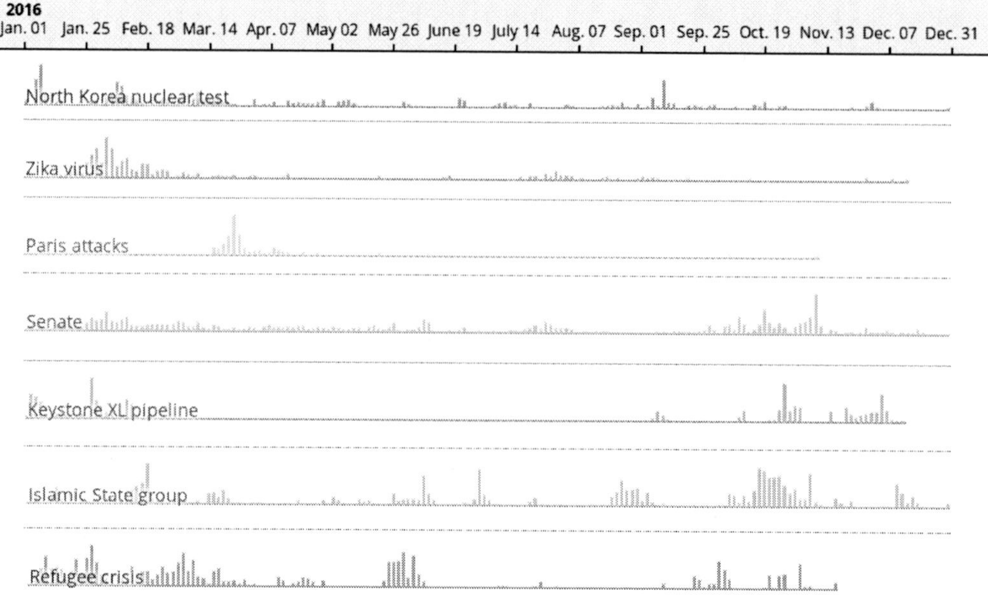

Figure 2: "lanes" interface. The 7 stories with most articles in 2016 are shown in timeline format.

Table 2: Timings of the pipeline. Time per unit, is a time per processed element. Total time is when running the pipeline on the entire dataset.

Process name	Time per unit	Total time
Internet Archive	4 min / source	80 min
Populating articles	0.05 sec / article	2.3 days
Extracting keywords	0.01 sec / article	12 hrs
Creating stories	2 sec / day	4 hours
Naming stories	0.02 sec / story	20 min

with the visualization challenge of displaying content in an understandable manner. The following section introduces *lanes*, the interface we propose to represent stories. Lanes is composed of three components: a timeline, article headlines and quotes tiles. Figure 3 presents two example lanes generated by our system.

4.1 Story timeline

The overall interface is framed on the x-axis representing time, each element added has a given x-position representing its occurrence within the story. We use a timeline as the main visual representation of the topic. The x-axis represents time, and the y-axis represents the number of articles in a given short period of time. This timeline creates a shape the user can identify the story with. Figure 2 shows the timelines of the 7 stories in year 2016 with most news articles. The assumption we

follow is that major events in a topic lead to more news articles in a following short period of time, which can be made prominent in the timeline of the overall topic by a peak. For example, in Figure 2, it appears that the most active periods for the story "Keystone XL pipeline" are in February, October and November 2016.

The timelines of Figure 2 help the user see "when" action occurred in a given story. The following two subsections present the annotations added when a user clicks on a chosen timeline. The annotations help understand the "what" and the "who" of the timeline, respectively.

4.2 Headline selection

Because we assume that peaks in the timeline of the story correspond to key times in the story, we propose to annotate these points for the reader. We sample news articles from peak periods of the story and add their headlines as annotation to the timeline. This allows the user to get an idea of what occurred during that period of the topic. The headline is clickable and takes the user to the article's original URL. This enables the user to access articles about a topic that can be several years old. When selecting which article to display for a given peak, we randomly sample an article. Added to the article headline is an image icon representing the logo of the news source, which helps the user

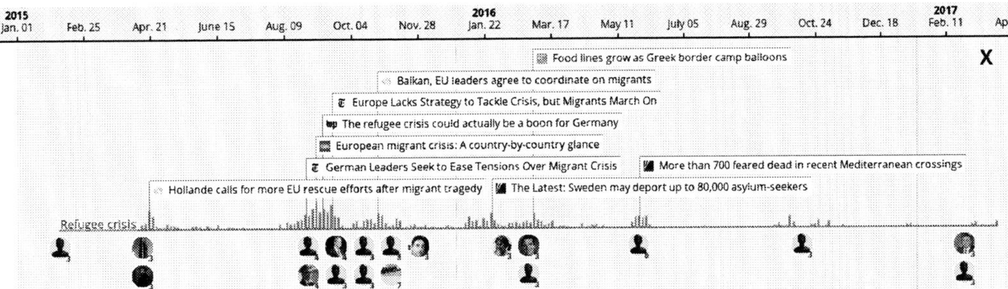

Figure 3: "Refugee crisis" story. Top to bottom: time legend, article headlines, timeline, and quote tiles.

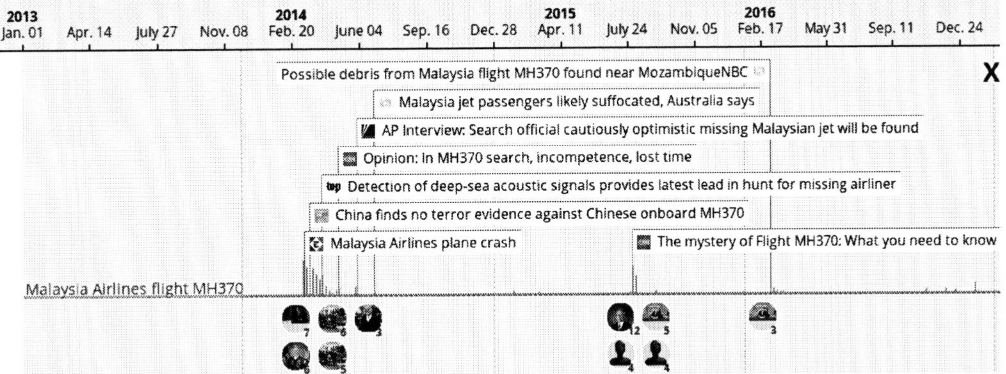

Figure 4: Timeline of the "Malaysia Airline flight MH370", it has large time gaps with no articles.

know the source of the headline at a glance.

There can be stories where many peaks happen in a short period of time, in which case the visualization would become cluttered. We impose a hard constraint in the visualization: headline annotations cannot overlap, and they are placed on a number of "rows" above the timeline. A maximum number of headline rows is allowed, and if a headline cannot be placed because of a lack of space, it is not displayed. Headlines are placed in decreasing order of their peak heights, so that more "more important" peaks get placed first.

4.3 Quote ranking and selection

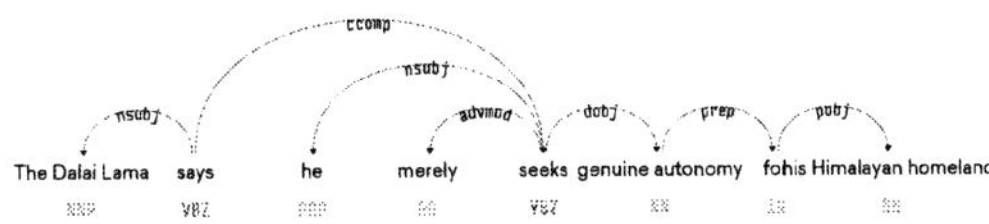

Figure 5: Dependency tree of a quote sentence illustrating how extraction process. This figure was generated using a modified version of displaCy.

We assume showing headlines annotations on the timeline helps the news reader answer the "what" of the story. We are experimenting with adding additional kinds of information to the interface. The first of these is quotations extracted from the article that are assumed to be important. Quote extraction is an active field of research (Pouliquen et al., 2007; O'Keefe et al., 2012). Our objective is to build a simple system to experiment with ranking and displaying the quotes. This process is done in 3 steps: entities are extracted, quotes for these entities are extracted and then grouped and scored for importance.

We extract entities from all articles using an NLP library named spaCy. In order to reduce entity duplication, we proceed with a simple entity linking process leveraging Wikidata (Vrandečić and Krötzsch, 2014). Each entity string is searched through Wikidata's search interface. Wikidata provides unique identifiers that match the search query. The first identifier in the query result is associated with the entity string. This allows us to merge entities such as: "Obama", "Barack Obama", "Mr. Obama", etc

Entity disambiguation is a complex task, and although Wikidata is a first step in resolving entities, it also introduces errors. For instance, many news articles mention "Washington" as the author of a quote. When searching for Washington in Wikidata, the first entry that appears is "George Washington" instead of the city of Washington D.C. Additional patterns verifying the span of life and entity types could be put in place, but overall, this is a complex task and we will introduce more sophisticated entity recognition in future work.

Once entities are extracted, the next step is to attribute quotes to the entities. To extract quotes, we look at each individual sentence in our corpus and determine whether it is a quote by a known entity. The method for quote extraction is the following:

1. The sentence is parsed into a dependency tree

2. Check if the subject (NSUBJ) of the root verb of the sentence is a known entity

3. Check if the lemma of the root verb is in a predefined list (say, tell, state, ...)

4. Check if the root has a complementary clause

5. If all checks are validated, extract the pair (entity, quote)

For example given the sentence from a Reuters article:

> The self-exiled Dalai Lama says he merely seeks genuine autonomy for his Himalayan homeland.

The dependency tree for this sentence is shown in Figure 5. We can see that for this sentence, all three conditions are met and the quote pair extracted is: (Dalai Lama, "he merely seeks genuine autonomy for his Himalayan homeland."). The dependency parsing is also achieved with the spaCy library.

This process does not extract all quotes as the pattern recognition we propose is fairly rigid. For now, we accept the low recall for a high precision in the quotes extracted, as we assume users would react more negatively to erroneous quotes than missing quotes. This produces on average 2 quotes per news article, which can represent thousands of quotes for a single story, which is too much to show to users. We propose a simple way to cluster quotes together to find important quotes.

Quotes are transformed into bag of words vectors, and the tf-idf transform is applied to the quote vector corpus. Quotes can then be compared using a cosine similarity measure. Two quotes are judged to be in the same "quote cluster" if they are from articles that are close in time, and they meet a minimum cosine similarity.

Once quote clusters are obtained, the size of the cluster is our measure for the quote cluster's importance. This assumes that a quote that is mentioned by several journalists from various sources has more importance in the story.

We can now rank quotes in order of importance and show a limited number of quotes in the "lanes interface". Each quote cluster is represented by an image tile of the entity speaking. When clicking on a tile, a frame showing the list of quotes in the cluster opens. Figure 6 shows one result of opening a quote tile: four quotes from the cluster are displayed, as well as the source from which the quote is extracted. Clicking on the quote opens the article from which the quote was extracted. In this

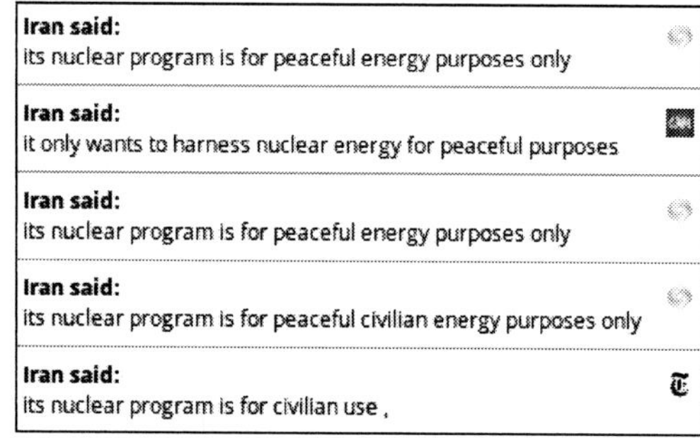

Figure 6: Interface that opens upon a user's click on a quote. Quotes shown were assigned to a common cluster in the story named "Iran nuclear talks"

example, we can see that the quote cluster contains quotes from Reuters, CNN and the NYTimes. The phrasing of each quote is slightly different, showing that sources modify and specify detail in their quote.

The lanes interface presents the stories as timelines annotated both with headlines at key times, as well as quotes representing main actors within the story.

5   Conclusion and Future Work

We have presented a method to build a dataset of news articles over a long range of time from several sources and an efficient, novel algorithm for organizing millions of articles into stories that span long time ranges, despite gaps in coverage. These stories are named with a simple but effective algorithm and visualized using a lanes metaphor, providing the user with a way to view each story in more detail.

Future work includes an assessment of the accuracy of the story creation algorithm: both the accuracy within stories, verifying that articles within a given story are related, and across stories, verifying that story humans would agree with the stories we propose. We also plan to continue refining the user interface and assess it with journalists, media analysts and other relevant end users: we will compare our interface with other news aggregator systems such as Google News, to assess the usability of this approach.

Future work will also leverage the considerable related work on event detection and event pattern understanding, and incorporating that into the story creation process.

Finally, source bias and information validity are important, in the context of alternative news sources and social media. An interface that presents the facts with the source of the information in a transparent way, as well as the results of calculating biases of news sources from a computational perspective is a future direction of interest.

References

Amr Ahmed, Qirong Ho, Jacob Eisenstein, Eric Xing, Alexander J Smola, and Choon Hui Teo. 2011. Unified analysis of streaming news. In *Proceedings of the 20th international conference on World wide web*. ACM, pages 267–276.

Vincent D Blondel, Jean-Loup Guillaume, Renaud Lambiotte, and Etienne Lefebvre. 2008. Fast unfolding of communities in large networks. *Journal of statistical mechanics: theory and experiment* 2008(10):P10008.

Makoto P. Kato, Hiroaki Ohshima, Satoshi Oyama, and Katsumi Tanaka. 2008. Can social tagging improve web image search? In *International Conference on Web Information Systems Engineering (WISE)*. Springer, pages 235–249.

Miloš Krstajić, Mohammad Najm-Araghi, Florian Mansmann, and Daniel A Keim. 2013. Story tracker: Incremental visual text analytics of news story development. *Information Visualization* 12(3-4):308–323.

Tim O'Keefe, Silvia Pareti, James R Curran, Irena Koprinska, and Matthew Honnibal. 2012. A sequence labelling approach to quote attribution. In *Proceedings of the 2012 Joint Conference on Empirical Methods in Natural Language Processing and Computational Natural Language Learning*. Association for Computational Linguistics, pages 790–799.

Gevorg Poghosyan and Georgiana Ifrim. 2016. Real time news story detection and tracking with hashtags. In *Computing News Storylines Workshop at EMNLP 2016, Austin, Texas*.

Bruno Pouliquen, Ralf Steinberger, and Clive Best. 2007. Automatic detection of quotations in multilingual news. In *Proceedings of Recent Advances in Natural Language Processing*. pages 487–492.

Bruno Pouliquen, Ralf Steinberger, and Olivier Deguernel. 2008. Story tracking: linking similar news over time and across languages. In *Proceedings of the workshop on Multi-source Multilingual Information Extraction and Summarization*. Association for Computational Linguistics, pages 49–56.

Dafna Shahaf, Carlos Guestrin, and Eric Horvitz. 2012. Trains of thought: Generating information maps. In *Proceedings of the 21st international conference on World Wide Web*. ACM, pages 899–908.

Russell Swan and James Allan. 2000. Automatic generation of overview timelines. In *Proceedings of the 23rd annual international ACM SIGIR conference on Research and development in information retrieval*. ACM, pages 49–56.

Xavier Tannier and Frdric Vernier. 2016. Creation, Visualization and Edition of Timelines for Journalistic Use. In *Proceedings of Natural Language meets Journalism Workshop at IJCAI 2016*. New York, USA.

Piek Vossen, Tommaso Caselli, and Yiota Kontzopoulou. 2015. Storylines for structuring massive streams of news. In *Proceedings of the First Workshop on Computing News Storylines*. pages 40–49.

Denny Vrandečić and Markus Krötzsch. 2014. Wikidata: a free collaborative knowledgebase. *Communications of the ACM* 57(10):78–85.

Detecting Changes in Twitter Streams using Temporal Clusters of Hashtags

Yunli Wang
Scientific Data Mining
Information & Communication
NRC Canada, Ottawa ON
`yunli.wang@nrc.ca`

Cyril Goutte
Multilingual Text Processing
Information & Communication
NRC Canada, Ottawa, ON
`cyril.goutte@nrc.ca`

Abstract

Detecting events from social media data has important applications in public security, political issues, and public health. Many studies have focused on detecting specific or unspecific events from Twitter streams. However, not much attention has been paid to detecting changes, and their impact, in online conversations related to an event. We propose methods for detecting such changes, using clustering of temporal profiles of hashtags, and three change point detection algorithms. The methods were tested on two Twitter datasets: one covering the 2014 Ottawa shooting event, and one covering the Sochi winter Olympics. We compare our approach to a baseline consisting of detecting change from raw counts in the conversation. We show that our method produces large gains in change detection accuracy on both datasets.

1 Introduction

Widespread data collection from news sources and microblogs has produced massive textual data streams that are challenging to process and analyze. The detection of emerging events from data streams such as Twitter has received growing attention from researchers. Many methods focus on detecting specific, "bursty" events such as natural disasters or major political and security crisis (Farzindar and Khreich, 2015), relying mostly on linguistic features (Sakaki et al., 2010). For detecting unspecific events, many approaches rely on applying clustering (Farzindar and Khreich, 2015) to temporal characteristics of tweets (Mathioudakis and Koudas, 2010). For example, Cordeiro (2012)

used hashtag peaks for unsupervised event detection.

Relatively little attention has been paid to detecting changes during events. Guralnik and Srivastava (1999) formulate the event detection problem from time series of sensor data as a *change point detection* problem. Change point detection (CPD) is the problem of detecting point where the underlying distribution changes in time series data. Several statistical models have been proposed to detect change points, such as Bayesian change point detection (`bcp`, Erdman and Emerson, 2007), E-Divisive change point detection (`ecp`, James and Matteson, 2015), or breakout detection (James et al., 2014). These methods use parametric (Wang and Emerson, 2015) or nonparametric statistical models, and are usually tested on time series of "counts", i.e. frequency of some feature or measurement.

We propose a novel method for detecting changes in document streams by combining the clustering of temporal profiles of hashtags with multivariate change point detection algorithms. The temporal profile clusters separate major events from unrelated events, while multivariate CPD is able to identify time points were important changes occurred in major events. We test our method on two datasets from Twitter, evaluate the performance of different CPD algorithms and the influence of several design choices.

2 Methods

Our method is based on the assumption that hashtags with similar temporal profiles are related to the same event or sub-event[1] within a document stream. In order to model that, we first build temporal profiles by counting the occurrences of

---

[1] We talk about *sub-events* here to refer to smaller events occurring within a larger event, e.g. a glitch happening within the opening ceremony at the Olympics.

Proceedings of the Events and Stories in the News Workshop, pages 10–14,
Vancouver, Canada, August 4, 2017. ©2017 Association for Computational Linguistics

each hashtag at each time interval. We then cluster the temporal profiles using hierarchical clustering. Each cluster represents a group of hashtags with similar temporal profiles, which we assume describe the same (sub-)events. We then build the temporal profiles of all clusters and input those into multivariate change point detection algorithms, in order to extract the locations where significant changes occur in the temporal profiles. The underlying assumption is that when something significant occurs, it will produce changes in some temporal profiles of clusters that are related to that sub-event. For example, in Fig. 1, we see that a sub-event late in Oct. 25 has produced a large impact on the profiles of both clusters. In earlier days, some sub-events have an impact of the profile for Cluster 1, but not for Cluster 2, for example on Oct 23rd, as Canadian prime minister lay a wreath in memory of the victim at the War Memorial.

There are two steps in our method: building hashtag temporal profiles and detecting change points from hashtag temporal profiles. The first step is described in Algorithm 1:

Algorithm 1: Hashtag profiles and clusters

Data: List of hashtags with time stamps
Parameters: Time interval I, #clusters C
Result: C hashtag clusters, with temporal profiles

Generate $K \times M$ hashtag-profile matrix by counting frequency of hashtags per interval;
Compute $K \times K$ hashtag similarity using Pearson correlation on hashtag profiles;
Run hierarchical clustering using the $K \times K$ hashtag similarity matrix
Cut the resulting hierarchy at C clusters.

In the second step, each cluster resulting from Algorithm 1 is a subset of the K hashtags we started with. For each of the C clusters, we build the temporal profile obtained from the frequency of all hashtags from that cluster at each time interval (e.g. Fig. 1). We use these temporal profiles as C time series on which we run multivariate change point detection algorithms bcp and ecp.[2] The single parameter used for change point detection is the number of change point locations to extract from the multivariate signal.

bcp implements the Bayesian change point

analysis of Barry and Hartigan (1993). It assumes that each block between two change points arises from a (multivariate) normal distribution, and outputs the posterior probability that a change point occurred at each time in the series. ecp uses a nonparametric, hierarchical divisive estimation method. E-Divisive estimates change points iteratively, by recursively dividing an existing segment using a divergence measure that estimates whether two random vectors are identically distributed. Although ecp can be used for univariate and multivariate time series without a priori knowledge of the number of change points, our experience is that it works better when a target number of change points is provided.

In order to evaluate the influence of the hashtag clusters, we also compare our method to change points directly detected from raw tweet counts. As this is a univariate time series, we test one additional CPD algorithm implemented in the R package breakout, which uses a robust *E-divisive with medians* algorithm to detect significant changes in data distribution.

3 Experiments

3.1 Datasets

We collected two datasets from the Twitter API. The *Ottawa Shooting* data was obtained by querying keywords like "Ottawa", "parliament shooting", "#CanadaStrong", "Zehaf-Bibeau" etc. during the period of Oct. 21st to Oct. 30th, 2014 and contains 694,017 tweets. Reference subevents to evaluate the detected change points for the Ottawa shooting data were collected from Macleans News[3] and include 32 change points. This small dataset is challenging because the number of both messages and subevents decreases sharply with time.

The *Olympics* dataset was collected during the Sochi 2014 winter Olympics during February 6th (opening ceremony) to 24th (closing ceremony) 2014 and contains 5,914,616 tweets. The reference subevents were collected from Wikipedia.[4] For our gold standard, we only included the final competitions in each discipline. More events (Quarterfinals, Semifinals, Bronze and Gold medal games) were included for Ice Hockey because they attracted more media attention. In

---

[2] From the R packages bcp and ecp.

[3] http://www.macleans.ca/news/canada/interactive-timeline-what-happened-in-ottawa/

[4] https://en.wikipedia.org/wiki/2014_Winter_Olympics

total, our gold standard contains 89 change points.

3.2 Evaluation

The performance of change point detection was evaluated against reference subevents using precision, recall and F-score (Goutte and Gaussier, 2005). A detected change point at time t is evaluated correct if there exists a reference change point between t and $t + \Delta t$, where Δt is a tolerance time window. We usually set Δt to a small multiplier of the time interval I used in the preprocessing. For Ottawa Shooting, $I = 30$min and $\Delta t = 1$h, while for the Olympics, $I = 1$h and $\Delta t = 2$h. To avoid duplication, we only consider one true detected change point if several detected change points fall in the same time window.

4 Results

We first show temporal profiles resulting from the hashtag clusters, we then evaluate the performance of our technique versus a few alternatives, and finally, we show the impact of design parameters. The number of clusters C is set to 10 in Ottawa shooting and 20 in the Olympics datasets. `bcp` uses all default parameter settings, returning the change points with highest posterior probability. `ecp` uses divisive hierarchical estimation with all default settings. The target number of change points is 30 for Ottawa Shooting and 90 for the Olympics data. `breakout` uses all default settings, picking the number of detected changes automatically.

4.1 Temporal Profile Clusters

Figure 1 shows the temporal profile of two clusters obtained from the Ottawa Shooting dataset. They clearly cover events from the first four days (Oct. 22–25) in different ways: Cluster 1 corresponds to the major shooting at the war memorial and parliament on Oct. 22, plus subsequent subevents on Oct. 23–25. Cluster 2 focuses on the victim, with small spikes on Oct. 24 when an official motorcade transported his body back to Hamilton, ON and a large peak on Oct. 25, when pre-game ceremonies were jointly held in Ottawa, Montreal, and Toronto to honour the deceased and first responders. This main peak in cluster 2 also appears in cluster 1 and is more localized than activities apparent in other days. This shows that hashtag clusters are able to capture documents related to different subevents in the collection.

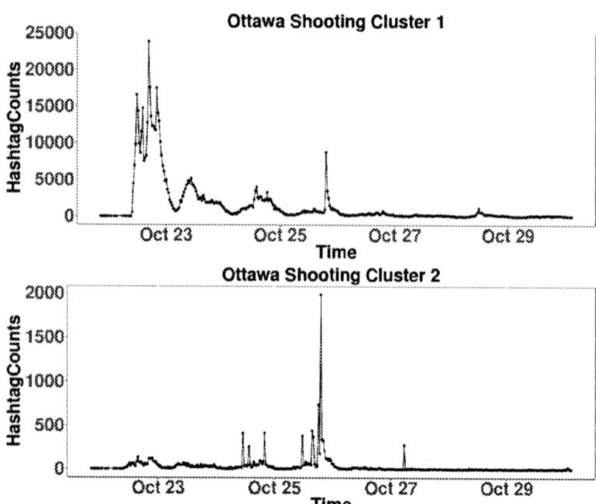

Figure 1: Temporal profiles for the two largest hashtag clusters for the Ottawa shooting data.

4.2 Change Points Results

We evaluate the performance of our change detection methods on both datasets and benchmark against two alternatives: running CPD on raw message counts (*Counts in Fig. 2), and running `bcp` or `ecp` on temporal profiles of the hashtags with highest volumes (*TopHashtags). Figure 2 shows that the change points detected from the temporal profiles of hashtag clusters (magenta and yellow bars) outperform those detected from either top hashtags or raw counts. On the Olympics dataset, `ecp` yields the same performance on raw counts as on hashtag clusters. The performance of breakout detection on raw counts varies greatly but clearly favours precision at the expense of recall. This suggests that it under-detects changes; unfortunately `breakout` does not allow to tune the number of change points detected to increase recall.

The fact that the performance of change point detection from hashtag cluster temporal profiles is higher than from a corresponding number of profiles of top hashtags suggests that the use of clusters is able to catch changes that are not apparent from the profile of large volume hashtags, but are reflected in clusters corresponding to significantly different patterns with lower volumes. This allows our proposed method to pick up weaker signals on time series from smaller clusters, instead of relying on the main, high-volume signals. Another situation where cluster profiles are useful is to handle the appearance of new hashtags after the main events. In the Ottawa Shooting dataset, for

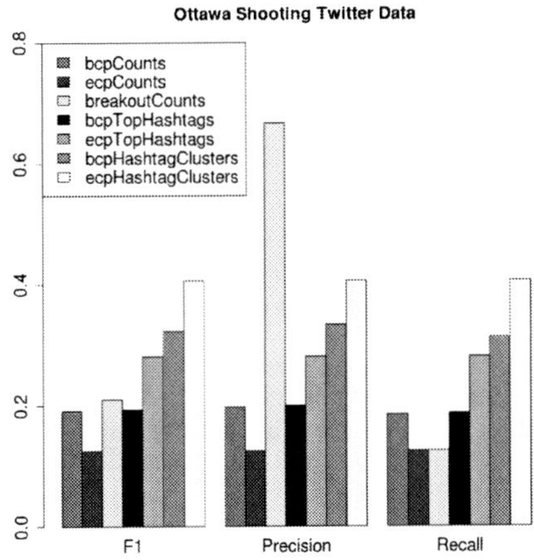

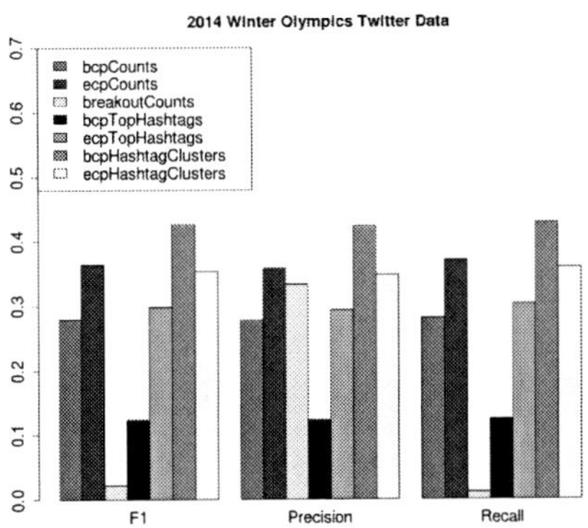

Figure 2: Performance of change detection from raw counts, top hashtags, and hashtag cluster temporal profiles on the Ottawa shooting (top) and Olympics (bottom) datasets.

example, hashtags #OttawaStrong and #CanadaStrong have high volume throughout the dataset and appear in cluster 1; other hashtags appear later, once the shooter (#ZehafBibeau) or victim (#CplCirillo) are identified, or when specific subevents unfold (#highwayofheroes, during the official motorcade on Oct. 24). Later hashtags are captured in different clusters with specific temporal profiles.

These results also show the benefits of using a multivariate change detection method, as opposed to a univariate method. Although `breakout` can efficiently identify breakouts in some univariate time series settings, the ability of `bcp` and `ecp` to handle multiple time series with different characteristics at the same time provides significant benefits on both datasets.

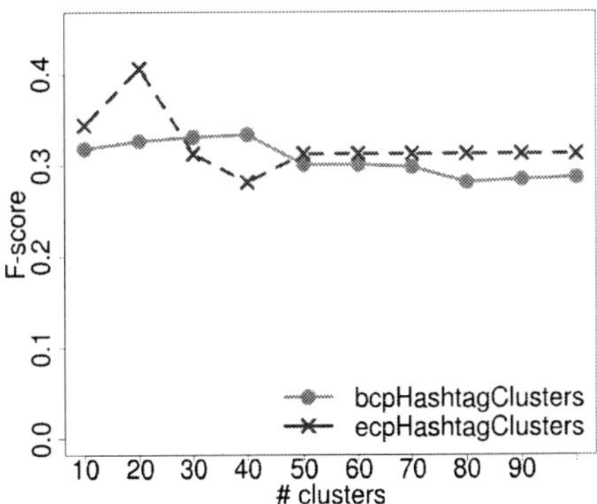

Figure 3: F-score for different numbers of clusters, on the Ottawa Shooting dataset.

4.3 Parameter Analysis

We investigate the impact of a few design parameters on our method's performance: the number of clusters, the time window used for evaluation, and the time interval. Figure 3 shows that performance is fairly stable across a range of cluster numbers. There is a small increase at $C = 20$ for `ecp`, and a slow decrease for `bcp` when C increases. Figure 4 shows that performance increases regularly with larger time windows Δt. This is expected, as increasing the time window systematically increases the number of reference events detected. Note that we use $I = 5$min. as time interval (instead of 30min in Figs. 1-3) so that we can more easily increase Δt. As a consequence, we also observe that performance is lower using this smaller time interval. This may be due to the increase is noise when counts are accumulated over a smaller time interval.

5 Discussion

In our work, we used different off-the-shelf changepoint detection algorithms in order to illustrate the benefits of using hashtag cluster profiles rather than raw counts. Theses different algorithms have different underlying assumptions, but both improve greatly when applied to multivariate temporal profiles. We could use different CPD methods. Our ongoing work actually focuses on developping an online variant that detects changes as events unfold rather that wait for *a posteriori* processing. A related point is that it is important to perform CPD on multivariate series as different clusters may represent different aspects of the

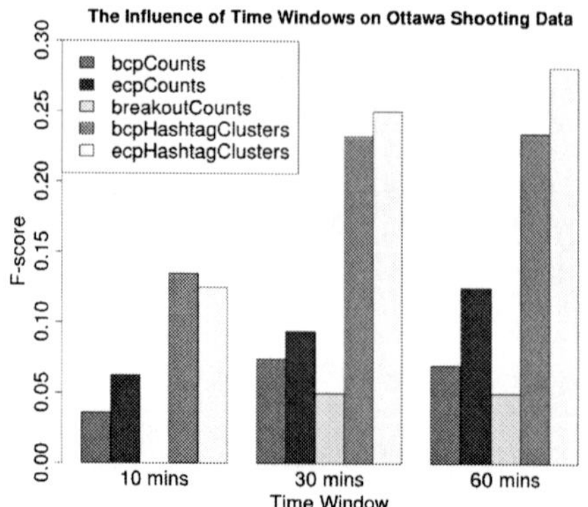

Figure 4: F-score for various time windows, with 5 min. time interval (Ottawa Shooting dataset).

data, and changes may be apparent in some profiles but not all, and be drowned when a single, global count is used.

Our method focuses on detecting sub-events using temporal profiles of hashtag clusters. As both datasets used here were acquired using query keywords, so most tweets in each dataset are related to the same events. The noise in these datasets is much lower than the real-time twitter stream. When focusing on specific events, we can filter the stream using a number of specific keywords. For unsupervised event detection, methods such as hashtag peaks (Cordeiro, 2012) can be used as pre-processing before applying our method.

6 Conclusions

We proposed a novel method for detecting changes related to sub-events in a Twitter stream, using temporal profiles from hashtag clusters. This is a combination of exploratory data analysis with quantitative data analysis. Clusters of hashtags identify a number of subevents within a major event, yielding distinctive temporal profiles. These temporal profiles can be visualized as an exploratory analysis of the message stream. They can also be used further downstream and combined with change point detection method in order to provide insight into significant changes in the stream. Our experiments on two datasets acquired from Twitter show that change points detected by our method identify up to 40% of reference subevents in these datasets, and clearly outperform the use of raw message or hashtag counts.

References

D. Barry and J.A. Hartigan. 1993. A bayesian analysis for change point problems. *Journal of the American Statistical Association* 35(3):309–319.

Mário Cordeiro. 2012. Twitter event detection: combining wavelet analysis and topic inference summarization. In *Doctoral Symposium on Informatics Engineering DSIE*. volume 8, pages 11–16.

Chandra Erdman and John Emerson. 2007. bcp: An R package for performing a bayesian analysis of change point problems. *Journal of Statistical Software* 23(1):1–13. https://doi.org/10.18637/jss.v023.i03.

Atefeh Farzindar and Wael Khreich. 2015. A survey of techniques for event detection in twitter. *Comput. Intell.* 31(1):132–164. https://doi.org/10.1111/coin.12017.

Cyril Goutte and Eric Gaussier. 2005. A probabilistic interpretation of precision, recall and f-score, with implication for evaluation. In D.E. Losada and J.M. Fernandez-Luna, editors, *Advances in Information Retrieval - 27th European Conference on IR Research*. pages 345–359. http://dx.doi.org/10.1007/978-3-540-31865-1_25.

Valery Guralnik and Jaideep Srivastava. 1999. Event detection from time series data. In *Proceedings of the Fifth ACM SIGKDD International Conference on Knowledge Discovery and Data Mining*. ACM, New York, NY, USA, KDD '99, pages 33–42. https://doi.org/10.1145/312129.312190.

Nicholas A. James, Arun Kejariwal, and David S. Matteson. 2014. Leveraging cloud data to mitigate user experience from "breaking bad". *eprint arXiv:1411.7955* .

Nicholas A. James and David Matteson. 2015. ecp: An R package for nonparametric multiple change point analysis of multivariate data. *Journal of Statistical Software* 62(1):1–25. https://doi.org/10.18637/jss.v062.i07.

Michael Mathioudakis and Nick Koudas. 2010. Twittermonitor: Trend detection over the twitter stream. In *Proceedings of the 2010 ACM SIGMOD International Conference on Management of Data*. ACM, New York, NY, USA, SIGMOD '10, pages 1155–1158. https://doi.org/10.1145/1807167.1807306.

Takeshi Sakaki, Makoto Okazaki, and Yutaka Matsuo. 2010. Earthquake shakes twitter users: Real-time event detection by social sensors. In *Proceedings of the 19th International Conference on World Wide Web*. ACM, New York, NY, USA, WWW '10, pages 851–860. https://doi.org/10.1145/1772690.1772777.

Xiaofei Wang and John W. Emerson. 2015. Bayesian change point analysis of linear models on graphs. *eprint arXiv:1509.00817* .

Event Detection Using Frame-Semantic Parser

Evangelia Spiliopoulou
Carnegie Mellon University
espiliop@cs.cmu.edu

Eduard Hovy
Carnegie Mellon University
hovy@cmu.edu

Teruko Mitamura
Carnegie Mellon University
teruko@cs.cmu.edu

Abstract

Recent methods for Event Detection focus on Deep Learning for automatic feature generation and feature ranking. However, most of those approaches fail to exploit rich semantic information, which results in relatively poor recall. This paper is a small & focused contribution, where we introduce an Event Detection and classification system, based on deep semantic information retrieved from a frame-semantic parser. Our experiments show that our system achieves higher recall than state-of-the-art systems. Further, we claim that enhancing our system with deep learning techniques like feature ranking can achieve even better results, as it can benefit from both approaches.

1 Introduction

Automatic Event Detection is an important and challenging task in Natural Language Processing and Information Extraction. According to the ACE 2005 Evaluations (ACE, 2005), an Event is defined as a specific occurrence that describes a change of state, the **Event Nugget**, and it involves a set of participants, the **Event Arguments**. The term Event Nugget (TAC, 2014) refers to a semantically meaningful unit of text that denotes some action (event), while the Event Arguments are Entity mentions or temporal expressions related to the Event Nugget. In this work, we focus on the task of Event Nugget Detection and its classification to types and subtypes of Events, according to the ACE 2005 guidelines.

Current Event Detection methods that achieve state-of-the-art results are based on Deep Learning techniques using shallow lexical features and word embeddings (Chen et al., 2015), (Nguyen and Gr-

ishman, 2015). Although these approaches open the door to automatically extracted features, they fail to exploit deeper semantic information. This results in a limited number of detected events and, consequently, in low recall/ high precision systems.

In this work, we investigate a different approach on the Event Detection task, that achieves higher recall by generating a large set of candidate events using a semantic-frame parser. Semantic-frame parsers output a variety of linguistic structures, including events, relations and entities. Similar to the approach followed by Liu et al. (2016), we exploit the similarities in structure between FrameNet and the ACE Ontology to create a mapping from the former to the latter. We use this mapping to refine the parser's output and classify the linguistic structures as event mentions. In this paper we show that this approach results in a high recall system (72.6%) which, if combined with a deep learning model, can achieve better recall without loss in precision.

2 Background

2.1 The ACE Dataset

According to the ACE 2005 Evaluations (ACE, 2005), an Event contains two spans: the Event Nugget and the Event Arguments. Although there are several types of events, the ACE annotations include only events that can be defined under a certain ontological structure. This structure contains 8 event types followed by a total of 33 event subtypes. The event types are: LIFE, MOVEMENT, TRANSACTION, BUSINESS, CONFLICT, CONTACT, PERSONNEL and JUSTICE. In this work, we focus on the Event Nugget detection and its classification to one type/subtype pair, as defined by the ACE guidelines.

Proceedings of the Events and Stories in the News Workshop, pages 15–20,
Vancouver, Canada, August 4, 2017. ©2017 Association for Computational Linguistics

2.2 FrameNet

FrameNet (Baker et al., 1998) is a taxonomy of more than 1,200 manually identified semantic frames, deriving from a corpus of 200,000 annotated sentences. The aim of the FrameNet semantic frames is to capture information about the type of a linguistic structure, which can be an event, entity or relation, and its participants. This type is called **Frame** and the participants are called **Frame Elements**. Each Frame is linked to a set of words that may trigger the Frame (**Lexical Units**).

Following the definition of FrameNet semantic frames and the ACE 2005 guidelines, it seems natural to assume a good correspondence between the two resources. This property implies that a mapping from FrameNet Frames to ACE types and subtypes can be extremely helpful in Event Detection (Liu et al., 2016).

2.3 Semafor

Semafor (Das et al., 2014) is a semantic frame parser based on the FrameNet taxonomy. Semafor follows a semi-supervised approach to detect words that are FrameNet triggers, which evoke some semantic frame(s). Semafor's output contains a set of FrameNet semantic frames, their trigger and their Frame Elements.

Since Semafor is based on FrameNet, its triggers can be events, entities or relations. This implies that Semafor cannot be directly applied on the Event Detection problem, since it has extremely low precision. However, in this paper we will present how Semafor can be used as an additional resource to enhance Event Detection recall.

2.4 Related Work

Recent research that achieves state-of-the-art results is primarily based on deep learning techniques. Chen et al. (2015) propose a dynamic multi-pooling convolutional neural network (DM-CNN), which automatically induces lexical-level and sentence-level features from text, achieving state-of-the-art results. Nguyen and Grishman (2015)'s work focuses on CNNs using word embeddings in order to achieve a more generalizable event detection system. Other approaches include Ghaeini et al. (2016)'s FBRNN, which is a modification of RNNs using word and branch embeddings, and Liu et al. (2016)'s ANN & Random ANN, which exploits the direct relationship between the FrameNet and the ACE Ontology in or-

der to construct an out-domain ANN model. Peng et al. (2016) showed that it is feasible to achieve state-of-the-art results with minimal supervision. In their approach, they use only a few examples and the SRL of a candidate event in order to construct a structured vector representation, which maps the event to an ontology.

3 Approach

In this paper, we present a system that uses a semantic-frame parser in order to generate event candidates, which are then filtered according to a mapping between ontologies. The main motivation behind this approach is that most systems based on deep learning methods do not exploit rich semantic information and therefore miss non-surface-level equivalences, which results in low recall. Furthermore, we claim that a combination of a semantically rich system with a deep learning approach can result in better overall performance than both traditional semantic-based approaches and pure deep learning methods.

3.1 Using Semafor

In order to generate a list of candidate events, we need a system with very high recall that contains semantic information about the event. A semantic-frame parser like Semafor, extracts a variety of semantic structures, as events, entities and relations. Furthermore, since it is based on FrameNet, it provides semantic information (Frame), which is essential for the classification of the structure as an event. In order to test the performance of Semafor on the ACE dataset and whether it is a reasonable choice for the system, we run experiments on the Newswire dataset and report the following: $Recall$ 82.53%, $Precision$ 6.8% and F_1 12.6%.

3.2 Defining Events

Based on the ACE 2005 guidelines, we define an event as a nominal or verbal phrase that can be mapped to a subtype of the ACE 2005 Ontology. Utilizing the structural similarity of ACE and FrameNet, we construct a mapping from a subset of FrameNet frames to ACE subtypes. We decided to create two different mappings, according to the POS tag of the trigger. This is because Event Nuggets can be either nominal or verbal phrases, each triggered by different sets of Frames.

In Table 1 we present the mapping of FrameNet Frames to ACE types for verbal mentions. Further, for a small number of frames, we use a set of lexically-based disambiguation rules to find the correct subtype. An example of such a rule is that the frame *Verdict* may correspond to both *Convict* and *Acquit* subtypes. Because FrameNet LUs do not include several words, this mapping does not cover the ACE Ontology. Thus, additional disambiguation rules may even further increase the precision and recall of the current model.

ACE Type	FrameNet Frame
Conflict	Invading, Attack, Explosion, Destroying, Hostile encounter, Use firearm, Shoot projectiles, Downing, Explosion, Destroying, Protest, Political actions
Life	Giving birth, Being born, Death, Killing, Forming relationships, Cause harm, Personal relationship, Cause harm, Dead or alive
Movement	Self motion, Inhibit movement, Travel, Departing, Arriving, Visiting, Motion, Cause motion, Bringing
Transaction	Import export scenario, Commerce buy, Commerce sell, Getting, Commerce pay, Borrowing, Giving
Business	Activity start, Conquering, Endeavor failure, Intentionally create, Business closure, Locale closure
Contact	Meet with, Discussion, Come together, Communication, Contacting, Communication means, Text creation, Request
Personnel	Take place of, Get a job, Hiring, Appointing, Removing, Firing, Quitting, Choosing, Becoming a member, Change of leadership
Justice	Arrest, Imprisonment, Detaining, Extradition, Breaking out captive, Try defendant, Pardon, Appeal, Verdict, Sentencing, Fining, Execution, Releasing, Notification of charges

Table 1: Mapping of FrameNet verbs to ACE Ontology.

3.3 System Architecture

We first use Semafor to generate a set of candidate Event Nuggets, their FrameNet frame and their Frame Elements. Then we use the POS tagger from Stanford CoreNLP (Manning et al., 2014) in order to distinguish the candidate events to verbal events and nominal events. For every trigger in the candidate events, we use the output FrameNet Frame in order to decide whether it is an event or not. If the Frame is in the domain of the FrameNet to ACE mapping, then it means that it corresponds to some subtype of the ACE Ontology and, thus, we accept it as an event. Furthermore, according to the mapping, we assign the type and subtype of the event. In Figure 1 we see an example output of the system for one article. The events are represented with green, red and black color if they are true positives, false positives and false negatives, respectively.

Type	Subtype	Event Nugget
Life	Die	killed
Life	Injure	wounded
Conflict	Attack	blast
Life	Die	death
Contact	Phone-Write	Radio
Life	Die	death
Transaction	Transfer-Money	giving
Life	Die	deaths
Life	Injure	wounded
Life	Injure	injured
Contact	Phone-Write	list
Conflict	Attack	bomb
Conflict	Attack	tore
Conflict	Attack	explosion
Conflict	Attack	hit
Life	Injure	injuries
Conflict	Attack	blast
Conflict	Attack	bomb
Conflict	Attack	exploded
Contact	Phone-Write	radio
Movement	Transport	carting
Life	Injure	wounded

Figure 1: Example output of Event Nuggets, Types and Subtypes.
Source: *ACE 2005, Newswire, AFP_ENG_20030304.0250*

4 Experiments

4.1 Dataset

The test dataset used for experiments is subset of the ACE 2005 corpus. It contains 106 Newswire articles and a total of 1557 event mentions. The methods we compare with are tested on a randomly selected subset of those articles (40 articles), as they needed to use some development data. Since our approach does not require training, we tested on the entire Newswire ACE 2005 corpus. In this way, our results show a more complete picture of the performance of our system on the corpus.

4.2 System Evaluation

Method	Recall	Precision	F1
Liu's ANN (2016)	60.7	79.5	68.8
Liu's Random ANN (2016)	49.5	**81.0**	61.5
Chen's DMCNN (2015)	67.7	80.4	**73.5**
Peng's MSEP (2016)	69.8	75.6	72.6
Proposed Model	**72.6**	43.3	54.2

Table 2: Evaluation on Event Nugget Detection.

For the Event Nugget Detection task, we report and compare the *Recall*, *Precision* and F_1 with the state-of-the-art methods discussed in Section 2.4. Out of a total of 1557 event mentions, the proposed system correctly recognizes 1131. As we see in Table 2, although the proposed system has relatively low precision, it achieves significantly higher recall than current state-of-the-art systems. This indicates that our model is a good candidate for integration with other systems, a hypothesis further discussed in the subsequent sections.

A second metric of evaluation is the classification of the Event Nuggets to types and subtypes. Out of a total of 1557 types and 1557 subtypes, our system correctly recognizes 1044 types and 1018 subtypes. This highlights that our system solves the problem of Event Detection simultanouesly with the event classification to types and subtypes. According to our results, 92.3% and 90.0% of the events that were correctly identified by our system were also correctly classified to types and subtypes, respectively. In Table 3, we report the *Recall*, *Precision* and F_1 measure of the ACE subtypes, viewed as a classification task without prior information about the Event Nuggets. We observe that our system still has the highest recall amongst the compared methods. Since precision on the Event Nugget Detection task was low, prior errors are also propagated to the event subtype classification.

Method	Recall	Precision	F1
Peng's MSEP (2013)	65.0	70.4	67.6
Chen's DMCNN (2015)	63.6	**75.6**	**69.1**
Proposed Model	**65.4**	39.0	48.35

Table 3: Evaluation on Event Subtype Classification.

4.3 Further Experiments

We claim that merging a high recall system based on rich semantic information with a deep learning classifier may achieve better results than current approaches on Event Detection, since it can benefit from both techniques. In a preliminary exploration of this hypothesis, we construct a dataset of candidate events based on our system's output and run classification experiments on them for the Event Nugget Detection task (binary classification). As described in previous approaches, we randomly split the ACE Newswire articles into 60% train and 40% test set. Each instance on those sets represents an extracted Event Nugget of our system for the corresponding article. The features of each instance are:

- **Shallow features:** Event Nugget textual representation & lemma, Part-of-Speech tag, Right Context & Left Context (one position away)

- **FrameNet Frame:** the Frame that Semafor extracted for this Event Nugget.

- **Frame Elements:** a list of the Frame Elements roles (eg Agent, Target) that Semafor extracted for this Event Nugget.

- **Predicted Type and Subtype:** the type and subtype that the our system predicted.

In table 4 we show the results of a Random Forest and a vanilla Neural Net (15 hidden layers) on this dataset. We compare those results with our system's output on the test set. Since the dataset contains only our system's output, the recall upper bound of any classifier is 73.43% (our system's recall).

Classifier	Recall	Precision	F1
None (system output)	73.43	39.2	51.11
Random Forest	52.8	72.6	61.1
Neural Net	51.53	65.0	57.49

Table 4: Classification of Events on our system's output.

Overall the classifiers behave in a similar way, since both of them show a drop in recall and a significant gain on precision. Further, we observe a significant increase on the F_1 score, which indicates that there is an actual system improvement instead of tweaking the precision/recall tradeoff.

A second interesting observation is that the Random Forest classifier gives better results than the Neural Net. We have identified two reasons for that. First, our dataset is extremely small (train: 1550 instances, test: 1045 instances), which results in insufficient training of the Neural Net. The second reason is the nature of the two classifiers. In general, Neural Nets are very strong at discovering new features, which is extremely important when there is a great bulk of hidden information not included as dataset features. On the other hand, Trees select and rank actual dataset features that give maximum entropy. Since each instance in our dataset has a small set of features that are either nominal classes or unigrams, Neural Nets fail to discover good new features. Instead, a good feature reranker as Random Forests, results in better feature selection and, consequently, higher precision.

5   Conclusion and Future Work

Our experiments indicate that our system achieves higher recall than current state-of-the-art systems, while maintaining a reasonable precision. This illustrates that semantically rich features give a great boost in recall that deep learning methods alone cannot reach, due to the inadequacy of shallow linguistic features to capture deep semantic information. On the other hand, deep learning methods are very good at automatic feature extraction and feature ranking, which leads in extremely high precision. We claim that merging the two approaches in one system can solve the current tradeoff between precision and recall, as the new sys-tem will benefit from both techniques.

As our preliminary experiments show, integrating our system with a classifier results in significantly better system performance. The fact that this is achieved with vanilla models which are not widely used for the Event Detection task, is a strong indicator that we can further improve the results by using more suitable models. Our next step is to investigate our system integration with a more sophisticated deep learning classifier instead of off-the-shelf vanilla models. Further, we plan to use an enlarged version of the dataset by including instances that our system did not recognize as Event Nuggets (e.g. all verbal and nominal mentions) with a lesser weight. In that way, we can reduce the previously unavoidable drop in recall, since we will add a bias but not enforce the candidate events to be part of our system's output.

An alternative approach to the system integration involves the construction of a collective output of multiple Event Detection systems with their corresponding confidence scores, if available. We plan to use this as input to a deep learning model, in a similar fashion with the approach discussed earlier. We claim that this classifier will capture more information about events, since it can learn from the strengths and weaknesses of the multiple Event Detection systems involved.

Acknowledgments

This research was supported in part by DARPA grant FA8750-12-2-0342 funded under the DEFT program.

References

2005. *ACE (Automatic Content Extraction) English Annotation Guidelines for Events.* Linguistic Data Consortium, 5.4.1 edition.

2014. *TAC KBP Event Detection Annotation Guidelines*, 1.7 edition.

Collin F. Baker, Charles J. Fillmore, and John B. Lowe. 1998. The berkeley framenet project. In *Proceedings of the 36th Annual Meeting of the Association for Computational Linguistics and 17th International Conference on Computational Linguistics - Volume 1*.

Yubo Chen, Liheng Xu, Kang Liu, Daojian Zeng, and Jun Zhao. 2015. Event extraction via dynamic multi-pooling convolutional neural networks. In *Proceedings of the 53rd Annual Meeting of the Association for Computational Linguistics and the*

7th International Joint Conference on Natural Language Processing (Volume 1: Long Papers).

Dipanjan Das, Desai Chen, André FT Martins, Nathan Schneider, and Noah A Smith. 2014. Frame-semantic parsing. *Computational Linguistics* .

Reza Ghaeini, Xiaoli Z Fern, Liang Huang, and Prasad Tadepalli. 2016. Event nugget detection with forward-backward recurrent neural networks. In *The 54th Annual Meeting of the Association for Computational Linguistics*.

Shulin Liu, Yubo Chen, Shizhu He, Kang Liu, and Jun Zhao. 2016. Leveraging framenet to improve automatic event detection. In *Proceedings of the 54th Annual Meeting of the Association for Computational Linguistics, ACL 2016, August 7-12, 2016, Berlin, Germany, Volume 1: Long Papers.*

Christopher D. Manning, Mihai Surdeanu, John Bauer, Jenny Finkel, Steven J. Bethard, and David McClosky. 2014. The Stanford CoreNLP natural language processing toolkit. In *Association for Computational Linguistics (ACL) System Demonstrations.*

Thien Huu Nguyen and Ralph Grishman. 2015. Event detection and domain adaptation with convolutional neural networks. In *ACL (2).*

Haoruo Peng, Yangqiu Song, and Dan Roth. 2016. Event detection and co-reference with minimal supervision. In *EMNLP.*

Improving Shared Argument Identification in Japanese Event Relation Knowledge Acquisition

Yin Jou Huang
Graduate School of Informatics
Kyoto University
`huang@nlp.ist.i.kyoto-u.ac.jp`

Sadao Kurohashi
Graduate School of Informatics
Kyoto University
`kuro@i.kyoto-u.ac.jp`

Abstract

Event relation knowledge represents the knowledge of causal and temporal relations between events. Shared arguments of event relation knowledge encode patterns of role shifting in successive events. A two-stage framework was proposed for the task of Japanese event relation knowledge acquisition, in which related event pairs are first extracted, and shared arguments are then identified to form the complete event relation knowledge. This paper focuses on the second stage of this framework, and proposes a method to improve the shared argument identification of related event pairs. We constructed a gold dataset for shared argument learning. By evaluating our system on this gold dataset, we found that our proposed model outperformed the baseline models by a large margin.

1 Introduction

Natural language understanding requires not only linguistic knowledge but also common knowledge about the real world. Event relation knowledge is a type of common knowledge of critical importance, representing the knowledge of the relation between events as well as the typical patterns of role shifting between events. Event relation knowledge is useful for natural language understanding tasks as well as natural language generation tasks which require modeling of the possible event sequences.

In this paper, we define an event to be a predicate argument structure (PAS), which consists of a

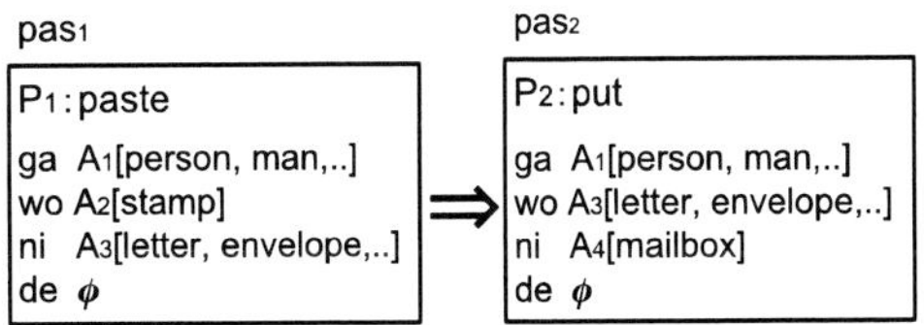

Figure 1: Event relation knowledge with shared arguments.[1]

predicate and its relevant arguments. In addition, we define one unit of event relation knowledge to be a pair of successive events with one or more shared arguments. Figure 1 represents an example of event relation knowledge, which consists of two events, pas_1 and pas_2.

The shared arguments correspond to the common participants of the two events, such as A_1 and A_3 in the above example. These shared arguments play an important role in the application of event relation knowledge since they encode the correspondence relations between case slots within a piece of event relation knowledge.

In this paper, we aim to improve the shared argument identification in Japanese event relation knowledge. Event relation knowledge acquisition in Japanese is a much more challenging task than its counterpart of English, due to several linguistic properties of Japanese. For example:

(1)   a. John attached a stamp to the letter, and he dropped it into the mailbox.

      b. John attached a stamp to the letter, and (ϕ_{he}) dropped (ϕ_{letter}) into the mailbox.

In the above example, (1-b) is the Japanese correspondence of (1-a), directly translated into English. We can observe that Japanese has an abundance of omitted arguments. In addition, Japanese lacks linguistic clues regarding the accordance in gender, number, etc., such as 'he' and 'it' in (1-a).

These linguistic properties hinder the performance of Japanese coreference resolution sys-

---

[1]In this paper we adopt the Japanese case marker, ga, wo, ni, and de, which roughly corresponds to nominative, accusative, dative, and instrumental/locative cases.

Proceedings of the Events and Stories in the News Workshop, pages 21–30,
Vancouver, Canada, August 4, 2017. ©2017 Association for Computational Linguistics

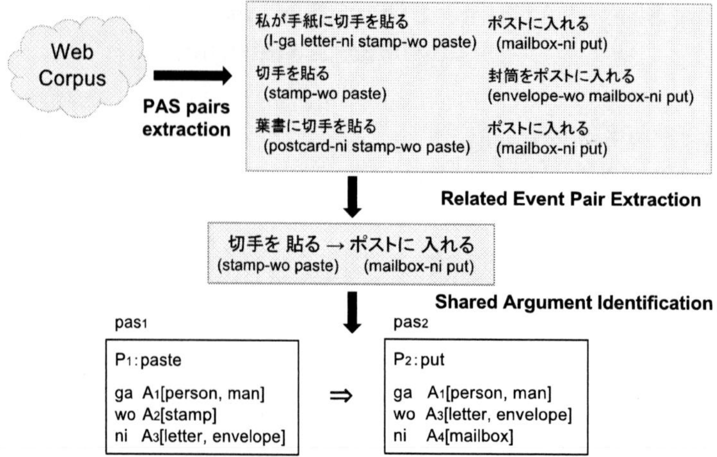

Figure 2: Two-stage approach for Japanese event relation knowledge acquisition.

tems, and make it unsuitable to apply coreference-based methods of English event relation knowledge acquisition (Chambers and Jurafsky, 2008) directly to Japanese.

On the other hand, event relation knowledge can benefit the task of the coreference resolution. The shared arguments within an event relation knowledge provide direct clues that the case slots sharing an argument should hold co-referring arguments. These clues are particularly critical in cases in which selectional preference is not helpful, such as coreference resolution problems presented in Winograd Schema Challenge (Levesque et al., 2012; Rahman and Ng, 2012). Consider the following example:

(2) a. グーグルが モトローラ を買収した。
    彼ら が破綻したからだ。
    (Google-ga acquired Motorola-wo, be-cause they-ga went bankrupt.)
   b. A_1-ga go bankrupt → A_2-ga A_1-wo acquire

In the example of (2-a), both precedents of 'they', 'Google' and 'Motorola', are of the same category. While selectional preference is not helpful in this case, the event relation knowledge in (2-b) can help us resolve (2-a) correctly.

In this work, we adopted the two-stage framework for Japanese event relation knowledge acquisition (Shibata and Kurohashi, 2011). In the first stage of related event pair extraction, we adopted the method proposed by Shibata and Kurohashi (2011); and in the second stage of shared argument identification, we extended the model of Kohama et al. (2015) to incorporate all types of

shared arguments in our gold dataset. We designed a richer feature representation for shared argument learning, which considers the interaction between shared arguments and the mechanism of argument omission in depth.

In addition, we manually constructed a gold dataset for shared argument learning. With the help of linguistic experts, we established an annotation scheme for shared argument. We classified the shared arguments into three types: standard shared argument, quasi shared argument, and multiple shared argument. We evaluated our method of shared argument identification on the gold dataset. By comparing our proposed methods with several baseline models, we observed a significant improvement for shared argument identification.

2   Related Work

As a resource-rich language, coreference resolution of English has achieved a satisfying performance. Thus, several works which utilize coreference information were proposed for English event relation knowledge acquisition.

Chambers and Jurafsky (2008) introduced the concept of narrative event chains as a representation of structured event relation knowledge. Their method utilizes the coreference chains within the input text to collect events involving the same entity, which they called the *protagonist*. Among the set of events involving the same entity, event sequences that are observed a significant number of times are extracted as typical event sequences.

pas_1		pas_2	Support sentences
切手を貼る (stamp-wo paste)	→	ポストに入れる (mailbox-ni put)	親宛に書いた葉書きに切手を貼ってポストに入れた。 (I pasted a stamp on the postcard to my parents, and put it into the mailbox.) 手紙を書いて、封をして、切手を貼って、ポストに入れる。 (I write a letter, seal it, paste a stamp, and put it into the mailbox.)
薬を飲む (medicine-wo take)	→	症状が軽くなる (symptom-ga alleviate)	薬を飲み続けていると、アレルギーの症状は大分軽くなってきている。 (Taking the medicine alleviates the allergy symptom significantly.) 抗ヒスタミン系の薬を処方され、飲めば症状は軽くなります。 (I was prescribed antihistamine, the symptom alleviated after taking it.)

Table 1: Related Event Pairs.

Pichotta and Mooney (2014) used a richer representation of event than in the work of Chambers et al. and achieved an improvement in predicting performance. Instead of representing an event as a (predicate, dependency) pair, they considered an event as a structure of a predicate and arguments with subject, object, direct object relations with the predicate. With this multi-argument event representation, their model performs better in the cases of ambiguous verbs, and is more capable of capturing complex interactions between multiple entities.

There are several works proposed for Japanese event relation knowledge acquisition utilizing the co-occurrences of events. Abe et al. (2008) proposed a pattern-based method which utilized a predefined set of lexico-syntactic co-occurrence patterns to perform bootstrapping for event relation learning. Their work focused on the acquisition of related event pairs, but not the relations between the arguments of the related events.

Shibata and Kurohashi (2011) proposed a two-stage approach for Japanese event relation knowledge acquisition (Figure 2). In the first stage, related event pairs are extracted from large-scale corpora by association rule mining. In the second stage, shared arguments of the event pairs are identified heuristically based on case slot similarity scores.

Kohama et al. (2015) improved the work of Shibata and Kurohashi (2011) by utilizing crowd-sourced data for shared argument learning. They proposed a joint model that simultaneously predicts the shared argument configuration and disambiguates the meaning of the predicates. However, their work failed to identify the shared arguments accurately for two reasons. First, the crowd-sourced data they used is very noisy and lacks a well-defined standard of labeling. Second, the features used in their model are not sufficient for capturing the characteristics of shared arguments.

3 Shared Argument Identification

In this section, we introduce our method of shared argument identification. In Section 3.1, we first introduce the acquisition of related event pairs, which are the inputs to our shared argument identification model. We introduce the gold dataset used for model learning in Section 3.2. In Section 3.3, we describe the selection of case frames. These case frames will be used to model different meanings of predicates in our model. The remaining of the section will be dedicated to the description of our proposed methods of shared argument identification.

3.1 Related Event Pairs

Our work is based on the two-stage framework of event relation knowledge proposed by Shibata and Kurohashi (2011). We adopt the first stage of related event pair extraction proposed in their work to obtain the related event pairs, which will be the input to our shared argument identification model.

Here, we briefly describe the first stage of related event pair extraction. Starting from the web corpus, we first extract the PAS pairs with syntactic dependency, and use the Apriori algorithm to pick out the related event pairs efficiently (Figure 2). In order to improve the quality of the extracted event pairs, we apply an additional filtering step based on the clause relations between event pairs as suggested in Kohama et al. (2015).

Table 1 shows several examples of related event pairs extracted in this process. Each event pair R consists of two PASs, pas_1 and pas_2, and the sentences containing both pas_1 and pas_2 are regarded as the support sentences of R. These support sentences contain many valuable clues for the task of shared argument identification. Thus, the event pair R along with its support sentences will serve as the input to our shared argument identification model.

Type	Event Pair	Shared Argument
Standard	切手を 手紙に 貼る → 手紙を ポストに 入れる (stamp-wo <u>letter-ni</u> paste) (<u>letter-wo</u> mailbox-ni put)	n-w
Quasi	牛を 飼う→ 牛乳で チーズを作る (<u>cow-wo</u> raise) (<u>milk-de</u> cheese-wo make)	w-d'
Multiple	観光客が 町を/に 訪れる→ 町が 賑わう (tourist-ga <u>town-wo/ni</u> visit) (<u>town-ga</u> be crowded)	w/n-g

Table 2: Types of Shared Arguments.

Type	Shared Argument	Standard Shared Argument Set
Standard	$n\text{-}w$	$\{n\text{-}w\}$
Quasi	$w\text{-}d$'	$\{w\text{-}d,\ \phi\}$
Multiple	$n\text{-}n/w$	$\{n\text{-}n,\ n\text{-}w\}$

Table 3: Transforming different types of shared arguments to their standard shared argument sets.

3.2 Gold Dataset

We manually constructed a gold dataset for learning shared argument identification model. In this work, we train and evaluate our proposed model on this gold dataset.

This dataset contains 809 related event pairs, with each of the event pair annotated with its shared argument configuration. Three annotators with linguistic background participated in the construction of this dataset.

Type of Shared Arguments

The gold dataset contains the following types of shared arguments (Table 2):

1. **Standard Shared Argument**:
   The arguments shared between one case slot of the first event and another case slot of the second event. This type of shared argument represents the fact that arguments of the two cases should correspond to an identical real world entity.

   In this work, we only consider the four main cases of ga (が), wo (を), ni (に), and de (で). From now on, we use the shorthand notation of g, w, n, and d to represent these four main cases. The first example in Table 2 has a standard shared argument between the first ni-case and the second wo-case, which both correspond to the entity 'letter'. we use the notation $n\text{-}w$ to represent it.

2. **Quasi Shared Argument**:
   Quasi shared argument is a pair of arguments which are closely related to each other in the context of the given event relation knowledge. As can be seen from the example in Table 2, the arguments of the first wo-case

and the second de-case are 'cow' and 'milk', respectively. These two arguments are considered to be closely related since the milk in the context corresponds to the specific milk which is produced by the cow in the same context.

We attached an apostrophe (') to denote a quasi shared argument.

3. **Multiple Shared Argument**:
   Multiple shared argument occurs when more than two case slots share the same argument. As can be seen from the example in Table 2, the argument 'town' is shared between three cases: wo-case or ni-case of the first event, and the ga-case of the second event.

We use the symbol '/' to separate different case slots of the same predicate which share arguments.

Preprocessing of Gold dataset

In this work, we only focus on the identification of standard shared arguments. For utilizing the gold dataset with other shared argument types, we perform a pre-processing to the gold annotation before model training. We transform each shared argument configuration into its corresponding standard configuration set.

First, we define the corresponding standard shared argument set for each shared argument in the following manner (Table 3):

1. For each standard shared argument, we transform it into the standard shared argument set containing only itself.

2. For each quasi shared argument, we transform it into the standard shared argument set containing a null shared argument (ϕ) and its

Shared Argument Configuration	Standard Configuration Set
$[g\text{-}g]$	$\{[g\text{-}g]\}$
$[g\text{-}g \; w\text{-}d']$	$\{[g\text{-}g, \; w\text{-}d], \; [g\text{-}g]\}$
$[g\text{-}g \; n\text{-}n/w]$	$\{[g\text{-}g, \; n\text{-}n], \; [g\text{-}g, \; n\text{-}w]\}$
$[g\text{-}g \; w\text{-}d' \; n\text{-}n/w]$	$\{[g\text{-}g, \; n\text{-}n], \; [g\text{-}g, \; n\text{-}w], \; [g\text{-}g, \; n\text{-}n, \; w\text{-}d], \; [g\text{-}g, \; n\text{-}w, \; w\text{-}d]\}$

Table 4: Transforming shared argument configuration to corresponding standard configuration set.

standard counterpart in which all the apostrophe (') mark is removed. See the second example in Table 3.

3. For each multiple shared argument, we transform it into the standard shared argument set containing all the shared arguments that could be entailed from it. See the third example in Table 3.

For a given shared argument configuration, we first transform each of its containing shared argument into its corresponding standard shared argument set in the above manner. By taking the product of these standard shared argument sets, we obtain the corresponding standard configuration set of the shared argument configuration. See Table 4 for examples.

3.3 Case Frame Selection

Selectional preferences provide important clues for the task of share argument identification. Case frames are good sources of selectional preference information, and it handles the issue of predicate ambiguity by clustering the usage of each predicate by their meanings. In turn, the meaning of a case frame is represented by the argument distribution in each case slot of its corresponding case frame.

In this work, we consider wide-coverage case frames constructed automatically from a huge raw corpus as the source of selectional preference information (Hayashibe et al., 2015). For each event pair $R(pas_1 \rightarrow pas_2)$, we select 10 relevant case frames for both pas_1 and pas_2 by utilizing the supporting sentences S of R. Here, we describe the method for selecting relevant case frames for each event pair, which are used in our proposed models.

Given a case frame cf, we denote the bag-of-words (BoW) representation of arguments within each case slot of cf as follows:

$$V^g, V^w, V^n, V^d$$

We denote the BoW representation of arguments appearing in the corresponding case slots of the support sentences S as follows:

$$U^g, U^w, U^n, U^d$$

We define the relevance score of cf with respect to R as follows:

$$rel(cf, R) = \sum_{x=\{g,w,n,d\}} cos(U^x, V^x) \quad (1)$$

which is the sum of cosine similarity scores between the BoW representation of case slots in the four main cases.

Finally, we rank all the case frames in descending order with respect to relevance score and take the top 10 of them as relevant case frames. Table 5 represents the first five relevant case frames of the predicate 訪れる (visit) of the following event pair:

$$観光客が訪れる \rightarrow 賑わう$$
(tourist-ga visit $\rightarrow$ be crowded)

3.4 Joint Prediction of Shared Argument and Case Frame

As mentioned in Section 3.3, case frames provide important information of selectional preferences. However, the gold data does not provide the appropriate case frame of each predicate. To tackle this problem, we propose a model of shared argument identification that simultaneously predicts the appropriate case frame for each predicate.

Model

We adopt a maximum entropy (MaxEnt) classifier model.

Given a related event pair $R(pas_1 \rightarrow pas_2)$ and its supporting sentences S, the conditional probability of a shared argument configuration $\mathbb{A}$ and case frame pair cf_1, cf_2 is modeled as:

$$P(\mathbb{A}, cf_1, cf_2 | R, S; \mathbf{w}) = \frac{exp\{\mathbf{w} \cdot \phi(\mathbb{A}, cf_1, cf_2, R, S)\}}{Z}$$
$$(2)$$

In the above equation, $\phi(\mathbb{A}, cf_1, cf_2, R, S)$ is the feature representation of the shared argument configuration, $\mathbf{w}$ is the model parameter, and Z is the normalization constant. In Table 6 we summarized the features used, under the example of shared argument $n\text{-}w$.

Rank	Case Frame	Relevance Score
1	[観光客, 人] が [地, 日本] を [実際] に 訪れる [tourist, person]-ga [place, Japan]-wo [practically]-ni visit	0.966
2	[数人, 人] が [事務所, 京都] を [激励, 視察] に 訪れる [people, person]-ga [office, Kyoto]-wo [encourage,inspection]-ni visit	0.807
3	[観光客, 大統領] が [中国, 台湾] を [視察, 見学] に 訪れる [tourist, president]-ga [China, Taiwan]-wo [inspection, field trip]-ni visit	0.760
4	[客, 観光客] が [店, ショップ] を [目当, 実際] に 訪れる [guest, tourist]-ga [store, shop]-wo [goal, practically]-ni visit	0.748
5	[人, 観光客] が [博物館, 美術館] を [見学] に 訪れる [person, tourist]-ga [museum, art museum]-wo [field trip]-ni visit	0.742

Table 5: Relevant case frames of 訪れる (visit).

Feature	Description
Configuration	Binary feature indicating the existence of the shared argument n-w.
Post-predicate	Binary feature indicating the existence of argument in w case of pas_2.
Core	Binary features indicating if n case of cf_1 and w case of cf_2 are core cases. If a case slot takes argument in more than 10% of the time in the selected case frame, we define it as a core case.
Case slot similarity	The cosine similarity between the vocabulary distribution of n case of cf_1 and w case of cf_2.
Normalized case slot similarity	Case slot similarity of n-w normalized over the similarities of all case slots of cf_1. Same for cf_2.
Conflict	The ratio of support sentences in S that holds different arguments in the first n case and the second w case.
Context	We collect words that appear in S but not within the event pair as context words. We calculate the relative probability of each context word to appear in the first n case compared to other main cases, and similar for the second w case. A tf-idf weighted sum of this probability is added as feature.

Table 6: Features for shared argument n-w.

Prediction

During the prediction phase, the shared argument configuration $\hat{\mathbb{A}}$ and case frame pair $\hat{cf_1}, \hat{cf_2}$ that gives the highest probability is chosen:

$$(\hat{\mathbb{A}}, \hat{cf_1}, \hat{cf_2}) = \underset{\mathbb{A},cf_1,cf_2}{\mathrm{argmax}} P(\mathbb{A}, cf_1, cf_2 | R, S; \mathbf{w}) \tag{3}$$

For each related event pair R, we choose 10 relevant case frames for each predicate of concern as candidate of cf_1 and cf_2, as described in Section 3.3.

Model Training

In the training phase, the most probable case frame pair $(\hat{cf_1}, \hat{cf_2})$ and the model parameter $\mathbf{w}$ are updated alternatively. Also, the most probable gold configuration $\hat{g}$ among the standard configuration set is also updated along with the case frame pair.

The training algorithm is summarized below:

1. Initialize model parameter $\mathbf{w}$ randomly.

2. Use the current parameter $\mathbf{w}$ to update the most probable gold configuration and the most probable case frame pair $(\hat{g}, \hat{cf_1}, \hat{cf_2})$:

$$\hat{g}, \hat{cf_1}, \hat{cf_2} = \underset{g,cf_1,cf_2}{\mathrm{argmax}} P(g, cf_1, cf_2 | R, S; \mathbf{w}) \tag{4}$$

3. Use $(\hat{g}, \hat{cf_1}, \hat{cf_2})$ to update model parameter $\mathbf{w}$. The following is the objective function, in which the superscripts of g, cf_1, and cf_2 denote the id of the event pairs, and N is the total number of training objects:

$$L = \sum_{n=1}^{N} logP(g^{(n)}, cf_1^{(n)}, cf_2^{(n)} | R, S; \mathbf{w}) - \alpha\|w\|^2 \tag{5}$$

$$\hat{\mathbf{w}} = \underset{\mathbf{w}}{\mathrm{argmax}} L \tag{6}$$

(Hyper-parameter α is set to 1.0.)

4. Back to 2 until convergence. The convergence condition is that the most probable $(\hat{g}, \hat{cf_1}, \hat{cf_2})$ for all event pairs are the same as the previous iteration. If the convergence condition is not satisfied after 15 iterations, we terminate the training process.

3.5 Shared Argument Learning with Combined Case Frame

Here, we introduce another model for learning shared arguments which uses the combined case frames.

The joint reference model (Section 3.4) picks exactly one case frame for each predicate. On the other hand, the combined case frame model combines the relevant case frames by taking the weighed sum of them by the relevance scores with respect to the event pair. This method does not decide the most appropriate case frame of each predicate. Instead, all of the relevant case frames are considered, and case frames with higher relevance scores have larger influence on the feature representation.

Combined Case Frame

A combined case frame is obtained by combining the relevant case frames according to their relevance scores. The calculation of the relevance scores of each case frame is described in Section 3.3.

Given a set of relevant case frames CF, we defined the combined case frame $\widetilde{cf}$ as follows:

$$\widetilde{cf} : \widetilde{V^g}, \widetilde{V^w}, \widetilde{V^n}, \widetilde{V^d} \tag{7}$$

$$\widetilde{V^x} = \sum_{cf \in CF} rel(cf, R) \times V_{cf}^x, \forall x \in \{g, w, n, d\} \tag{8}$$

in which V_{cf}^x is the vocabulary distribution vector of cf.

Model

Similar to the joint prediction model presented in section 3.4, we adopt a MaxEnt classifier model. Given an event pair $R(pas_1 \rightarrow pas_2)$ and its supporting sentences S, we model the conditional probability of shared argument configuration $\mathbb{A}$ as:

$$P(\mathbb{A}|R, S; \mathbf{w}) = \frac{exp\{\mathbf{w} \cdot \phi(\mathbb{A}, \widetilde{cf_1}, \widetilde{cf_2}, R, S)\}}{Z} \tag{9}$$

In the above equation, ϕ is the feature representation as summarized in Table 6, $\mathbf{w}$ is the model parameter, and Z is the normalization constant.

The training algorithm is similar to the one described in Section 3.4. In the training phase, the most probable gold configuration $\hat{g}$ and the model parameter $\mathbf{w}$ are updated alternatively until convergence.

4 Experiments

4.1 Settings

The case frames used in the experiments are built from a web corpus of four billion sentences, with the method proposed by Hayashibe et al. (2015).

We use Classias (Okazaki, 2009) as the implementation of maximum entropy classifier and L-BFGS (Nocedal, 1980) as the optimization algorithm for learning. We train and evaluate our proposed models by a 5-fold cross-validation test on the gold shared argument dataset.

4.2 Evaluation and Result

We apply three evaluation metrics: precision, recall, and F-score (F_1) for the evaluation of our shared argument identification models.

Model	Precision	Recall	F_1
Baseline[g-g]	0.731	0.717	0.724
Baseline[Kohama+15]	0.729	0.733	0.731
Joint	0.747	**0.786**	**0.766**
Combined	**0.753**	0.748	0.750

Table 7: Evaluation result.

We compared our proposed models with two baseline models. The first baseline model, denoted as Baseline[g-g] in Table 7, is the majority classifier which gives the output of g-g regardless of the event pair given. The second baseline model, denoted as Baseline[Kohama+15], is the model proposed by Kohama et al. (2015).

The experiment results are summarized in Table 7. In addition, several event relation knowledge acquired are shown in Table 8.

4.3 Discussion

Comparison with Baseline Models

As can be observed from Table 7, both of our proposed models outperformed the baseline models by a large margin.

Compared to the model proposed by Kohama et al. (2015), we use a richer feature representation for shared argument configuration. In their work, a shared argument is represented by the vocabulary distribution similarity between two case slots, such as the similarity between case frames, or the similarity between arguments in the supporting sentences. However, by considering only the distributional similarities between two case slots, their method overlooked two important intrinsic properties of the shared argument identification task:

Event Pair	Gold Annotation	System Output	Error Type
熟成させる→出荷される (ripen) (ship)	w-g	w-g	-
ジュースが安くなる→買う (juice-ga become cheaper) (buy)	g-w	g-w	-
肌に与える→若返らせる (skin-ni give) (rejuvenate)	w/g-g n-w	g-g n-w	-
切手を貼る→ポストに入れる (stamp-wo paste) (mailbox-ni put)	g-g n-w	g-g	1
迫害される→殺される (suffer persecution) (be killed)	g-g n-n	n-g	2
明るくなる→太陽が顔を出す (become brighter) (sun-ga face-wo appear)	ϕ	g-w	3

Table 8: Evaluation results of the proposed and baseline models for shared argument identification.

Case	Arguments
ga	私, 誰, 人, ママ, 夫, 自分, 母, .. (I, who, people, mom, self, mother, ..)
wo	茶, 私, 子供, 花, 模様, .., 手紙, .., 封筒, .. (tea, I, child, flower, pattern, .., <u>letter</u>, .., envelope, ..)
ni	中, 風呂, 部屋, 手, 家, ポスト, .. (interior, bathroom, room, hand, house, mailbox)
de	〈数量〉+人, 〈時間〉, 急須, 白, 湯, 鉛筆, .. (〈number〉+people, 〈time〉, teapot, white, hot water, pencil)

Table 9: Example of bad case frame

1. Interaction of shared arguments:
   Different pieces of shared arguments are not independent, and shared arguments that share a case slot have repulsive effects on each other. For example, if a shared argument configuration already includes g-g, then it would be unlikely that g-w also exists in the same configuration. We add the normalized case slot similarity feature which considers not only the case slot similarity of a pair of case slots, but also the relative similarity of them, to account for this property.

2. The mechanism of argument omission in related event pairs:
   High vocabulary distribution similarity indicates the existence of shared arguments, but not vice versa. Consider the following example:

   <u>ジュースが</u> 安くなる→ <u>ジュースを</u> 買う
   (<u>juice-ga</u> become cheaper → <u>juice-wo</u> buy)

   Although there exists a shared argument of g-w, the vocabulary distributions of the two corresponding case slots are quite different. To address this property, we add the context feature which considers each context word and the relative probability of them to appear in each of the main case slots.

Comparison Between Proposed Models

The major difference between the two proposed models lies in how case frames for feature construction are decided.

As can be observed from Table 7, the joint prediction model achieved a better F-score than the combined case frame model. We conclude that deciding one best case frame is a better way for modeling the selectional preference of a predicate, compared to combining case frames with respect to the relevance scores. The result also verified the effectiveness of the joint model of case frames and shared arguments.

Error Analysis

In the following are several patterns of error observed in the system output. Examples of each error type are presented in Table 8.

1. **Error due to case frame granularity (Error Type 1):**
   Our proposed model jointly predicts the most appropriate case frame along with the shared argument configuration. By selecting a single case frame for each predicate, we are able to model the selectional preference of the predicates accurately. However, the automatically constructed case frames do not always provide the granularity suitable for our task. If a coarse-grained case frame is selected dur-

ing prediction phase, the prediction of shared argument will also be affected.

For the example shown in Table 8, an appropriate case frame of the second predicate 'put' should contain words that supports n-w shared argument in the wo-case. Table 9 represents the most appropriate case frame of the predicate 'put' among all the case frames of this predicate. It can be observed that although the wo-case contains words relevant to the n-w shared argument, such as 'letter' and 'envelope', there are other irrelevant words dominating this case. These kind of broad, somewhat noisy case frames hinder the performance of our shared argument identification model.

2. **Error due to event participants with similar characteristics (Error Type 2):**
Our method relies largely on selectional preference information for identifying shared arguments. Thus, the prediction performance of our system is not very good for event pairs containing multiple participants with similar characteristics.

For the example shown in Table 8, our model wrongly identified the shared argument n-g. Although both cases are expected to hold human participants, the entity in the first ni-case should correspond to the victim of both actions 'persecute' and 'kill', while the second ga-case should hold the entity of the perpetrator of the two actions. In the scenario of the above event pair, there are two participants of similar characteristics, which are both expected to be human. Since selectional preference cannot effectively distinguish between these similar participants, our model often has difficulty dealing with event pairs with multiple similar participants.

3. **Error due to fixed expression (Error Type 3)**
In a fixed expression, an argument often takes on a different meaning than it usually does. Fixed expressions within events sometimes cause problems in shared argument identification. For the example shown in Table 8, the system output is as follows:

顔が 明るくなる→太陽が 顔を 出す

(face-ga become brighter → sun-ga <u>face-wo</u> appear)

Independently, both PASs shown above are plausible. However, the first PAS, 'face-ga become brighter', means showing a cheerful look; while the second PAS, 'sun-ga face-wo appear', means sun rising. Although both expression contains the argument 'face', the shared argument of g-w does not exist.

5 Conclusion

This paper proposed a method for shared argument identification in event relation knowledge acquisition. By addressing several problems of the previous works, we improved the shared argument identification model significantly. We proposed a richer feature representation of shared argument configuration which is more suitable for model learning. In order to incorporate different types of shared argument in the gold dataset, we update the most appropriate gold configuration along with case frames during the training process. We evaluated our model on a manually annotated gold dataset, and our model outperformed the baseline models by a large margin.

Our proposed model jointly predicts the shared argument configuration and the appropriate case frames. By comparing the result of our proposed model with the combined case frame model, we verified the effectiveness of this joint model to predict the appropriate case frames.

References

Shuya Abe, Kentaro Inui, and Yuji Matsumoto. 2008. Acquiring event relation knowledge by learning cooccurrence patterns and fertilizing cooccurrence samples. *Proceedings of the 3rd International Joint Conference on Natural Language Processing* pages 479–504.

Nathanael Chambers and Dan Jurafsky. 2008. Unsupervised learning of narrative event chains. In *Proceedings of the 46th Annual Meeting of the Association of Computational Linguistics*. Association for Computational Linguistics, Columbus, Ohio, pages 789–797.

Yuta Hayashibe, Daisuke Kawahara, and Sadao Kurohashi. 2015. Japanese case frame construction considering varieties of case patterns. Technical report.

Shotaro Kohama, Tomohide Shibata, and Sadao Kurohashi. 2015. Argument alignment learning in event knowledge. In *Proceedings of the 21th Annual Meeting of the Association for Natural Language Processing (In Japanese)*. Association for Natural Language Processing, Kyoto, Japan, pages 1065–1067.

Hector Levesque, Ernest Davis, and Leora Morgenstern. 2012. The winograd schema challenge. In *13th International Conference on the Principles of Knowledge Representation and Reasoning*. Association for the Advancement of Artificial Intelligence, pages 552–561.

Jorge Nocedal. 1980. Updating quasi-newton matrices with limited storage. *Mathematics of computation* 35(151):773–782.

Naoaki Okazaki. 2009. Classias: a collection of machine-learning algorithms for classification.

Karl Pichotta and Raymond Mooney. 2014. Statistical script learning with multi-argument events. In *Proceedings of the 14th Conference of the European Chapter of the Association for Computational Linguistics*. Association for Computational Linguistics, Gothenburg, Sweden, pages 220–229.

Altaf Rahman and Vincent Ng. 2012. Resolving complex cases of definite pronouns: The winograd schema challenge. In *Proceedings of the 2012 Joint Conference on Empirical Methods in Natural Language Processing and Computational Natural Language Learning*. Association for Computational Linguistics, Jeju Island, Korea, pages 777–789.

Tomohide Shibata and Sadao Kurohashi. 2011. Acquiring strongly-related events using predicate-argument co-occurring statistics and case frames. In *Proceedings of 5th International Joint Conference on Natural Language Processing*. Asian Federation of Natural Language Processing, Chiang Mai, Thailand, pages 1028–1036.

Tracing armed conflicts with diachronic word embedding models

Andrey Kutuzov
Department of Informatics
University of Oslo
andreku@ifi.uio.no

Erik Velldal
Department of Informatics
University of Oslo
erikve@ifi.uio.no

Lilja Øvrelid
Department of Informatics
University of Oslo
liljao@ifi.uio.no

Abstract

Recent studies have shown that word embedding models can be used to trace time-related (diachronic) semantic shifts for particular words. In this paper, we evaluate some of these approaches on the new task of predicting the dynamics of global armed conflicts on a year-to-year basis, using a dataset from the field of conflict research as the gold standard and the Gigaword news corpus as the training data. The results show that much work still remains in extracting 'cultural' semantic shifts from diachronic word embedding models. At the same time, we present a new task complete with an evaluation set and introduce the 'anchor words' method which outperforms previous approaches on this data.

1 Introduction

Several recent studies have investigated how distributional word embeddings can be used for modeling language change, and particularly lexical semantic shifts. This includes tracing perspective change through time, usually for periods equal to centuries or decades; see (Hamilton et al., 2016b) among others. One of the main problems in these studies is the lack of proper ground truth resources describing the degree and direction of semantic change for particular words. Unfortunately, there is no such manually compiled compendium of all the semantic shifts that English words underwent in the last two centuries. The problem is even more severe for studies using more fine-grained time units spanning days or years, rather than decades, like in (Kulkarni et al., 2015) or (Kutuzov and Kuzmenko, 2016): When trying to uncover subtle changes of perspective (for example, *'Trump'*

moving towards being associated with *'president'* rather than *'millionaire'*), it is difficult to find gold standard annotations for rigorous evaluation of the proposed methods.

In this paper, we make use of a social science dataset which to the best of our knowledge has not been introduced in the NLP field before. This dataset is described in section 3 and comprises a manually annotated history of armed conflicts starting from 1946 up to now. Together with word embedding models trained on temporal slices of the *Gigaword* news corpus (Parker et al., 2011), this allows us to properly evaluate several methods for tracing semantic shifts. We monitor changes in the local semantic neighborhoods of country names, applying it to the downstream task of predicting changes in the state of conflict for 52 countries at the year-level. This is essentially a classification task with 3 classes:

1. Nothing has changed in the country conflict state year-to-year (class **'stable'**);

2. Armed conflicts have escalated in the country year-to-year (class **'war'**);

3. Armed conflicts have calmed down in the country year-to-year (class **'peace'**).

The results of this evaluation provide some insights into the performance of current semantic shift detection techniques and describe the best combinations of hyperparameters. We also propose the 'anchor words' method and show that it outperforms previous approaches when applied to this classification task.

2 Related work

Significant results have already been achieved in employing word embeddings to study diachronic

Proceedings of the Events and Stories in the News Workshop, pages 31–36,
Vancouver, Canada, August 4, 2017. ©2017 Association for Computational Linguistics

language change. Hamilton et al. (2016a) proposed an important distinction between cultural shifts and linguistic drifts. They showed that global embedding-based measures, like comparing the similarities of words to all other words in the lexicon in (Eger and Mehler, 2016), are sensitive to regular processes of linguistic drift, while local measures (comparing restricted lists of nearest associates) are a better fit for more irregular cultural shifts in word meaning. We here follow this latter path, because our downstream task (detecting armed conflicts dynamics from semantic representations of country names) certainly presupposes cultural shifts in the associations for these country names (not a real change of dictionary meaning). Additionally, local neighborhood measures of change are more sensitive to nouns, which makes them even better for our purpose.

It is important to note that in (Hamilton et al., 2016b) and other previous work on the subject, proper names were mostly filtered out: their authors were interested in more global semantic shifts for common nouns. In contrast to this, for the practical task of monitoring news streams, we here make proper names (countries and other toponyms) our main target. We are mostly interested in what is happening to this or that named entity, not in whether there were subtle changes in the meaning of some common noun. Another difference between the previous work and ours is that our time span is much smaller: not decades but years.

3 Data description

In this section we provide some background on the conflict dataset that forms the basis of our experiments, and the modifications we have applied to extract the gold standard to evaluate diachronic embeddings models.

The UCDP/PRIO Armed Conflict Dataset[1] maintained by the Uppsala Conflict Data Program[2] and the Peace Research Institute Oslo[3] is a manually annotated geographical and temporal dataset with information on armed conflicts, in the time period from 1946 to the present (Gleditsch et al., 2002). It encodes both internal and external conflicts, where at least one party is the government of a state. The Armed Conflict Dataset is widely used in conflict research; thus, this can be the beginning of a fruitful collaboration between social scientists and computational linguists.

The collection of the dataset started in the mid-1980s under the name *Conflict Data Project*, but has since then evolved constantly. In the autumn of 2003 the amount of work on conflict data collection led to a change in the name of the project and it was thus turned into the *Uppsala Conflict Data Program*.

An essential notion in the UCDP project is that of *armed conflict*, defined as 'a contested incompatibility concerning government and/or territory where the use of armed force between 2 parties results in at least 25 battle-related deaths' (Sundberg and Melander, 2013). Note that *armed force* here means the use of arms in order to promote the parties general position in the conflict, resulting in deaths. In turn, *arms* means any material means, e.g. manufactured weapons but also sticks, stones, fire, water etc. *Organized actor* can mean a government of an independent state, or a formally or informally organized group according to UCDP criteria [Ibid.].

The subset of the data that we employ is the *UCDP Conflict Termination dataset*.[4] It contains entries on starting and ending dates of about 2000 conflicts. We limited ourselves to the conflicts taking place between 1994 and 2010. We omitted the conflicts where both sides were governments (about 2% of the entries), for example, the 1998 conflict between India and Pakistan in Kashmir. The reason for this is that with these entries, distributional models have a hard time telling the name of the state (conflict actor) from the name of the territory (conflict location). Thus, we analyzed only the conflicts between a government and an insurgent armed group of some kind (these conflicts constitute the majority of the UCDP dataset anyway).

Another group of the omitted conflicts is where at least one of the sides was mentioned in the full *Gigaword* less than 100 times. The rationale for this decision was that these conflicts have too little contextual coverage in the corpus for our models to learn meaningful representations for them. These cases constitute about 1% of the entries.

In total, the resulting test set mentions 52 unique

---

[1]http://ucdp.uu.se/

[2]http://www.pcr.uu.se/research/ucdp/program_overview/about_ucdp/

[3]https://www.prio.org/Data/Armed-Conflict

[4]http://www.ucdp.uu.se/downloads/monadterm/ucdp-term-conf-2015.xlsx

locations and 673 unique armed conflicts. It also includes the UCDP intensity level of the conflict in the current year: 493 conflicts are tagged with the intensity level 1 (between 25 and 999 battle-related deaths), and 180 conflicts with the intensity level 2 (at least 1,000 battle-related deaths). For location–year pairs with no records in the UCDP dataset we assign the tag 0, indicating that there were no armed conflicts in this location at that time.

We then represented this data as a set of data points equal to the *differences* (δ) between the location's conflict state in the current year and in the previous year, 832 points in total (52 locations $\times$ 16 years). If there were several conflicts in the location in this particular year, we used the average of their intensities. As an example, for Congo, the transition from 2001 to 2002 was accompanied by the ending of armed conflicts. Thus, for the data point 'congo_2002' we have $\delta = 0 - 1 = -1$. Then, there were no changes (each new δ has the value of 0) until 2006, when armed conflicts resumed with the intensity of 1. Thus, for the 'congo_2006' data point, $\delta = 1 - 0 = 1$.

However, for practical reasons it is more useful to predict a human-interpretable class of the conflict state change, rather than a scalar value. A version of this test set was produced where δ values were transformed to classes:

$$class = \begin{cases} war & \text{if } \delta \geq 0.5 \\ peace & \text{if } \delta \leq -0.5 \\ stable & \text{otherwise} \end{cases}$$

The 'shifting' classes **War** and **Peace** constitute 10% and 11% of the data points respectively. Thus, they are minority classes and we are mostly interested in how good the evaluated models are in predicting them. Below we describe the evaluated approaches.

4 Evaluated approaches

For training distributional word embedding models, we employed the *Continuous Bag-of-Words*[5] algorithm proposed in (Mikolov et al., 2013), as implemented in the Gensim toolkit (Řehůřek and Sojka, 2010). This was chosen because it allows us to straightforwardly update the models incrementally with new data, unlike, for example,

with *GloVe* (Pennington et al., 2014) or traditional PPMI+SVD matrices.

4.1 Representing time in the models

As we are dealing with temporal data, we experiment with different methods for representing chronological information in word embedding models. All *Gigaword* texts are annotated with publishing date, so it is trivial to compile yearly corpora starting from 1994. Then, we trained three sets of word embedding models, differing in the way they represent time:

1. yearly models, each trained from scratch on the corpora containing news texts from a particular year only (dubbed **separate** hereafter);

2. yearly models trained from scratch on the texts from the particular year and all the previous years (**cumulative** hereafter);

3. incrementally trained models (**incremental**).

The last type is most interesting: here we actually 'update' one and the same model with new data, expanding the vocabulary if needed. Our hypothesis was that this can help coping with the inherently stochastic nature of predictive distributional models. However, this turned out to be not entirely true (see Section 5).

4.2 Detecting and quantifying semantic shifts

Once the sets of models are there, one can detect semantic shifts in a given query word w_q (in our case, always a location name), with two major existing approaches:

1. align two models (current and previous year, M_{cur} and M_{prev}) using the orthogonal Procrustes transformation, and then measure cosine similarity between the w_q vectors in both models, as proposed in (Hamilton et al., 2016b);

2. alternatively, define a set of *anchor words* related to the semantic categories we are interested in, and then measure the 'drift' of w_q towards or away from these 'anchors' in M_{cur} compared against M_{prev}. This is the method we propose in this paper.

The first approach outputs one value of cosine similarity for each data point, representing the degree of the semantic shift, but not its direction. In

<hr>

[5]*Continuous Skipgram* showed comparable but slightly worse results, thus we report only those for CBOW.

contrast, the *anchor words* method can potentially provide information about the exact direction of the shift. This can be quantified in two ways:

1. for each anchor, calculate its *cosine similarity* against w_q in M_{cur} and M_{prev} (dubbed **Sim** hereafter);

2. as above, but instead of using the cosine, find the *position of each anchor in the models' vocabulary* sorted by similarity to w_q; we normalize by the size of the vocabulary so that rank 1 means the the anchor is the most similar word to w_q while rank 0 means it is the least similar (we dub this approach **Rank**).

The selection of anchor words is further described in Section 5, but for now note that both methods produce two vectors $\vec{R}_{prev}$ and $\vec{R}_{cur}$, corresponding to the models M_{cur} and M_{prev}. Their size is equal to the number of the anchor words, and each component of these vectors represents the relation of w_q to a particular anchor word in a particular time period.

To compute the differences between these vectors, one can either:

1. calculate the *cosine distance between these 'second-order vectors'*, as described in (Hamilton et al., 2016a); we dub this **SimDist** or **RankDist**, depending on whether **Sim** or **Rank** was used;

2. element-wise *subtract $\vec{R}_{prev}$ from $\vec{R}_{cur}$* to get the idea of whether w_q drifted towards or away from the anchors; we dub this **SimSub** or **RankSub**.

In the first case, the output is again one value, and in the second case it is the vector of diachronic differences, with the size equal to the number of the anchor words. These 'features' can then be fed into any classifier algorithm.

5 Results

To predict the actual 'direction' of the semantic shift (whether armed conflicts are escalating in the location or vice versa), one needs to perform classification into 3 classes: **war**, **peace** and **stable**.

To evaluate the approaches described in Section 4, we need a set of anchor words strongly related to the topic of armed conflicts. For this we adopted the list of search strings used within

Approach	Separ.	Cumul.	Increm.
Procrustes	0.15	0.24	0.29
Basic word list			
SimDist	0.27	0.17	0.25
SimSub	0.31	0.26	0.26
RankDist	0.28	0.19	0.23
RankSub	0.26	0.22	0.21
Expanded word list			
SimDist	0.25	0.18	0.23
SimSub	0.35	0.31	0.29
RankDist	0.24	0.20	0.28
RankSub	**0.36**	0.30	0.32

Table 1: Macro-F1 measure of predicting conflict state changes (ternary classification)

UCDP to filter the news texts for subsequent manual coding (Croicu and Sundberg, 2015): *kill, die, injury, dead, death, wound, massacre*. Additionally, an expanded version of this list was created, where every initial anchor word is accompanied with its 5 nearest associates (belonging to the same part of speech) in the *CBOW* model trained on the full *Gigaword*. This resulted in a set of 26 words (some nearest associates overlap).

The classification itself was done using a one-vs-rest SVM (Boser et al., 1992) with balanced class weights. The features used were either the cosine distance between $\vec{R}_{prev}$ and $\vec{R}_{cur}$ (in the case of **SimDist** and **RankDist**) or the result of $\vec{R}_{cur} - \vec{R}_{prev}$ (in the case of **SimSub** and **RankSub**). In the first case we have only one feature, while in the second case the number of features depends on the number of the anchor words.

The results for CBOW, evaluated with 10-fold stratified cross-validation, are presented in Table 1 in the form of macro-averaged F1.

The labels for approaches are the same as in section 4. *Procrustes* is our baseline: it does not use any anchor words, only the cosine distances between w_q in aligned models.

Overall, one can see that more words in the anchor sets is beneficial, and using $\vec{R}_{cur} - \vec{R}_{prev}$ (**Sub**) is almost always better than $\cos(\vec{R}_{cur}, \vec{R}_{prev})$ (**Dist**). As for the using of either cosine similarities (**Sim**) or ranks (**Rank**) as $\vec{R}$ values, there does not seem to be a clear winner. We also tried to concatenate similarities and ranks

Class	Precision	Recall	F1
Peace	**0.13** (0.06)	**0.29** (0.06)	**0.18** (0.06)
Stable	0.80 (0.79)	0.58 (**0.82**)	0.67 (**0.80**)
War	**0.17** (0.12)	**0.33** (0.08)	**0.22** (0.10)

Table 2: Detailed performance of the best model (results of weighted random guess in parenthesis)

to produce the feature vector of size 52. However, this did not improve the classifier performance.

It is interesting that the best results are shown by the **separate** models: at least for this particular task, it does not make sense to employ schemes of updating the models with new data or concatenating new corpora with the previous ones. It seems that the models trained from scratch on yearly corpora are more 'focused' on the events happening in this particular year, and thus are more useful.

Note that for the Procrustes alignment baseline it is vice versa: separate models are the worst choice for alignment, probably because they are too different from each other (each initialized independently and with independent collection of training texts). Anyway, the anchor words approach outperforms the Procrustes alignment baseline in all types of models. Hamilton et al. (2016b) report almost perfect accuracy for the Procrustes transformation when detecting the direction of semantic change (for example, the meaning of the word '*gay*' moving away from '*happy*' and towards '*homosexual*'). However, our task and data is different: the time periods are much more granular and we attempt to detect subtle associative drifts (often pendulum-like) rather than full-scale shifts of the meaning.

Table 2 provides the detailed per-class performance of the best model (**separate** CBOW with the expanded word list, using differences in anchor ranks as features). In parenthesis, we give the performance values for the stratified random guess baseline. Detecting stability breaks seems to be more difficult than detecting the 'no changes' state. The performance for the '**war**' and '**peace**' minority classes is far from ideal. However, it is significantly better than chance.

6   Conclusion

In this paper, we evaluated several approaches for extracting diachronic semantic shifts from word embedding models trained on texts from differ-

ent time periods. We have focused on time spans equal to one year, using the Gigaword news collection as the training corpus. As the gold standard for testing, we adapted a dataset from the field of conflict research provided by the UCDP and containing manually annotated data about the dates of armed conflicts starting and ending all over the world. Thus, we applied diachronic word embedding models to the task of predicting the events of conflicts escalating or calming down in 52 geographical locations, spanning over 16 years (1994–2010)[6].

The conclusion is that tracing actual real-world events by detecting 'cultural' semantic shifts in distributional semantic models is a difficult task, and much work is still to be done here. The approaches proposed in the previous work – mainly for large-scale shifts observed over decades or even centuries – are not very successful in this more fine-grained task. Our proposed '*anchor words*' method outperforms them by large margin, but its performance is still not entirely satisfactory, achieving a macro F1 measure of 0.36 on the task of ternary classification ('stable', 'escalating', 'calming down').

We plan to further study ways to improve the performance of diachronic word embedding models in the area of armed conflicts and other types of events. If successful, these techniques can be used to semi-automate the labor-intensive process of manually annotating the social science data, as well as to mine news text streams for emerging events and trends. It can also be interesting to trace differences in diachronic representations relative to the source of the training texts (for example, the NYT newspaper against the Xinhua news agency).

References

Bernhard E Boser, Isabelle M Guyon, and Vladimir N Vapnik. 1992. A training algorithm for optimal margin classifiers. In *Proceedings of the fifth annual workshop on Computational learning theory*. ACM, pages 144–152.

Mihai Croicu and Ralph Sundberg. 2015. UCDP georeferenced event dataset codebook version 4.0. *Journal of Peace Research* 50(4):523–532.

Steffen Eger and Alexander Mehler. 2016. On the linearity of semantic change: Investigating mean-

---

[6]The test set is available here: `http://ltr.uio.no/~andreku/armedconflicts/ucdp_conflicts_1994_2010_testset.tsv`.

ing variation via dynamic graph models. In *Proceedings of the 54th Annual Meeting of the Association for Computational Linguistics (Volume 2: Short Papers)*. Association for Computational Linguistics, pages 52–58.

Nils Petter Gleditsch, Peter Wallensteen, Mikael Eriksson, Margareta Sollenberg, and Håvard Strand. 2002. Armed conflict 1946-2001: A new dataset. *Journal of peace research* 39(5):615–637.

L. William Hamilton, Jure Leskovec, and Dan Jurafsky. 2016a. Cultural shift or linguistic drift? Comparing two computational measures of semantic change. In *Proceedings of the 2016 Conference on Empirical Methods in Natural Language Processing*. Association for Computational Linguistics, pages 2116–2121.

L. William Hamilton, Jure Leskovec, and Dan Jurafsky. 2016b. Diachronic word embeddings reveal statistical laws of semantic change. In *Proceedings of the 54th Annual Meeting of the Association for Computational Linguistics (Volume 1: Long Papers)*. Association for Computational Linguistics, pages 1489–1501.

Vivek Kulkarni, Rami Al-Rfou, Bryan Perozzi, and Steven Skiena. 2015. Statistically significant detection of linguistic change. In *Proceedings of the 24th International Conference on World Wide Web*. Florence, Italy, pages 625–635.

Andrey Kutuzov and Elizaveta Kuzmenko. 2016. Cross-lingual trends detection for named entities in news texts with dynamic neural embedding models. In *First International Workshop on Recent Trends in News Information Retrieval co-located with 38th European Conference on Information Retrieval (ECIR 2016)*. Technical University of Aachen, pages 27–32.

Tomas Mikolov, Ilya Sutskever, Kai Chen, Greg S Corrado, and Jeff Dean. 2013. Distributed representations of words and phrases and their compositionality. *Advances in Neural Information Processing Systems 26* pages 3111–3119.

Robert Parker, David Graff, Junbo Kong, Ke Chen, and Kazuaki Maeda. 2011. English Gigaword Fifth Edition LDC2011T07. Technical report, Linguistic Data Consortium, Philadelphia.

Jeffrey Pennington, Richard Socher, and Christopher D. Manning. 2014. Glove: Global vectors for word representation. In *Empirical Methods in Natural Language Processing (EMNLP)*. pages 1532–1543.

Radim Řehůřek and Petr Sojka. 2010. Software Framework for Topic Modelling with Large Corpora. In *Proceedings of the LREC 2010 Workshop on New Challenges for NLP Frameworks*. Valletta, Malta, pages 45–50.

Ralph Sundberg and Erik Melander. 2013. Introducing the UCDP georeferenced event dataset. *Journal of Peace Research* 50(4):523–532.

The Circumstantial Event Ontology (CEO)

Roxane Segers and **Tommaso Caselli** and **Piek Vossen**
Vrije Universiteit Amsterdam
De Boelelaan 1105 1081 HV Amsterdam (NL)
{r.h.segers,t.caselli;p.t.j.m.vossen}@vu.nl

Abstract

In this paper we describe the ongoing work on the Circumstantial Event Ontology (CEO), a newly developed ontology for calamity events that models semantic circumstantial relations between event classes, where we define circumstantial as explicit and implicit causal relations. The circumstantial relations are defined manually in the ontology for classes of events that involve a change to the same property of a participant. We discuss and contrast two types of circumstantial relations: semantic and episodic circumstantial relations. Further, we describe the meta-model and the current contents of the ontology and outline the future evaluation of the CEO.

1 Introduction

Suppose we read a sentence such as *"Helen was crossing the street; she was hit by a truck"*. As it is clear to most readers, but implicit in this sentence, there must be some relation between "crossing the street" (A) and "being hit by a truck" (B). First, the two events, A and B, share the same participant ("Helen" - "she") and they stand in a temporal relation of inclusion.However, the interpretation of this sentence as a text, i.e. a unitary message, requires some additional coherence relation between the two events that is not explicitly expressed. In the context of this occurrence, it is normal for a human reader to interpret event B, "hit" as a *consequence* of the event A, "crossing".

We consider this type of relations between event pairs as a case of a *circumstantial relation*. A circumstantial relation can be best described as a coherence relation between events which allows to interpret and understand their occurrence in the world in terms of a coherent unitary message. It explains to human readers "why" something happened, without necessarily explaining it. Circumstantial relations are a set of relations which includes temporal, causal, entailment, prevention and contingency relations, among others.

We distinguish two types of circumstantial relations: episodic and semantic. An *episodic* circumstantial relation is a relation that holds between a pair of specific actual event instances in a specific context, where their connection is necessary to understand what is described in a meaningful and coherent way. For instance, the relation between events A and B is a case of an episodic circumstantial relation: A and B may happen independently without implying the other necessarily, but when described in the same context, or circumstance, a connection is created that explains their occurrence as a dependent relation.[1]

On the other hand, we define *semantic* circumstantial relations as a relation that holds between event classes (abstracting from actual events), where an event of class C gives rise to another event of class D or vice versa, based on shared properties in the formalization of the classes. For instance: the class "Shooting" has a semantic circumstantial relation with the class "Impacting", because they both share the property of translocation of an object from location Y to Z. Modeling these relations provides a means to track chains of logically related events and their shared participants within and across documents.

Semantic circumstantial relations thus define possible explanatory sequences of events but not the actual explanatory sequences. Episodic relations define actual circumstantial sequences that fit the semantic model. The Circumstantial Event

---

[1]Of course, not all events can have an explanation. For instance, there is no episodic circumstantial relation that tells us why Helen is crossing the street.

Proceedings of the Events and Stories in the News Workshop, pages 37–41,
Vancouver, Canada, August 4, 2017. ©2017 Association for Computational Linguistics

Ontology (CEO), described in this paper, models the semantic relations, based on *shared properties* of the event classes with the intention to support detecting episodic circumstantial relations in texts.

We specify the methodology used in section 2.1. Modeling the relations in an ontology will allow us to 1.) abstract over the different lexical realizations of the same concept (i.e. at an event mention level); 2.) facilitate reasoning between event classes and enrich the extraction of information for event knowledge and event sequences. [2]

Existing ontologies and models such as SUMO (Niles and Pease, 2001) and FrameNet(Ruppenhofer et al., 2006) do provide explicit causal relations between event classes (SUMO) or preceding and causal relations (FrameNet). These causal relations are strict, meaning that if A happens, then B must happen as well. However, our relations are circumstantial, meaning that some instance of event class C and D can happen independently, but given the circumstance that they coincide, C implies D or D is implied by C. The implication is however not necessary.

Previous work on the encoding of semantic relations between event pairs has focused on specific subsets of circumstantial relations. For instance, one example is the encoding of the entailment relations in WordNet (Fellbaum, 1998). With respect to the WordNet approach in this work, we abstract from various event types (i.e. lexical items) and do not depend on relations defined at a synset level by formalizing event knowledge and relations in an ontology. Another related approach are narrative chains as described in (Chambers and Jurafsky, 2010) that provide chains of various event mentions. However, the relation between these mentions is not specified explicitly but based on co-occurrence of participants and a basic precedence relation. Manual inspection of these chains revealed that dissimilar relations are implied within these chains, varying from temporal ordering, to episodic, up to causal. The Penn Discourse Tree-Bank (PDTB) (Prasad et al., 2007) annotates contingency relations, of which causal relations are a subclass. In PDTB, the focus of the annotation is between two Abstract Objects (called Arg1 and Arg2), corresponding to discourse units, rather than event mentions. The contingency relation is

annotated either in presence of an explicit connective, i.e. a lexical item, connecting the two abstract objects or implicitly by adjacency in discourse. In our approach, contingency relations are one of the possible values which express circumstantial relations, and, most importantly, they are independent of the presence of connectives or adjacency in discourse but grounded on (shared) properties of events.

A resource such as the CEO is envisioned to be of added value for several NLP tasks such as script mining, question answering, information extraction and textual entailment, among others. Furthermore, the explicitly defined relations between events can be of help in reconstructing storylines (Vossen et al., 2015), (van den Akker et al., 2010) and improve the coherence of the narrative chain models (Chambers and Jurafsky, 2010).

The remainder of this paper is organized as follows: in section 2 we describe the meta model and the development of CEO; in section 3 we report on plans and current work to evaluate CEO; in section 4 we conclude with final remarks and future work.

2 The Circumstantial Event Ontology

The CEO builds upon an existing event ontology called the Event and Implied Situation Ontology (ESO) (Segers et al., 2016). ESO is designed to run over the output of Semantic Role Labeling systems by making explicit the ontological type of the predicative element and the situation that holds before, during and after the predicate. Each so called pre-, post- and during situation consists of a set of properties and roles that define what holds true. For instance, as can be seen in Figure 2 the pre- and post-situations of the event class "Damaging" define:

- that something is in a "relatively plus" state (pre-situation);

- that this something is in a "relatively less" state, i.e. it underwent a loss or a negative change, relatively to the state before the damaging ("+") (post-situation);

- that some object is in a state 'damaged' after the event (post-situation);

- that something has some damage which has some negative effect on some activity (post-situation).

```
pre situation:    damaging-undergoer    inState              damaging-state-1
                  damaging-state-1      hasRelativeValue     "+"

post situation:   damaging-undergoer    inState              damaging-state-2
                  damaging-state-2      hasRelativeValue     "-"
                  damaging-undergoer    isDamaged            true
                  damaging-undergoer    hasDamage            damaging-damage
                  damaging-damage       hasNegativeEffectOn  activity
```

Figure 1: The ESO assertions for the class Damaging

ESO allows to track chains of states and changes over time, whether explicitly reported or inferred. However, ESO does not provide any explicit definition on what event class logically precedes or follows some other event class, i.e. the pre-, post- and during situations provide only descriptions of properties of the participants of the event in analysis. CEO aims at extending ESO, by further developing the event hierarchy, the expressiveness of the pre-, post-, and during situations, and, finally, the definition of the circumstantial semantic relations between the classes.

2.1 The CEO Meta Model

CEO is an OWL2 ontology, still under development, which currently consists of 250 event classes, 65 roles, and 58 unique properties that model the pre-, post- and during situations of the event classes.

The CEO meta model fully adopts and extends the ESO model (Segers et al., 2016). The reasons to reuse and extend it are twofold: 1) The ESO classes and roles are mapped to FrameNet, therefore we can rely on existing SRL techniques and models to instantiate CEO (Björkelund et al., 2009; de Lacalle et al., 2016); 2) ESO provides a model that defines what situation, or state, is true before and after an event, thereby already providing the initial hooks to define the circumstantial semantic relations. Event classes are connected by checking if a shared property holds in one of the following conditions:

- between a post-situation of class X and the pre-situation of class Y;

- between the post-situation of class X and the during situation of class Y;

- between the during situation of class X and the pre-situation of class Y.

Figure 2.1 illustrates this approach and the CEO meta model. In the Figure, the class "Damaging" has a post-situation where is stated that some object is damaged (X isDamaged true). For the static class "BeingDamaged", the same statement is defined as a during situation, meaning that during the state "BeingDamaged", some object is in a damaged state. As such, both classes are tied together, based on a shared property. Further, the role of the entity that undergoes the change (here: X) is mapped to several FrameNet frame elements while the class, e.g. "Damaging", is mapped to both a SUMO class and FrameNet frames.

For relating the classes we investigate two options. Either we leave the relation between the classes implicit and track possible paths connecting the classes based on the shared properties. Another possibility is that we define explicit relations between the classes. For the latter case, we propose to define two properties: 1.) "hasCircumstantialPreEvent" (HCPrE), which expresses that an event class (e.g. "Shooting") is elicited by another one (e.g. "BeingArmed"); and 2.) "hasCircumstantialPostEvent" (HCPoE) which expresses that an event class (e.g. "Shooting") elicits another one ('Impacting"). Both properties are modeled as a non-inverse property of each other and as non-propagational. This implies that the relation only holds between two event classes and does not inherit to any of its subclasses. Also, if there is a "hasCircumstantialPostEvent" property between event class A and B, this does not imply that there is a relation from B back to A, unless specified otherwise. However, at this moment the pre-, post- and during situations, which are used to connect the classes, do not provide the information to determine the directionality of the HCPrE and HCPoE relations.

Figure 2.1 illustrates a chaining of calamity events and their relations. On the left, we show the event classes and on the right the pre–, post– and during situations. Note that we do not show the subclass hierarchy here, but only the binding of a subset of event classes based on shared properties. For instance, the class "Shooting" has a HCPoE relation to "Impacting", while the class "BeingArmed" has a HCPrE relation to "HavingAPurpose".

2.2 Building the CEO

CEO is designed to capture chains of events in newswire, more specifically calamity events. We define a calamity event as any event where some

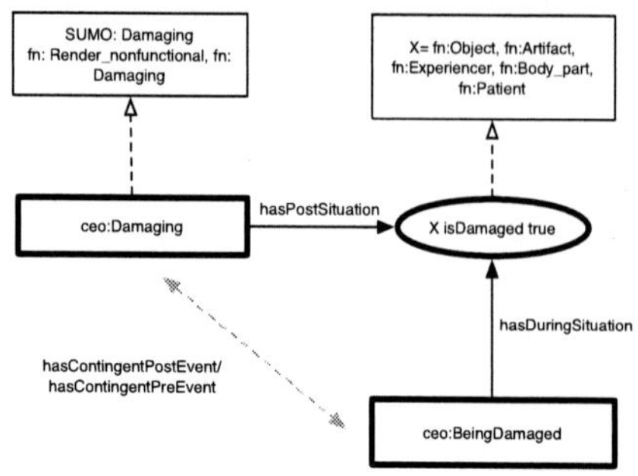

Figure 2: The meta model of CEO and the mappings to the external resources FrameNet (fn) and SUMO at class and at role levels.

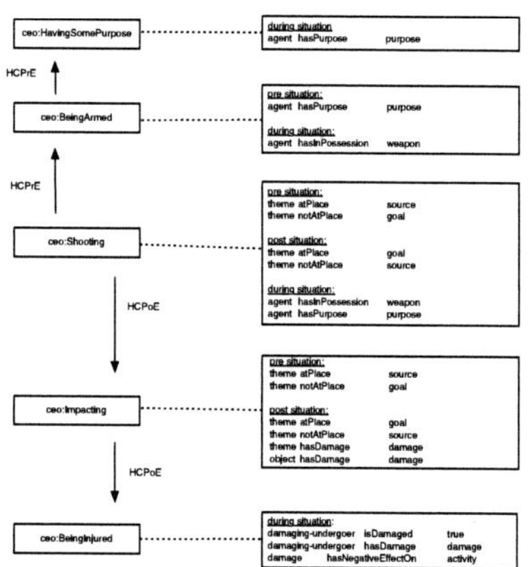

Figure 3: Explicit chaining of event classes (left) and their shared properties in the pre, post and during situation (right).

situation turns from relatively positive to some relatively negative state due to some changes in the world. Event classes that define processes are also modeled in CEO, where some agent tries to improve some situation in reaction to some calamity, i.e. going from a relatively negative situation back to a relatively positive situation. Examples of calamity event classes are "CyberAttack" and "Earthquake". Examples of event classes where an attempt to some improvement of a situation is made are "Repairing" and "Evacuation".

ESO already provides us with some event classes for calamities, though the coverage is rather limited as ESO was designed for the economic-financial domain. As such, we massively extended the hierarchy from the initial 63 event classes in ESO to the 250 event classes currently in CEO. To the best of our knowledge, no formal ontology specific for calamities and the inter-event relations exist. Some thesauri such as the IPTC [3] contain terms for calamities but these are not formalized and provide few relations. Therefore, we decided to define a new model, reusing existing resources as much as possible.

As an input for the calamity classes defined in CEO, we partially were able to reuse Chamber's narrative chains (Chambers and Jurafsky, 2010) for as far as these pertained to calamities of some sort. This selection was made manually, based on at least three calamity events per event chain. Further, we manually selected FrameNet frames that capture calamity events. We used the SUMO ontology as a backbone for modeling our initial list of of verbs and frames. Finally, we defined SKOS mappings from each CEO event class to FrameNet and SUMO. [4] thus providing the opportunity to use CEO on SRL labeled text as well as to find the vocabulary expressing calamities by means of the lexical units mapped to frames in FrameNet and the mappings to Princeton WordNet that are defined in SUMO.

3 Evaluation

The CEO will be evaluated against a benchmark corpus to determine precision and recall for both the classes and the semantic circumstantial relations. For this, we plug the CEO into an existing NLP pipeline for text annotation and analysis (Vossen et al., 2016) For this, we are cur-

[3]https://iptc.org/
[4]https://www.w3.org/2004/02/skos/

rently annotating part of the ECB+ corpus (Cybulska and Vossen, 2014). We selected 24 topics that describe a calamity event. In our annotation, we only use the existing event mention annotations and add new mentions if they realize an event calamity class. In addition to this, the annotators define co-reference sets among event mentions and the semantic circumstantial relations. As such, we can evaluate what events are captured by our ontology and what relations can be successfully reconstructed. For the annotation, we use the CAT annotation tool (Bartalesi Lenzi et al., 2012). Additionally, we are designing a Question-Answering task, where systems will have to provide answers to questions "why" a certain event has taken place rather than factoid questions by providing the most relevant and direct preceding event that can be seen as an explanation.

4   Conclusion and Future Work

We have described current ongoing work on an event ontology that captures calamity events in newswire and the semantic circumstantial relations that hold between event classes, based on shared properties in the pre-, post- or during situations defined for each class. Future work includes the further development of the ontology with a focus on defining the circumstantial semantic relations between the classes and an extension of the expressivity of the pre-, post- and during situations of the event classes. Further, we will evaluate the added value of our model both intrinsically, against a manually annotated corpus, and extrinsically, by means of a QA task.

5   Acknowledgements

This research was funded by the NWO Spinoza Prize project "Understanding Language by Machines.

References

V. Bartalesi Lenzi, G. Moretti, and R. Sprugnoli. 2012. Cat: the celct annotation tool. In *LREC*. pages 333–338.

A. Björkelund, L. Hafdell, and P. Nugues. 2009. Multilingual semantic role labeling. In *Proceedings of CoNLL-2009*. Boulder, CO, USA.

N. Chambers and D. Jurafsky. 2010. A database of narrative schemas. In *Proceedings of the 9th Language Resources and Evaluation Conference (LREC2010)*.

A. Cybulska and P. Vossen. 2014. Using a sledgehammer to crack a nut? lexical diversity and event coreference resolution. In *Proceedings of the 9th Language Resources and Evaluation Conference (LREC2014)*. Reykjavik, Iceland. http://www.lrec-conf.org/proceedings/lrec2014/pdf/840_Paper.pdf.

M. Lopez de Lacalle, E. Laparra, I. Aldabe, and G. Rigau. 2016. A multilingual predicate matrix. In *Proceedings of Language Resources and Evaluation Conference (LREC 2016)*.

C. Fellbaum. 1998. *WordNet: an electronic lexical database*. MIT Press.

I. Niles and A. Pease. 2001. Towards a standard upper ontology. In *Proceedings of FOIS-Volume 2001*. ACM.

R. Prasad, E. Miltsakaki, N. Dinesh, A. Lee, A. Joshi, L. Robaldo, and Bonnie L Webber. 2007. The penn discourse treebank 2.0 annotation manual .

J. Ruppenhofer, M. Ellsworth, M. Petruck, C.R. Johnson, and J. Scheffczyk. 2006. *FrameNet II: Extended Theory and Practice*. International Computer Science Institute, Berkeley, California.

R. Segers, M. Rospocher, P. Vossen, E. Laparra, G. Rigau, and A.L. Minard. 2016. The event and implied situation ontology: Application and evaluation. In *Proceedings of Language Resources and Evaluation Conference (LREC 2016)*.

C. van den Akker, L.M. Aroyo, A.K. Cybulska, M.G.J. van Erp, P. Gorgels, L. Hollink, C. Jager, S. Ległne, L. van der Meij, J. Oomen, J. van Ossenbruggen, G. Schreiber, R. Segers, P.T.J.M. Vossen, and B. Wielinga. 2010. *Historical Event-based Access to Museum Collections*, CEUR-WS (online), pages 1–9.

P. Vossen, R. Agerri, I. Aldabe, A. Cybulska, M. van Erp, A. Fokkens, E. Laparra, A. Minard, A. Palmero Aprosio, G. Rigau, M. Rospocher, and R. Segers. 2016. Newsreader: Using knowledge resources in a cross-lingual reading machine to generate more knowledge from massive streams of news. *Special Issue Knowledge-Based Systems, Elsevier* https://doi.org/dx.doi.org/10.1016/j.knosys.2016.07.013.

P. Vossen, T. Caselli, and Y. Kontzopoulou. 2015. Storylines for structuring massive streams of news. In *Proceedings of the 1st Workshop on Computing News StoryLines (CNewS 2015) at the 53rd Annual Meeting of the Association for Computational Linguistics and the 7th International Joint Conference on Natural Language Processing (ACL-IJCNLP 2015)*. Bejing, China.

Event Detection and Semantic Storytelling:
Generating a Travelogue from a large Collection of Personal Letters

Georg Rehm[*], **Julian Moreno Schneider**[*], **Peter Bourgonje**[*], **Ankit Srivastava**[*],
Jan Nehring[*], **Armin Berger**[+], **Luca König**[+], **Sören Räuchle**[+], **Jens Gerth**[+]

DFKI GmbH, Language Technology Lab[*]   3pc GmbH Neue Kommunikation[+]
Alt-Moabit 91c, 10559 Berlin, Germany   Prinzessinnenstraße 1, 10969 Berlin, Germany
Corresponding author: georg.rehm@dfki.de

Abstract

We present an approach at identifying a specific class of events, movement action events (MAEs), in ca. 2,800 personal letters exchanged by the German architect Erich Mendelsohn and his wife, Luise. A backend system uses these and other semantic analysis results as input for an authoring environment that curators can use to produce new pieces of content. The human expert will receive recommendations from the system with the goal of putting together a travelogue, i. e., a description of the trips and journeys undertaken by the couple. We describe the components and also apply the system to news data.

1   Introduction

Robust event detection coupled with text analytics can lead to a multitude of innovative solutions to contribute to the decades-old "information overflow" challenge, but also to address more specialised, sector-specific needs. While many researchers concentrate on identifying meaningful stories, story paths or storylines in collections of news documents we propose an approach that bundles a flexible set of semantic services for the *production of digital content*, especially to recommend interesting storylines to human experts who process large collections of documents. We call this approach *Semantic Storytelling*.

The activities reported in this paper are carried out in the context of the research and technology transfer project Digital Curation Technologies, in which a research centre collaborates with four SME companies that operate in four sectors. We develop and deploy, in prototypically implemented use cases, a flexible platform that provides generic curation services such as, e. g.,

summarisation, named entity recognition, entity linking and machine translation (Bourgonje et al., 2016a,b). These are integrated into the in-house systems of the partner companies and customised to their domains so that the knowledge workers, journalists, experts, museum planners and digital curators who use these systems can do their jobs more efficiently, more easily and with higher quality. Their tasks involve the processing, analysis, skimming, sorting, summarising, evaluating and making sense of large amounts of digital content, out of which a new piece of digital content is created, e. g., an exhibition catalogue, a news article or an investigative report. The curation technology platform is meant to simplify the content curation task significantly.

This paper is structured as follows: Section 2 describes the Semantic Storytelling use case in more detail, i. e., the authoring environment and the data set.Section 3 focuses upon the approach, defines Movement Action Events (MAEs), and describes the curation services, e. g., temporal analysis, entity recognition, and event detection. Section 4 sketches the results of initial experiments on news data, while Section 5 summarises related work. Section 6 concludes the paper.

2   Use Case: Semantic Storytelling

The generic Semantic Storytelling use case involves processing a coherent and self-contained collection of documents in order to identify and to suggest, to the human expert, one or more potential story paths that can then be used to structure an actual story around them or, generally, a new piece of content (Schneider et al., 2016). One example are millions of leaked documents, in which an investigative journalist wants to find the interesting nuggets of information, i. e., surprising relations between different entities, say, politicians and off-

Proceedings of the Events and Stories in the News Workshop, pages 42–51,
Vancouver, Canada, August 4, 2017. ©2017 Association for Computational Linguistics

shore banks. The semantic technologies involved do not necessarily have to exhibit perfect performance because, in our use cases, humans are always in the loop. We want to provide, ideally, robust and generic technologies with broad coverage. For some services this goal can be fulfilled while for others, it must be considered ambitious.

2.1 Smart Authoring Environment

One of the partner companies is currently designing and developing an authoring environment, enabled by the curation technology platform and its semantic services.[1] Many of its projects involve a client, e. g., a company, a museum or a political party, that approaches the company with a set of digital content and a rough conception how to structure and visualise these assets in the form of a website or app. An authoring environment that can semantically process such a collection to enable the efficient authoring of flexible, professional, convincing, visually appealing content products that provide engaging stories would significantly reduce the effort on the side of the agency and, at the same time, improve their flexibility. From the same set of semantically enhanced content different output formats could be generated (e. g., web app, iOS or Androis app, ebook etc.). Example screens of the authoring environment's user interface ("Redaktionstool" in German) are shown in Figure 3. With regard to the look and feel, it was a conscious design decision to move beyond the typical notion of a "web page" that is broken up into different "modules" using templates. The clear focus are engaging stories told through the content.

With this tool the curator can interactively put together a story based on the content that has previously been enriched through the curation services and that act as building blocks. Figure 3 shows examples from the set of ca. 2,800 letters exchanged between the German architect Erich Mendelsohn (1887-1953) and his wife Luise, both of whom travelled frequently. We decided to focus upon the use case of identifying all *movement action events*, i. e., all trips undertaken by the author of the respective letter from location A to location B using a specific mode of transport. We want to construct, ideally automatically, a *travelogue* from this analysis layer, that provides an engaging story to the reader and that also enables ad-

ditional modes of access, e. g., through map-based or timeline-based visualisations. The goal is to process multiple interconnected instances of the text type *letter* in order to generate one instance of the text type *travelogue*.

2.2 Data Set: The Mendelsohn Letters

The collection contains 2,796 letters, written between 1910 and 1953, with a total of 1,002,742 words (avg. number of words per letter: 358.6, incl. addresses) on more than 11,000 sheets of paper; 1,410 of the letters were written by Erich and 1,328 by Luise Mendelsohn.[2] Most are in German (2,481), the rest is written in English (312) and French (3). The letters were scanned, transcribed and critically edited; photos and metadata are available. This research was carried out in a project that the authors of the present paper are not affiliated with (Bienert and de Wit, 2014). In the letters the Mendelsohns discuss their private and professional lives, their relationship, meetings with friends and business partners, and also their travels. One result of (Bienert and de Wit, 2014) is an online version of the Mendelsohn collection. In the present project we explore to what extent it is possible to automate the production of an online version of an arbitrary document collection.

3 Approach

We attempt to detect movement events to generate the backbone of a travelogue. Typically, in linguistics, the definition of "event" (vs. "state") is so broad and implicit that it is, for the time being, not feasible to implement a corresponding general-purpose event detection system. In NLP, on the other hand, events are usually defined as words or phrases (typically verbs, sometimes nouns) that clearly signal, on the linguistic surface, the existence of a specific action, activity, or change of state. Event detection is related to information and relation extraction (IE, RE). While IE and RE are focused on specific relations or template-like IE, event detection is more general. As open domain event detection is not feasible yet, we focus on Movement Action Events (MAEs). With regard to the text type "letter", an MAE mention relates to a currently happening or upcoming trip or journey announced or mentioned in a letter. A few examples, taken from two letters from Erich to Luise,

---

[1]This company, 3pc GmbH, is a digital agency, founded in 1995, that has completed more than 2,000 projects.

[2]There are also several duplicates and letters without any textual content in the collection.

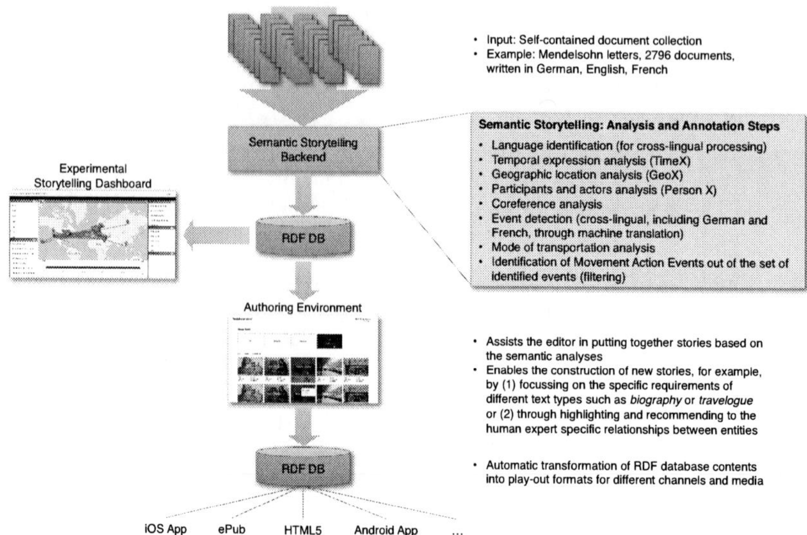

Figure 1: The Semantic Storytelling architecture and workflow

written on March 14, 1944, and March 10, 1949, respectively:

> "The hectic days of St. Louis, my beloved, are drawing to their close. *I am leaving tonight for Davenport.*"

> "Temple Washington affair promising. Have been there on Tuesday night from 9.30 to 1, *returned to Baltimore at 2 A.M.* [...] *Due in St. Louis around midnight.*"

MAEs imply physical motion events that occur when a person is travelling from one location (e. g., town, city) to another using a medium or long distance mode of transport. An MAE consists of the six-tuple MAE = $< P, L_O, L_D, t_d, t_a, m >$ with P a reference to the participant (E. or L. Mendelsohn), L_O and L_D references to the origin and destination locations (named locations, GPS coordinates), t_d and t_a the time of departure and arrival and m the mode of transport. Each component is optional as long as the MAE contains at least one participant and a destination. If multiple people travel together P can refer to a set of persons. For consecutive MAEs, we assume that L_D is L_O of the next trip:

$$\text{MAE}_1 = < P, L_a, L_b, t_i, t_j, m_x >$$
$$\text{MAE}_2 = < P, L_b, L_c, t_k, t_l, m_y >$$
$$\text{MAE}_3 = < P, L_c, L_d, t_m, t_n, m_z >$$

We detect MAEs through triggers, locations, temporal expressions, participants and the mode of transport. Out of the instantiated sets of six-tuples we attempt to construct a travelogue as a list of six-tuples (see Figure 1).

Many researchers working on, among others, text linguistics have emphasised the relationship between generalised text structure patterns and their respective text types or genres. Recently, (Caselli and Vossen, 2016) proposed the Storyline Annotation and Representation Scheme, which is primarily aimed at news articles to "identify salient events (climax events) as the central elements around which a specific topic develops". With regard to the travelogue example, the notion of one "climax event", "rising actions" and "falling actions" is not applicable, also see (Pang et al., 2011; Ye et al., 2011). Storyline applications tailored to specific text types (*news articles* vs. *letters* and *travelogue*) have different requirements regarding their storyline abstraction models. Accordingly, we focus on the identification of consecutive instantiations of MAE six-tuples.

3.1 Temporal Expressions

We use two tools for extracting temporal expressions: TimeX and HeidelTime. TimeX is our own implementation for recognising and normalising temporal expressions. It is based on a regular expression grammar and available for English and German. TimeX covers concrete ("11th of March, 2014") and relative mentions ("last week"). All expressions are normalised into a machine-readable format.

	TimeX			HeidelTime		
WikiwarsDE	P: 0.72	R: **0.90**	F: 0.80	P: **0.98**	R: 0.85	F: **0.91**
Mendelsohn letters	P: **0.91**	R: **0.60**	F: **0.72**	P: 0.71	R: 0.44	F: 0.54

Table 1: Comparison of the performance of TimeX and HeidelTime

A typical date notation used in the letters is "12.IV.26" ("12 April 1926"), with roman-style numerals for the number of the month; the extraction grammar can be adapted to cover alternative notations. A brief comparison of the performance of TimeX and HeidelTime on two data sets is shown in Table 1. TimeX achieves reasonable results but is outperformed by HeidelTime (Strötgen and Gertz, 2010) on the general domain corpus. TimeX scores better on the Mendelsohn collection. The WikiwarsDE corpus (Strötgen and Gertz, 2011) consists of German documents describing military conflicts. Customising HeidelTime's grammar requires significant modifications on different levels; having direct control over our own system worked better for us regarding the Mendelsohn collection and other data sets. After recognising and normalising temporal expressions, we also want to position documents on a timeline. This requires calculation of the average time stamp of a document including the spread over the timeline. The time stamp is computed on the basis of average milliseconds before or after java epoch (1st January 1970); standard deviation is also calculated. For the Mendelsohn experiments we use TimeX. For processing general domain texts and languages not covered by TimeX, we integrated HeidelTime into our platform.

3.2 Geolocations

Our geolocation extraction tool, GeoX, is based upon the OpenNLP NameFinder (Apache Software Foundation, 2016) trained on Wikipedia locations (Nothman et al., 2012). After the identification of locations we use DBPedia Spotlight or a domain-specific ontology (GeoNamesfor the Mendelsohn experiments) to retrieve a URI for every location entity. Once a URI is available, latitude and longitude can be obtained. Similar to TimeX, the average latitude and longitude value is calculated for every document, so that documents (rather than locations mentioned in them) can be pinpointed on a map. Adaptability to new domains is an important requirement. In addition to a general model, we allow uploading key-value-based dictionaries for pattern-based entity spotting. The key is the pattern to look for, the value a URI in an ontology. If it allows SPARQL queries, we can include ontology-specific queries to retrieve related information (e. g., latitude, longitude, country etc.). For the Mendelsohn experiments we had access to a database that includes a list of location names and their GeoNames URIs. Table 2 shows GeoX's performance using the Wikipedia model, based on 10-fold cross-validation on part of the data from (Nothman et al., 2012) using 120,000 sentences with 101,540 locations.

	GeoX	PersonX
Precision	93.68	96.89
Recall	69.50	74.00
F-score	79.80	83.91

Table 2: Performance of GeoX and PersonX

3.3 Participants and Actors

Similar to GeoX, we implemented a tool (PersonX) for extracting persons by training a corresponding model. For the general model, the same data is used as for the location model as it was also annotated for person-type entities. We also perform entity linking to retrieve an ontology URI (DBPedia by default, unless a domain-specific ontology is plugged in). For the Mendelsohn experiments we had access to a list of persons linked to a URI at Deutsche Nationalibliothek. Table 2 shows evaluation results using the same procedure as for the location model, using 120,000 sentences containing 56.086 persons.

3.4 Crosslingual Event Detection

The Mendelsohn data set is multilingual with the majority of the letters written in German. Most of our processing tools are language dependent, several are available for English only. Therefore, we implemented a crosslingual event detection system, i. e., translating German and French documents into English through Moses Statistical Machine Translation (Koehn et al., 2007) and detecting events in the translated documents. We implemented a dedicated pre-processing module for cleaning the German letters before we were able to send them to the MT engine. Approximately 30% of the words remained untranslated but an analysis showed these to be mainly named entities (people, locations) and abbreviations. The documents were then processed by the event detection system.

3.5 Generic Event and MAE Detection

We implemented a state-of-the-art event extraction system based on (Yang and Mitchell, 2016) to pinpoint words or phrases in a sentence that refer to events involving participants and locations, affected by other events and spatio-temporal aspects. The system is trained on the ACE 2005 data (Doddington et al., 2004), consisting of 529 documents from a variety of sources (newswire reports, blogs, discussion forums). We apply the tool to extract generic events in an ACE 2005 test set (30 news documents consisting of 672 sentences with 4,184 entity mentions and 438 triggers) and to detect MAEs in the Mendelsohn letters.

After processing the Mendelsohn letters, the English data set consisting of 295 documents and 7,899 sentences yielded 1,600 event triggers. The German (translated into English, see Section 3.4) data set consisting of 2,450 documents and 76,350 sentences yielded 6,950 event triggers. For MAE detection, the most relevant event type is the ACE "Transport" event. According to the ACE guidelines[3] a transport event occurs whenever an entity (person, vehicle, weapon) is moved from one place (GPE, facility, location) to another; a Transport Event contains seven slots (agent, entity, vehicle, price, origin, destination, time). Circa 45% and 40% of the labelled events in the English and German Mendelsohn letters respectively are Transport events. After detection, the events are passed to the next step in the workflow.

(Yang and Mitchell, 2016) decompose the learning problem into three subproblems: learning within-event structures, learning event-event relations, and learning for entity extraction. These learned models are then integrated into a single model that performs joint inference of all event triggers, semantic roles for events, and also entities across the whole document. With a precision of 82.4, recall of 79.2 and F-score of 80.8

we achieve comparable results to those reported by (Yang and Mitchell, 2016). As there is no gold standard available for the Mendelsohn data set, we manually evaluated a small subset and discovered that several events could not be detected due to data formatting issues and the fact that the system is trained on news documents from the early 21st century. After normalising the statistics and comparing with the ACE 2005 test data, we found that the Mendelsohn data set (out-of-domain) yielded 5 times and 7 times less events in the English and German letters than in the ACE 2005 test data.

3.6 Mode of Transportation

In the MAE six-tuple, m refers to the mode of travel, e. g., plane, train, car etc. An obvious approach is to look for linguistic cues, i. e., for corresponding nouns in sentences like "Tomorrow I'll go to New York by *train*". Often, the event's trigger verb provides the mode ("I'm *flying* to Los Angeles tonight."). For these two sets of cues, we can rely on a set of rules to cover all means of transportation. If there is no linguistic evidence available, we can attempt to deduce the mode. As we retrieve a URI for locations we can also retrieve related geographical location information using SPARQL. Using latitude and longitude of the origin and destination, we can calculate the distance using Vincenty's formulae.[4] From the distance, we attempt to deduce the mode using a set of threshold values. For short trips (from San Francisco to Palo Alto, say), typically the train, bus or car is used, but not a plane. We can also divide the time difference between departure and arrival and deduce the mode. For distances of more than 5,000km and a time of less than 10 hours, a plane is likely. For trips of more than 3,000km spanning different continents and taking more than a week, a cruise ship is more likely. Based on this approach we can identify 369 modes of transportation in the (English) Mendelsohn letters and 5,152 in the Obama corpus (Section 4).

3.7 Instantiation of MAE Six-Tuples

The following approach iterates over all documents. First, temporal expressions (Section 3.1), geolocations (Section 3.2), participants (Section 3.3) and trigger elements are annotated; we use two types of trigger elements, a motion-type

---

[3]ACE English Events guidelines, `https://www.ldc.upenn.edu/sites/www.ldc.upenn.edu/files/english-events-guidelines-v5.4.3.pdf`

[4]`https://en.wikipedia.org/wiki/Vincenty%27s_formulae`

verb class and a list of modes of transport (Section 3.6).[5] Afterwards, event detection is performed (Section 3.5). Finally, we filter for MAEs. This algorithm operates on the sentence level; for this we segment the letters into individual sentences. A rule set determines if an event is a MAE:
1) If a general candidate event does not contain a trigger element it is deleted.
2) If the event does not contain a participant, location, or temporal expression, we include, in the six-tuple, the author, location, or date – as noted by the author in the letter head – as P, L_O or t_d of the MAE candidate.
3) We generate all combinations of MAE candidate six-tuples by filling the six-tuple with the available entities. Every candidate receives a score that is computed as a weighted linear combination of the existence of the six-tuple components:

$$\begin{aligned} sc_{MAE} \ = \ & w_P * sc_P + \\ & w_{L_O} * sc_{L_O} + \\ & w_{L_D} * sc_{L_D} + \\ & w_{t_d} * sc_{t_d} + \\ & w_{t_a} * sc_{t_a} + \\ & w_m * sc_m \end{aligned} \qquad (1)$$

where sc_i is the score of the ith feature (in this case these scores are always 1), w_i is the weight of the ith feature and $\sum_i w_i = 1$.
4) The MAE candidates with a score greater than a certain threshold th are processed further.

For the evaluation we use a quantitative and a qualitative measurement: the number of MAEs annotated and a manual evaluation of the MAEs of some randomly selected documents. We apply five different approaches to generate MAE candidates: (**A1**) using all entities available in a candidate event; (**A2**) like A1 but also including the metadata of the letters as entities (author, location, date); (**A3**) using all entities available in a candidate event but avoiding similar locations for L_O and L_D as well as similar dates for t_d and t_a; (**A4**) like A3 but also including the metadata of the letters as entities; (**A5**) like A3 but only including the MAEs that appear in sentences that also include a trigger element. The number of MAE candidates in the Mendelsohn letters are shown in Table 3.

The approaches that include the metadata of the letters generate much more MAE candidates. This is to be expected because the inclusion of the

[5]The verb cues are based on (Levin, 1993), Chapter 51.

	th=0	th=.25	th=.5	th=.75	th=1
A1	591	328	98	0	0
A2	6386	4831	3554	736	0
A3	563	253	54	0	0
A4	5640	3166	1260	53	0
A5	116	60	11	0	0

Table 3: Generating MAE candidates

metadata makes three entities (person, date, location) available in each candidate. We tried the approaches including the letters' metadata because the author often uses "I" instead of her/his name, of course, which is why the author is often not included as an extracted entity. All candidatesthat do not make sense have to be filtered in a post-processing step. We tried to determine the best threshold value by using five values between 0 and 1. The respective score is directly related to the amount of features they are composed of: the higher the number of included features, the higher the score. This is why the different thresholds can be seen as a "proof" of the number of MAE candidates including the needed amount of information.

We also performed a qualitative evaluation selecting randomly 10 MAE candidates. While 9 out of 10 inspected candidates were extracted correctly and refer to proper MAEs, the instantiation of the six-tuples (esp. t_d and t_a) needs further improvement: 5 correct departure times, 1 correct arrival time, 3 correct persons, 8 correct origins, 1 correct destination and 0 correct transportation modes.

George Downs, Santa Crux, Carmel, [], [], [].

[George Downs will pick us up tomorrow at 9.30 a.m. and we intend to drive skyline to Los Gatos to see Kate Ostwald for a moment and then via Santa Crux [sic] to Carmel!]

A general problem is the huge number of MAE candidates, much higher than the actual number of genuine complete MAEs, due to the combination of all possible entities existing in an event. Some common errors appear in many MAEs candidates. Sometimes, regarding departure and arrival time, the current time (i. e., execution time/date) is used, because the date is underspecified and the anchor year "now" is used. In some cases the arrival times are *before* the departure time, which can be taken care of easily by making the instantiation algorithm time-aware. In some cases we had false MAE positives due to misinterpreted triggers such as, for example, "Drive" (referring to street names). These errors are more common on MAE candidates with higher scores because they contain more features, even if some of them are incorrect. Some MAE candidates with a lower score have better features, or a higher number of correct features. In the following we present two MAE candidates that are correct MAEs with less features. With the inclusion of additional metadata from the letters the results could be improved considerably because in both cases the subject "I" was not identified as an entity and, thus, not included in the six-tuple (see above with regard to the incorrectly identified arrival and departure times).

> [], [], Cleveland, Sat May 06 12:00:00 CEST 2017, [], [].
>
> [*My discussion here will, I hope, be finished before I leave for Cleveland tomorrow night.*]
>
> [], [], New York, , [], [].
>
> [*I left Sunday – soon after the pleasant meeting – for New York.*]

We also performed more traditional relation extraction experiments by using the Stanford Dependency Parser to extract relation triples (subject, verb, object) to collect the information for filling the six-tuple slots. In the dependency graph we extract sub-root level nodes (typically verbs) that connect two noun phrases or other candidates. The extracted relations are then filtered for motion-type verbs (Levin, 1993). Typically, the subject would be the P in the MAE, and the object of the relation any of the other slots (L_O, L_D, t_d, t_a, m). Applying this approach on the English subset of the Mendelsohn collection resulted in only 10 triples that met the criteria of having a movement action at the core of the relation.[6]

3.8 Semantic Storytelling Dashboard

To get a better understanding of the data set, the analysis results, the extracted MAEs and to prepare attaching the Semantic Storytelling backend to the authoring environment (see Figure 1), we implemented an experimental dashboard (Figure 2). The upper left window shows a list of the documents in the data set; extracted MAE candidates, visualised in the map, can be filtered by document. The bottom left window shows the list of annotated named entities. The map visualises the locations involved in the MAE candidates with highlighted annotations. The slider below the map can be used to filter MAEs by time. The windows on the right hand side show all location names, temporal expressions and modes of transportation. Additional details and case studies can be found in (Rehm et al., 2017; Schneider et al., 2017)

4   MAE Detection in News Data

Our primary data set in this paper is the Mendelsohn collection but we also see multiple application scenarios for the news domain – the Semantic Storytelling backend and authoring environment are meant to be applied to arbitrary data sets after all. We performed an initial evaluation of our system applied to a data set that consists of news articles on the multiple trips of Barack Obama.[7] The corpus contains 487 files with 24,387 sentences and 897,630 tokens. We annotated 17,241 persons, 21,569 locations, 19,572 temporal expressions, 5,104 transport modes and 3,537 trigger verbs. The event extraction system annotated 61,718 entity mentions and 6,752 event triggers, 31% of which were "Transport" events. We found that in-domain data (the Obama data set) produced three times more event triggers than out-of-domain data (Mendelsohn letters). We plan to close this gap through domain adaptation.

For the evaluation we applied three of the approaches mentioned in Section 3.7: (**A1**) using all entities available in a sentence; (**A3**) using all entities in a sentence but avoiding similar locations in L_O and L_D and similar dates in t_d and t_a; and (**A5**) the same as A3 but only including the MAEs that appear in sentences that also include a trigger element (see Table 4).

	th=0	th=.25	th=.5	th=.75	th=1
A1	13030	9700	5314	0	0
A3	7841	4511	2784	0	0
A5	2545	1768	1328	0	0

Table 4: Generating MAE candidates (Obama)

While, in our manual evaluation, many MAE candidates turned out to be genuine MAEs, we also found instances of false positives, which contained information extracted from non-article contents such as, for example, the imprint and copy-

---

[6]This approach performed better on the Obama news corpus (Section 4).

[7]Based on a list of links to news articles in `https://en.wikipedia.org/wiki/List_of_ international_presidential_trips_made_ by_Barack_Obama`

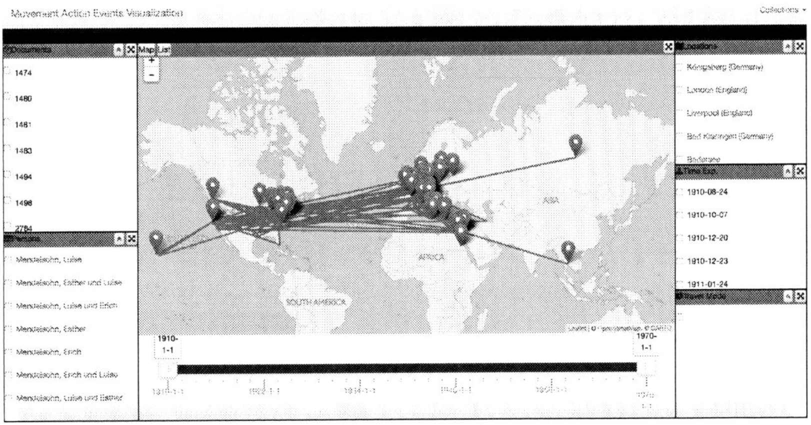

Figure 2: The storytelling dashboard showing Movement Action Events annotations

right information; we tried to remove all HTML boilerplates and templates using a dedicated tool but in some instances these pieces of text were kept. Sometimes, organisations were incorrectly annotated as person entities, which lead to several incorrect MAEs. In some cases the locations used for the six-tuple were too generic (e. g., continent names). Nevertheless, many candidates are genuine MAEs, for example:

Obama, Brasilia, Rio de Janeiro, [], [], [].

[Mr Obama arrived in Rio de Janeiro after a day of talks in the capital, Brasilia, with Ms Rousseff and business leaders.]

5 Related Work

Most approaches in the event detection literature are machine learning-based and adhere to a modular approach (Ahn, 2006), i. e., they use the output from constituency and dependency parsers, named entity recognisers, coreference resolution systems, and part-of-speech taggers to build classifiers for subtasks of trigger labelling and argument labelling. However, recently, state-of-the-art results have been achieved by joint entity and event extraction systems (Yang and Mitchell, 2016; Li et al., 2013), i. e., approaches which compute joint inference in one combined model to minimise the errors introduced by sub-modules.

Several approaches are related to our Semantic Storytelling concept, all of them concentrating on their own objectives and providing solutions for their respective challenges. A few systems focus on providing content for entertainment purposes (Wood, 2008). Other researchers focus on specific domains, for example, storytelling in gaming

(Gervás, 2013), for recipes (Cimiano et al., 2013; Dale, 1989) or for weather reports (Belz, 2008; Goldberg et al., 1994; Reiter et al., 2005; Turner et al., 2006), requiring knowledge about characters, actions, locations, events, or objects that exist in this particular domain (Gervás et al., 2005; Riedl and Young, 2010; Turner, 2014). The most closely related approach is the one developed by (Poulakos et al., 2015), which presents "an accessible graphical platform for content creators and even end users to create their own story worlds, populate it with smart characters and objects, and define narrative events that can be used by existing tools for automated narrative synthesis".

6 Summary and Future Work

We present an approach at identifying a specific class of events, movement action events, in the Mendelsohn data set. The goal is to expose these and other semantic analysis results through the Semantic Storytelling backend to an authoring environment that curators can use to produce new pieces of content based on this data collection. The authoring environment can provide recommendations, ideas, suggestions or potential story paths to the human expert, in this case, with the goal of producing a travelogue, i. e., a vivid description of the multiple trips and journeys undertaken by the Mendelsohns.

The evaluations show that the task of processing the Mendelsohn data set to identify MAEs is an ambitious challenge. This is especially due to the rather old-fashioned, highly abbreviated, partially poetic, spoken-style language employed and also due to the fact that most actual MAE mentions are contained only implicitly, making their automatic extraction difficult. Initial results from applying our system to the Obama corpus are more promising as MAEs are contained in news articles in a more explicit way. We assume that our approach can be applied to contemporary news documents more effectively than to personal letters that are, partially, almost 100 years old and belong to a genre and register that is notoriously difficult to process automatically.

In terms of future work, we will connect the storytelling backend to the authoring environment and we will integrate additional components to arrive at an integrated working prototype.

Acknowledgments

The project "Digitale Kuratierungstechnologien" (DKT) is supported by the German Federal Ministry of Education and Research (BMBF), "Unternehmen Region", instrument Wachstumskern-Potenzial (no. 03WKP45). More information: http://www.digitale-kuratierung.de. The authors would also like to thank the anonymous reviewers for their valuable comments.

References

David Ahn. 2006. The stages of event extraction. In *Proc. of the Workshop on Annotating and Reasoning About Time and Events (ARTE 06)*. ACL, Stroudsburg, PA, USA, pages 1–8.

Apache Software Foundation. 2016. Apache OpenNLP. http://opennlp.apache.org.

Anja Belz. 2008. Automatic Generation of Weather Forecast Texts Using Comprehensive Probabilistic Generation-space Models. *Nat. Lang. Eng.* 14(4):431–455.

Andreas Bienert and Wim de Wit, editors. 2014. *EMA – Erich Mendelsohn Archiv. Der Briefwechsel von Erich und Luise Mendelsohn 1910-1953*. Kunstbibliothek – Staatliche Museen zu Berlin and The Getty Research Institute, Los Angeles. With contributions from Regina Stephan and Moritz Wullen, Version March 2014. http://ema.smb.museum.

Peter Bourgonje, Julian Moreno-Schneider, Jan Nehring, Georg Rehm, Felix Sasaki, and Ankit Srivastava. 2016a. Towards a Platform for Curation Technologies: Enriching Text Collections with a Semantic-Web Layer. In H. Sack, G. Rizzo, N. Steinmetz, D. Mladeni, S. Auer, and C. Lange, editors, *The Semantic Web*. Springer, number 9989 in Lecture Notes in Computer Science, pages 65–68. ESWC 2016 Satellite Events. Heraklion, Crete, Greece, May 29 – June 2, 2016 Revised Selected Papers.

Peter Bourgonje, Julin Moreno Schneider, Georg Rehm, and Felix Sasaki. 2016b. Processing Document Collections to Automatically Extract Linked Data: Semantic Storytelling Technologies for Smart Curation Workflows. In A. Gangemi and C. Gardent, editors, *Proc. of the 2nd Int.*

Create new story from a document collection:

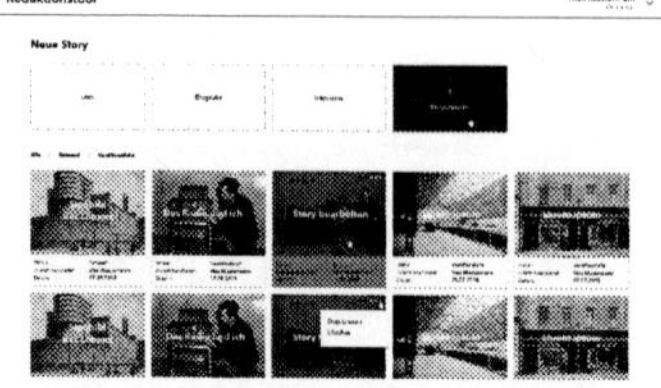

Dragging and dropping content into the story:

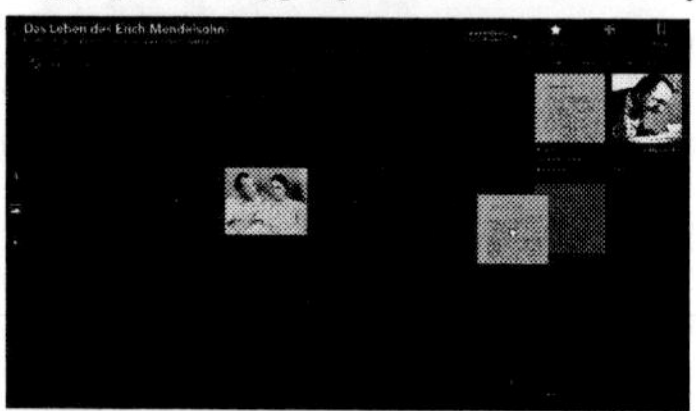

Annotating and arranging the story:

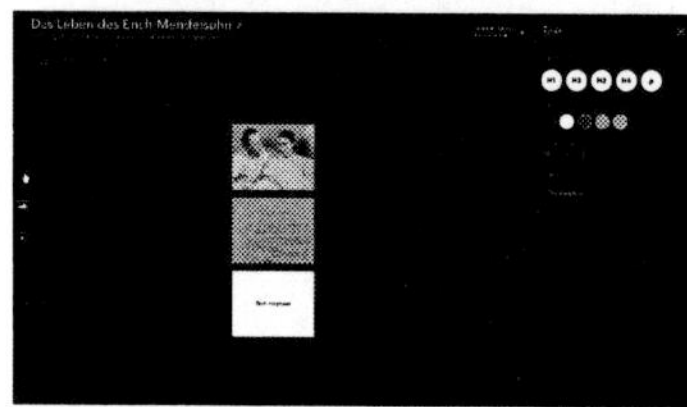

Searching content pieces:

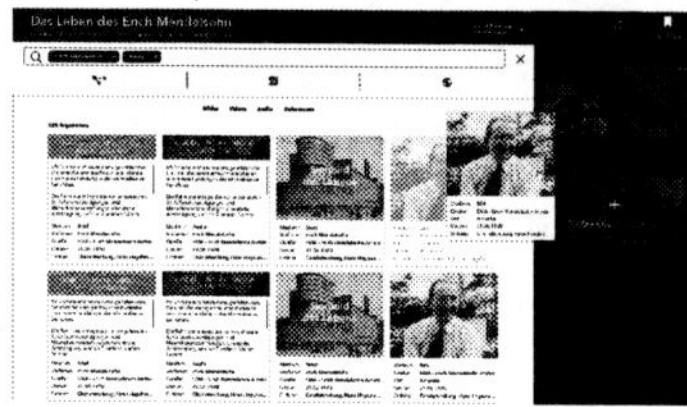

Examining relations between entities:

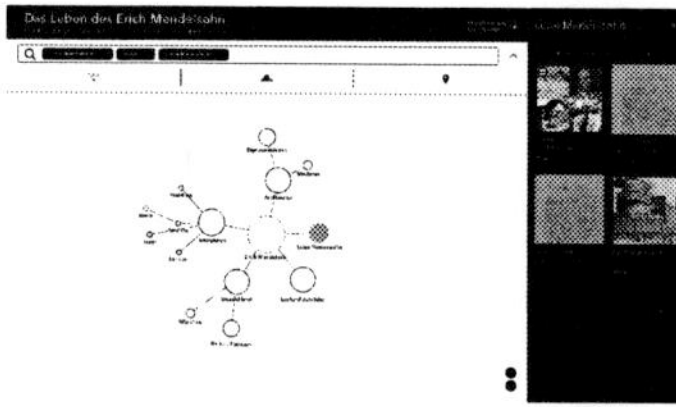

The final story, ready to be deployed:

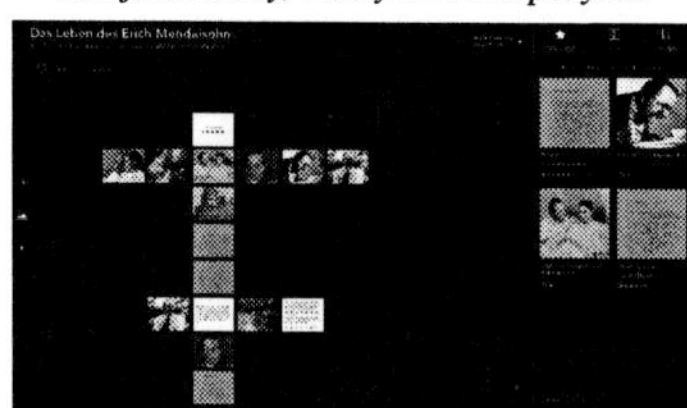

Figure 3: The smart authoring environment

Workshop on Natural Language Generation and the Semantic Web (WebNLG 2016). ACL, Edinburgh, UK, pages 13–16.

Tommaso Caselli and Piek Vossen. 2016. The Storyline Annotation and Representation Scheme (StaR): A Proposal. In T. Caselli, B. Miller, M. van Erp, P. Vossen, and D. Caswell, editors, *Proc. of the 2nd Workshop on Computing News Storylines*. Austin, Texas, pages 67–71.

Philipp Cimiano, Janna Lüker, David Nagel, and Christina Unger. 2013. Exploiting Ontology Lexica for Generating Natural Language Texts from RDF Data. In *Proc. of the 14th European Workshop on Natural Language Generation*. ACL, Sofia, Bulgaria, pages 10–19.

Robert Dale. 1989. Cooking Up Referring Expressions. In *Proc. of the 27th Annual Meeting of the ACL*. Stroudsburg, PA, USA, ACL '89, pages 68–75.

George Doddington, Alexis Mitchell, Mark Przybocki, Lance Ramshaw, Stephanie Strassel, and Ralph Weischedel. 2004. The automatic content extraction (ace) program – tasks, data, and evaluation. In *Proc. of the Fourth Int. Conf. on Language Resources and Evaluation (LREC 2004)*. ELRA, Lisbon, Portugal.

Pablo Gervás. 2013. Stories from Games: Content and Focalization Selection in Narrative Composition. In *I Spanish Symposium on Entertainment Computing*. Universidad Complutense de Madrid, Madrid, Spain.

Pablo Gervás, Belén Díaz-Agudo, Federico Peinado, and Raquel Hervás. 2005. Story Plot Generation based on CBR. In A. Macintosh, R. Ellis, and T. Allen, editors, *Applications and Innovations in Intelligent Systems XII: Proc. of AI-2004, the 24th SGAI Int. Conf. on Innovative Techniques and Applications of Artificial Intelligence*. Springer, London, pages 33–46.

Eli Goldberg, Norbert Driedger, and Richard I. Kittredge. 1994. Using Natural-Language Processing to Produce Weather Forecasts. *IEEE Expert: Intelligent Systems and Their Applications* 9(2):45–53.

Philipp Koehn, Hieu Hoang, Alexandra Birch, Chris Callison-burch, Richard Zens, Marcello Federico, Nicola Bertoldi, Chris Dyer, Brooke Cowan, Wade Shen, Christine Moran, Ondrej Bojar, Alexandra Constantin, and Evan Herbst. 2007. Moses: Open source toolkit for statistical machine translation. ACL, Prague, Czech Republic, pages 177–180.

Beth Levin. 1993. *English Verb Classes and Alternations: A Preliminary Investigation*. Chicago Press, University.

Qi Li, Heng Ji, and Liang Huang. 2013. Joint event extraction via structured prediction with global features. In *Proceedings of the 51st Annual Meeting of the ACL (Volume 1: Long Papers)*. Association for Computational Linguistics, Sofia, Bulgaria, pages 73–82.

Joel Nothman, Nicky Ringland, Will Radford, Tara Murphy, and James R. Curran. 2012. Learning multilingual named entity recognition from Wikipedia. *Artificial Intelligence* 194.151–175.

Yanwei Pang, Xin Lu, Yuan Yuan, and Xuelong Li. 2011. Travelogue enriching and scenic spot overview based on textual and visual topic models. *International Journal of Pattern Recognition and Artificial Intelligence* 25(3).

Steven Poulakos, Mubbasir Kapadia, Andrea Schüpfer, Fabio Zünd, Robert Sumner, and Markus Gross. 2015. Towards an Accessible Interface for Story World Building. In *AAAI Conference on Artificial Intelligence and Interactive Digital Entertainment*. pages 42–48.

Georg Rehm, Jing He, Julian Moreno Schneider, Jan Nehring, and Joachim Quantz. 2017. Designing User Interfaces for Curation Technologies. In *19th Int. Conf. on Human-Computer Interaction – HCI Int. 2017*. In print, Vancouver, Canada.

Ehud Reiter, Somayajulu Sripada, Jim Hunter, and Ian Davy. 2005. Choosing words in computer-generated weather forecasts. *Artificial Intelligence* 167:137–169.

Mark Owen Riedl and Robert Michael Young. 2010. Narrative Planning: Balancing Plot and Character. *J. Artif. Int. Res.* 39(1):217–268.

Julian Moreno Schneider, Peter Bourgonje, Jan Nehring, Georg Rehm, Felix Sasaki, and Ankit Srivastava. 2016. Towards Semantic Story Telling with Digital Curation Technologies. In L. Birnbaum, O. Popescuk, and C. Strapparava, editors, *Proc. of NLP meets Journalism – IJCAI-16 Workshop (NLPMJ 2016)*. New York.

Julian Moreno Schneider, Peter Bourgonje, and Georg Rehm. 2017. Towards User Interfaces for Semantic Storytelling. In *19th Int. Conf. on Human-Computer Interaction – HCI Int. 2017*. In print, Vancouver, Canada.

Jannik Strötgen and Michael Gertz. 2010. Heideltime: High quality rule-based extraction and normalization of temporal expressions. In *Proc. of the Int. Workshop on Semantic Evaluation*. ACL, Stroudsburg, PA, USA, SemEval '10, pages 321–324.

Jannik Strötgen and Michael Gertz. 2011. Wikiwarsde: A german corpus of narratives annotated with temporal expressions. In *Proceedings of the Conference of the German Society for Computational Linguistics and Language Technology (GSCL 2011)*. Hamburg, Germany, pages 129–134.

Ross Turner, Somayajulu Sripada, Ehud Reiter, and Ian P. Davy. 2006. Generating Spatio-temporal Descriptions in Pollen Forecasts. In *Proc. of the 11th Conf. of the European Chapter of the ACL: Posters & Demonstrations*. ACL, Stroudsburg, PA, USA, EACL '06, pages 163–166.

S.R. Turner. 2014. *The Creative Process: A Computer Model of Storytelling and Creativity*. Taylor & Francis.

Mark D. Wood. 2008. Exploiting Semantics for Personalized Story Creation. In *Proc. of the 2008 IEEE Int. Conf. on Semantic Computing*. IEEE Computer Society, Washington, DC, USA, ICSC '08, pages 402–409.

Bishan Yang and Tom Mitchell. 2016. Joint extraction of events and entities within a document context. In *Proc. of the 2016 Conf. of the North American Chapter of the ACL: Human Language Technologies*. ACL, pages 289–299.

Mao Ye, Rong Xiao, Wang-Chien Lee, and Xing Xie. 2011. On theme location discovery for travelogue services. In *Proc. of the 34th Int. ACM SIGIR Conf. on Research and development in IR*. ACM, Beijing, China, pages 465–474.

Inference of Fine-Grained Event Causality from Blogs and Films

Zhichao Hu, Elahe Rahimtoroghi and Marilyn A Walker
Natural Language and Dialogue Systems Lab
Department of Computer Science, University of California Santa Cruz
Santa Cruz, CA 95064, USA
`zhu@soe.ucsc.edu, elahe@soe.ucsc.edu, mawalker@ucsc.edu`

Abstract

Human understanding of narrative is mainly driven by reasoning about causal relations between events and thus recognizing them is a key capability for computational models of language understanding. Computational work in this area has approached this via two different routes: by focusing on acquiring a knowledge base of common causal relations between events, or by attempting to understand a particular story or macro-event, along with its storyline. In this position paper, we focus on knowledge acquisition approach and claim that newswire is a relatively poor source for learning fine-grained causal relations between everyday events. We describe experiments using an unsupervised method to learn causal relations between events in the narrative genres of first-person narratives and film scene descriptions. We show that our method learns fine-grained causal relations, judged by humans as likely to be causal over 80% of the time. We also demonstrate that the learned event pairs do not exist in publicly available event-pair datasets extracted from newswire.

1 Introduction

Computational models of language understanding must recognize narrative structure because many types of natural language texts are narratively structured, e.g. news, reviews, film scripts, conversations, and personal blogs (Polanyi, 1989; Jurafsky et al., 2014; Bell, 2005; Gordon et al., 2011a). Human understanding of narrative is driven by reasoning about causal relations between the events and states in the story (Ger-

---

> **We packed all our things** on the night before Thu (24 Jul) except for frozen food. We brought a lot of things along. **We woke up** early on Thu and JS started **packing the frozen marinatinated food** inside the small cooler... In the end, we decided the best place to set up the tent was the squarish ground that's located on the right. Prior to setting up our tent, **we placed a tarp on the ground**. In this way, the underneaths of the tent would be kept clean. After that, **we set the tent up**.

Figure 1: Part of a blog story about camping

rig, 1993; Graesser et al., 1994; Lehnert, 1981; Goyal et al., 2010). Thus previous work has aimed to learn a knowledge base of semantic relations between events from text (Chklovski and Pantel, 2004; Gordon et al., 2011a; Chambers and Jurafsky, 2008; Balasubramanian et al., 2013; Pichotta and Mooney, 2014; Do et al., 2011), with the long-term aim of using this knowledge for understanding. Some of this work explicitly models causality; other work characterizes the semantic relations more loosely as "events that tend to co-occur". Related work points out that causality is granular in nature, and that humans flexibly move back and forth between different levels of granularity of causal knowledge (Hobbs, 1985). Thus methods are needed to learn causal relations and reason about them at different levels of granularity (Mulkar-Mehta et al., 2011).

One limitation of prior work is that it has primarily focused on newswire, thus have only learned relations about newsworthy topics, and likely the most frequent, highly common (coarse-grained) news events. But news articles are not the only resource for learning about relations between events. Much of the content on social media in personal blogs is written by ordinary people about their daily lives (Burton et al., 2009), and these blogs contain a large variety of everyday events (Gordon et al., 2012). Film scene descriptions

Proceedings of the Events and Stories in the News Workshop, pages 52–58,
Vancouver, Canada, August 4, 2017. ©2017 Association for Computational Linguistics

are also action-rich and told in fine-grained detail (Beamer and Girju, 2009; Hu et al., 2013). Moreover, both of these genres typically report events in temporal order, which is a primary cue to causality. In this position paper, we claim that knowledge about fine-grained causal relations between everyday events is often not available in news, and can be better learned from other narrative genres.

For example, Figure 1 shows a part of a personal narrative written in a blog about a camping trip (Burton et al., 2009). The major event in this story is *camping*, which is contingent upon several finer-grained events, such as *packing things the night before, waking up in the morning, packing frozen food*, and later on at the campground, *placing a tarp* and *setting up the tent*. Similarly film scene descriptions, such as the one shown in Figure 2, typically contain fine-grained causality. In this scene from Lord of the Rings, *grabbing* leads to *spilling*, and *pushing* leads to *stumbling* and *falling*.

We show that unsupervised methods for modeling causality can learn fine-grained event relations from personal narratives and film scenes, even when the corpus is relatively small compared to those that have been used for newswire. We learn high-quality causal relations, with over 80% judged as causal by humans. We claim that these fine-grained causal relations are much closer in spirit to those motivating earlier work on scripts (Lehnert, 1981; Schank et al., 1977; Wilensky, 1982; de Jong, 1979), and we show that the causal knowledge we learn is not found in causal knowledge bases learned from news.

Section 2 first summarizes previous work on learning causal knowledge. We then present our experiments and results on modeling event causality in blogs and film scenes in Section 3. Conclusions and future directions are discussed in Section 4.

2 Background and Related Work

Cognitive theories of narrative understanding define narrative coherence in terms of four different sources of causal inferences between events A and B (Trabasso and van den Broek, 1985; Warren et al., 1979; Trabasso et al., 1989; Van den Broek, 1990). (1) Physical: A physically causes event B. (2) Motivational: A happens with B as a motivation. (3) Psychological: A brings about emotions expressed by event B. (4) Enabling: A creates a

Pippin, sitting at the bar, chatting with Locals. Frodo leaps to his feet and pushes his way towards the bar. Frodo **grabs** Pippin's sleeve, **spilling** his beer. Pippin **pushes** Frodo away...he **stumbles** backwards, and **falls** to the floor.

Figure 2: Film Scene from Lord of the Rings, Fantasy Genre

state or condition for B to happen.

There has been a great deal of interest in learning narrative relations or narrative schema in an unsupervised or weakly supervised manner from text. Here we focus on work where the resulting knowledge bases have been made publicly available, allowing us to compare the learned knowledge directly.

The VerbOcean project learned five different semantic relations between event types (verbs) from newswire, with the HAPPENS-BEFORE relation defined as "indicating that the two verbs refer to two temporally disjoint intervals or instances". WordNet's cause relation, between a causative and a resultative verb (as in buy::own) is tagged as an instance of HAPPENS-BEFORE in VerbOcean, consistent with the heuristic that temporal ordering is a major component of causality. Other examples of the HAPPENS-BEFORE relation in the VerbOcean knowledge base include marry::divorce, detain::prosecute, enroll::graduate, schedule::reschedule, and tie::untie (Chklovski and Pantel, 2004).

Balasubramanian et al. (2013) generate pairs of event relational tuples, called *Rel-grams*. The Rel-grams are publicly available through an online search interface[1]. Rel-gram tuples are extracted using a co-occurrence statistical metric, Symmetric Conditional Probability (SCP), which combines Bigram probability in both directions as follows:

$$SCP(e_1, e_2) = P(e_2|e_1) \times P(e_1|e_2) \quad (1)$$

Their evaluation experiments directly compared the knowledge learned in Rel-grams to the previous work on narrative schemas (Chambers and Jurafsky, 2008, 2009), showing that they achieve better results, thus our work compares directly to the tuples available in Rel-grams.

Other work focuses more directly on learning **causal** or **contingency** relations between events.

---

[1]http://relgrams.cs.washington.edu:10000/relgrams

Beamer and Girju (2009) introduced a distributional measure called *Causal Potential* to assess the likelihood of a causal relation holding between two events. This measure is based on Suppes' probabilistic theory of causality (Suppes, 1970).

$$CP(e_1, e_2) = PMI(e_1, e_2) + \log \frac{P(e_1 \rightarrow e_2)}{P(e_2 \rightarrow e_1)}$$

$$(2)$$

$$\text{where } PMI(e_1, e_2) = \log \frac{P(e_1, e_2)}{P(e_1)P(e_2)}$$

where the arrow notation means ordered event pairs, i.e. event e_1 occurs before event e_2. CP consists of two terms: the first is pair-wise mutual information (PMI) and the second is relative ordering of bigrams. PMI measures how often events occur as a pair (without considering their order); whereas relative ordering accounts for the order of the event pairs because temporal order is one of the strongest cues to causality (Beamer and Girju, 2009; Riaz and Girju, 2010, 2013). This work explicitly links their definitions to research using the Penn Discourse Treebank (PDTB) definition of CONTINGENCY.

Beamer and Girju (2009) applied the CP measure to 173 film scripts, resulting in a high correlation between human-judged causality and the CP measure. Their paper provides a list of 90 verb pairs, selected from the high, middle and low CP ranges in their learned causal pairs. We compare their 30 highest CP events with causal event pairs that we learn from film.

Riaz and Girju (2010) apply a similar measure to topic-sorted news stories about Hurricane Katrina and the Iraq War and present ranked causality relations between events for these topics, suggesting that topic-sorted corpora can produce better causal knowledge. Other work has also used CP to measure the contingency relation between two events, reporting better results than achieved with PMI or bigrams alone (Hu et al., 2013; Rahimtoroghi et al., 2016).

3 Methods and Evaluations

Our primary goal is simply to show that fine-grained causal relations can be learned from film scripts and blogs, and that these are not found in causal knowledge bases learned from newswire. In this section we describe our datasets and methods, and the present two evaluations. First, we evaluate whether the relations learned are causal

Corpus	Number	Word Count
Drama	579	6,680,749
Fantasy	113	1,186,587
Mystery	107	1,346,496
Camping	1,062	2,207,458

Table 1: Number of documents and word count for each dataset

using human judgment HITs on Amazon Mechanical Turk. Second, we directly compare to event pair collections from other publicly available sources learned from news genre.

3.1 Datasets

Topical coherence and similarity of events within the corpus used for learning event relations can be as important as the size of the corpus (Riaz and Girju, 2010; Rahimtoroghi et al., 2016). We use two datasets for learning causal event pairs: first-person narratives from blogs (Burton et al., 2009; Rahimtoroghi et al., 2016), and film scene descriptions (excluding dialogs because dialogs are not as action-rich) (Walker et al., 2012; Hu et al., 2013). Our experiment on blogs learns causal relations from a topic-sorted corpus of ~1000 camping stories. We also posit that the genre of a film may select for similar types of events. However genres can be defined broadly or narrowly, e.g. the Drama genre overlaps with many other genres. We thus compare two narrow film genres of Fantasy and Mystery with the Drama genre from an existing corpus (Walker et al., 2012; Hu et al., 2013). The raw numbers for each subcorpus are shown in Table 1. Note that Camping corpus consists of blog posts which are much shorter compared to movie scripts. Thus their word count is much smaller compared to films corpus despite the larger number of documents.

3.2 Methods

In the blogs, related event pairs are more frequently separated by utterances that provide state descriptions or affective reactions to events (Swanson et al., 2014). As a result, we use Causal Potential (CP) measure to assess the causal relation between events and apply skip-2 bigram method for modeling event pairs. But in film scenes, events are very densely distributed, thus related event pairs are often adjacent to one another and therefore nearby events are more likely to be causal. So, for event pairs extracted from

54

Camping Event Pairs
person - pack up $\rightarrow$ person - go - home
person - wake up $\rightarrow$ person - pack up - backpack
person - eat - breakfast $\rightarrow$ person - pack up - campsite
person - head $\rightarrow$ hike up
person - pack up - car $\rightarrow$ head out

Fantasy Event Pairs
person - slam - something $\rightarrow$ shut
send - something $\rightarrow$ fly - something
person - watch $\rightarrow$ something - disappear
person - pick up - something $\rightarrow$ carry - something
person - turn $\rightarrow$ face - person

Mystery Event Pairs
bind $\rightarrow$ gag
person - reach $\rightarrow$ touch - something
person - pull - something $\rightarrow$ reveal - something
person - look $\rightarrow$ confuse
person - come $\rightarrow$ rest

Drama Event Pairs
person - slam - something $\rightarrow$ shut
person - offer - something $\rightarrow$ something - decline
person - rummage $\rightarrow$ person - find - something
send - something $\rightarrow$ something - fly
send - something $\rightarrow$ sprawl

Table 2: High-CP pairs from Camping, Fantasy and Mystery datasets

films we use a variant of CP measure, shown in Eq. 3, that accounts for different window sizes and punishes event pairs from larger window sizes (Riaz and Girju, 2010, 2013; Do et al., 2011; Pichotta and Mooney, 2014).

$$CP_{variant}(e_1, e_2) = \sum_{i=1}^{w_{max}} \frac{CP_i(e_1, e_2)}{i} \qquad (3)$$

where w_{max} is the max window size (how many events after the current event are paired with the current event). $CP_i(e_1; e_2)$ is the CP score for event pair $e_1; e_2$ calculated using window size i.

3.3 Experiments and Results

We process the data in each dataset and calculate causal potential score for each extracted event pair, resulting in a rank-ordered list of causal event pairs. We evaluate the top 100 event pairs for camping, and the top 684 event pairs for films. We take a number of event pairs from each film genre (proportional to the number of films in that genre, see Table 1 and 3), then remove duplicate event pairs, which result in the 684 event pairs from film. Table 2 presents examples of learned high-

Genre	# High-CP Pairs	% Causality
Drama	655	82.6
Fantasy	127	90.7
Mystery	122	87.7

Table 3: Percentage of high-CP pairs labeled as causal by AMT worker, comparing with low-PC pairs, in film genres Drama, Fantasy and Mystery.

CP event pairs from each corpus. In our following Mechanical Turk experiments, Turkers have to pass qualification tests similar to the actual HITs to be able to participate in our task.

In a study on each genre of films, we compare high-CP pairs to a random sample of low-CP pairs on Mechanical Turk to see if pairs with high CP score more strongly encode causal relations that ones with low CP. For every event pair in the 684 high pairs, we randomly select a low pair in order to collect human judgments on Mechanical Turk. The task first defines events and event pairs, then gives examples of event pairs with causal relations. Turkers are asked to select the event pair that is more likely to manifest a causal relation. The results, summarized in Table 3, show that humans judge a large majority of the high-CP pairs to have a causal relation and the results vary by genre. The causality rate is achieved for more focused genres, Fantasy (90.7%) and Mystery (87.7%), despite their smaller size, and the lowest for Drama (82.6%). We believe this result is further evidence that topical coherence improves causal relation learning (Rahimtoroghi et al., 2016; Riaz and Girju, 2010).

In our second evaluation method, we compare the learned CP event pairs to the existing causal knowledge collections. First, we compare our results to the Rel-grams data (learned from newswire) (Balasubramanian et al., 2013). For event pairs from films, we randomly sample 100 high-CP event pairs ensuring that each of the first events of the pairs are distinct. We use the publicly available search interface for Rel-grams to find tuples with the same first event for direct comparison of content of the learned knowledge. We set the co-occurrence window to 5, and select the Rel-gram tuples with the highest # 50 (FS) (frequency of first statement occurring before second statement within a window of 50) to choose high-quality tuples. We evaluate the extracted Rel-gram tuples using the same Mechanical Turk HIT described above. Table 4 shows Mechanical Turk evaluation results for our method on films vs. Rel-grams: in 81% questions, humans judge the high-CP pairs to be more likely to manifest a causal relation. We believe this is because the fine-grained event pairs we learn do not exist in the Rel-gram collections and thus the Rel-gram tuples that matched our first events are not highly coherent, despite the filtering we applied.

Dataset	Film	Rel-gram Tuples
Percentage of causal relation	81 %	19 %

Table 4: Percentage of pairs judged as causal by AMT workers. Film vs. Rel-Grams.

For event pairs from camping blogs, we evaluate all 100 high-CP pairs in a Mechanical Turk study where Turkers are asked to choose whether an event pair has causal relation or not. We also evaluate Rel-gram tuples using the same task. However, Rel-grams are not sorted by topic. To find tuples relevant to Camping Trip, we use our top 10 indicative events and extracted all the Rel-gram tuples that included at least one event corresponding to one of the Camping indicative events, e.g. *go camp*. We remove any tuple with frequency less than 25 and sort the rest by the total symmetrical conditional probability. The evaluation results presented in Table 5 show that 82% of the blog paurs were labeled as causal, where as only 42% of the Rel-gram pairs were labeled as causal. We argue that this is mainly due to the limitations of the newswire data which does not contain the fine-grained everyday events that we have extracted from our corpus.

Dataset	Camping	Rel-gram Tuples
Percentage of causal relation	82 %	42 %

Table 5: Percentage of pairs judged as causal by AMT workers. Camping blogs vs. Rel-Grams.

Next, we compare our results to the event pairs in VerbOcean (learned from newswire) with the HAPPENS-BEFORE relation (Chklovski and Pantel, 2004). We use all 6497 event pairs from VerbOcean, comparing with our 684 event pairs from films and 100 event pairs from camping blogs with high CP scores. Our result shows that there are 12 event pairs that exist in both VerbOcean and films, e.g. *turn - leave* and *slow - stop*, and there is only one event pair that exist in both VerbOcean and camping blogs: *pack - leave*. This confirms that most causal relations learned from other narrative genres do not exist in the currently available knowledge bases extracted from newswire. A number of event pairs from these collections share the first event, e.g. *dig - find* and *scan - spot* from films vs. *dig - repair* and *scan - upload* from VerbOcean; *drive - park* and *pick - eat* from blogs vs. *drive - drag* and *pick - plunk* from VerbOcean.

Finally, we compare our high-CP pairs learned from film to the high-CP event pairs from Beamer and Girju (2009), learned from only 173 films. There is no public release of Beamer and Girju's event pairs, thus we take the 29 event pairs with high CP score presented in the paper. A total of 14 of their 29 pairs are also in our top 684 film pairs. These include pairs such as *swerve - avoid*, *leave - stand* and *unlock - open*. However on our larger genre-sorted corpus we also learn pairs such as *grab - haul*, *scratch - claw* and *saddle- mount* that do not exist in their collection.

4 Conclusions and Future Work

Causality is often granular in nature with major events related to the occurrence of finer-grained events. In this position paper, we argue that the focus on newswire has inhibited attempts to learn fine-grained causal relations between everyday events, and that other narrative genres better support such learning. We use unsupervised methods to extract fine-grained causal event relations from films and blog posts about camping.

We show that more than 80% of the relations we learn are evaluated as causal, and that topical coherence plays an important role in modeling event relations. We also show that the causal knowledge we learn from other narrative genres does not exist in current event collections induced from newswire. We plan to expand our genre-specific experiments on the films corpus in future, as well as using other narrative datasets, like restaurant reviews, to extract fine-grained causal knowledge about events.

References

Niranjan Balasubramanian, Stephen Soderland, Mausam, and Oren Etzioni. 2013. Generating coherent event schemas at scale. In *EMNLP*. pages 1721–1731.

Brandon Beamer and Roxana Girju. 2009. Using a bigram event model to predict causal potential. In *Computational Linguistics and Intelligent Text Processing*, Springer, pages 430–441.

Allan Bell. 2005. News stories as narratives. *The Language of Time: A Reader* page 397.

Kevin Burton, Akshay Java, and Ian Soboroff. 2009. The ICWSM 2009 Spinn3r dataset. In *Proceedings of the Third Annual Conference on Weblogs and Social Media (ICWSM 2009)*.

Nathanael Chambers and Dan Jurafsky. 2008. Unsupervised learning of narrative event chains. *Proceedings of ACL-08: HLT* pages 789–797.

Nathanael Chambers and Dan Jurafsky. 2009. Unsupervised learning of narrative schemas and their participants. In *Proceedings of the 47th Annual Meeting of the ACL*. pages 602–610.

Timothy Chklovski and Patrick Pantel. 2004. Verbocean: Mining the web for fine-grained semantic verb relations. In *EMNLP*. volume 4, pages 33–40.

G. F. de Jong. 1979. *Skimming Stories in Real Time: An Experiment in Integrated Understanding*. Ph.D. thesis, Computer Science Department, Yale University.

Quang Xuan Do, Yee Seng Chan, and Dan Roth. 2011. Minimally supervised event causality identification. In *Proceedings of the Conference on Empirical Methods in Natural Language Processing*. Association for Computational Linguistics, pages 294–303.

R.J. Gerrig. 1993. *Experiencing narrative worlds: On the psychological activities of reading*. Yale Univ Pr.

Andrew Gordon, Cosmin Bejan, and Kenji Sagae. 2011a. Commonsense causal reasoning using millions of personal stories. In *Twenty-Fifth Conference on Artificial Intelligence (AAAI-11)*.

Andrew S Gordon, Cosmin Adrian Bejan, and Kenji Sagae. 2011b. Commonsense causal reasoning using millions of personal stories. In *AAAI*.

Andrew S Gordon, Christopher Wienberg, and Sara Owsley Sood. 2012. Different strokes of different folks: Searching for health narratives in weblogs. In *Privacy, Security, Risk and Trust (PASSAT), 2012 International Conference on and 2012 International Confernece on Social Computing (SocialCom)*. IEEE, pages 490–495.

Amit Goyal, Ellen Riloff, and Hal Daumé III. 2010. Automatically producing plot unit representations for narrative text. In *Proceedings of the 2010 Conference on Empirical Methods in Natural Language Processing*. pages 77–86.

Arthur C Graesser, Murray Singer, and Tom Trabasso. 1994. Constructing inferences during narrative text comprehension. *Psychological review* 101(3):371.

Jerry R Hobbs. 1985. Granularity. In *Proceedings of the 9th international joint conference on Artificial intelligence-Volume 1*. Morgan Kaufmann Publishers Inc., pages 432–435.

Zhichao Hu, Elahe Rahimtoroghi, Larissa Munishkina, Reid Swanson, and Marilyn A Walker. 2013. Unsupervised induction of contingent event pairs from film scenes. In *Proceedings of Conference on Empirical Methods in Natural Language Processing*. pages 370–379.

Dan Jurafsky, Victor Chahuneau, Bryan R Routledge, and Noah A Smith. 2014. Narrative framing of consumer sentiment in online restaurant reviews. *First Monday* 19(4).

Wendy G Lehnert. 1981. Plot units and narrative summarization. *Cognitive Science* 5(4):293–331.

Rutu Mulkar-Mehta, Christopher Welty, Jerry R Hoobs, and Eduard Hovy. 2011. Using granularity concepts for discovering causal relations. In *Proceedings of the FLAIRS conference*.

Karl Pichotta and Raymond J Mooney. 2014. Statistical script learning with multi-argument events. *EACL 2014* page 220.

Livia Polanyi. 1989. *Telling the American Story: A Structural and Cultural Analysis of Conversational Storytelling*. MIT Press.

Elahe Rahimtoroghi, Ernesto Hernandez, and Marilyn A. Walker. 2016. Learning fine-grained knowledge about contingent relations between everyday events. In *Proceedings of SIGDIAL 2016*. pages 350–359.

Mehwish Riaz and Roxana Girju. 2010. Another look at causality: Discovering scenario-specific contingency relationships with no supervision. In *Semantic Computing (ICSC), 2010 IEEE Fourth International Conference on*. IEEE, pages 361–368.

Mehwish Riaz and Roxana Girju. 2013. Toward a better understanding of causality between verbal events: Extraction and analysis of the causal power of verb-verb associations. In *Proceedings of the annual SIGdial Meeting on Discourse and Dialogue (SIGDIAL)*. Citeseer.

R Schank, Robert Abelson, and Roger C Schank. 1977. *Scripts Plans Goals*. Lea.

Patrick Suppes. 1970. *A probabilistic theory of causality*. North-Holland Publishing Company Amsterdam.

Reid Swanson, Elahe Rahimtoroghi, Thomas Corcoran, and Marilyn A Walker. 2014. Identifying narrative clause types in personal stories. In *15th Annual Meeting of the Special Interest Group on Discourse and Dialogue*.

Tom Trabasso and Paul van den Broek. 1985. Causal thinking and the representation of narrative events. *Journal of Memory and Language* 24:612–630.

Tom Trabasso, Paul Van den Broek, and So Young Suh. 1989. Logical necessity and transitivity of causal relations in stories. *Discourse processes* 12(1):1–25.

Paul Van den Broek. 1990. The causal inference maker: Towards a process model of inference generation in text comprehension. *Comprehension processes in reading* pages 423–445.

Marilyn Walker, Grace Lin, and Jennifer Sawyer. 2012. An annotated corpus of film dialogue for learning and characterizing character style. In *Language Resources and Evaluation Conference, LREC2012*.

William H Warren, David W Nicholas, and Tom Trabasso. 1979. Event chains and inferences in understanding narratives. *New directions in discourse processing* 2:23–52.

Robert Wilensky. 1982. Points: A theory of the structure of stories in memory. In Wendy G. Lehnert and Martin H. Ringle, editors, *Strategies for Natural Language Processing*.

On the Creation of a Security-Related Event Corpus

Martin Atkinson, Jakub Piskorski, Hristo Tanev, Vanni Zavarella
Text and Data Mining Unit, Directorate I: Competencies
Joint Research Centre of the European Commission
Via Enrico Fermi 2749, 21027 Ispra (VA), Italy
`firstname.lastname@ec.europa.eu`

Abstract

This paper reports on an effort of creating a corpus of structured information on security-related events automatically extracted from on-line news, part of which has been manually curated. The main motivation behind this effort is to provide material to the NLP community working on event extraction that could be used both for training and evaluation purposes.

1 Introduction

Due to a rapid proliferation of textual information in digital form various security-related organisations have recently acknowledged the benefits of deploying techniques to automate the process of extraction of structured information on events from free texts (Appelt, 1999; Ashish et al., 2006; Ji et al., 2009; Piskorski and Yangarber, 2013). Examples of current capabilities of such techniques for the extraction of disease outbreaks, crisis situations, cross-border crimes and computer security events from on-line sources are given in (Grishman et al., 2002; King and Lowe, 2003; Tanev et al., 2008; Yangarber et al., 2008; Atkinson et al., 2011; Gao et al., 2013; Danilova and Popova, 2014; Ritter et al., 2015).

This paper reports on the creation of a corpus of structured information on security-related events automatically extracted from online news over a period of 8 years, part of which has been manually curated. The main drive behind this endeavour is to provide material to theNLP community working on event extraction, which could be used in various ways, e.g., for: (a) carrying out evaluations of detection and extraction of security-related events from online news (human-curated data), (b) training event type classifiers, (c) learning domain-specific terminology, (d) creating full-fledged inline or stand-off annotations with event-centric information based on the automatically extracted event templates.

Other efforts on the creation of corpora with event-related annotation of various nature include: GDELT (Leetaru and Schrodt, 2013), FactBank (Saurí and Pustejovsky, 2009), ICEWS (Ward et al., 2013), EventCorefBank (Cybulska and Vossen, 2014), ASTRE (Nguyen et al., 2016) and (Hong et al., 2016). Contrary to most other initiatives our corpus contains aggregated information on events extracted at news cluster level without provision of links to concrete phrases in news articles from which the information was inferred.

Section 2 briefly presents our news event extraction system. Section 3 reports on an evaluation thereof to provide insights on the quality of extraction. Section 4 provides some corpus statistics.

2 Event Extraction System Description

Our event extraction system has been primarily designed to help analysts from international institutions to automate the process of gathering intelligence on security-related events from online news. It is capable of extracting information on different types of crises, such as political violence, social turmoil, natural and man-made disasters. We briefly describe the core elements of the event extraction system, while a more detailed description can be found in (Tanev et al., 2008; Piskorski et al., 2008; Tanev et al., 2009).

The event extraction system runs on top of Europe Media Monitor (EMM), a large-scale news aggregation engine that gathers articles from ca. 7000 sources in 60 languages on a 24/7 basis (Atkinson and Van Der Goot, 2009). The system takes as input a set of news articles on the same topic, called a *news cluster* which are pro-

Proceedings of the Events and Stories in the News Workshop, pages 59–65,
Vancouver, Canada, August 4, 2017. ©2017 Association for Computational Linguistics

duced every 10 minutes by the news aggregation engine. The output of the event extraction is an event description template corresponding to the main event reported in the cluster and includes two main slots: *Event type* and *Geolocation*, and other event-type specific descriptive and numerical slots, e.g., *Perpetrators, Dead victims, Number injured, Displaced, Targeted infrastructure*.

In the first step, each article in the cluster is linguistically pre-processed to produce a more abstract representation of the text, including, i.a., tokenization, sentence splitting, NER, and labeling of key terms like action words (e.g. *kill, shoot*).

Our event extraction system is applied only on the title and lead sentences of each article assuming that articles are written using the *inverted pyramid style*, the dominant paradigm in modern journalism (Pöttker, 2003). Although one might potentially report on a relevant event in the final paragraphs of an article, our system has not been designed to capture them.

Next lexico-semantic patterns for the extraction of one or two slots in the event template are applied to parse more complex phrases, which express different actions and situations whose results are death, injury or other effects on people, e.g. *five people were injured, the boss of Cosa Nostra was found dead*. These patterns (several hundreds) were semi-automatically acquired using a bootstrapping approach (Riloff, 1996; Yangarber et al., 2000) described in more detail in (Tanev et al., 2008, 2009).

Since information about events is scattered over different articles, in the next step cross-document information validation and fusion heuristics are deployed, e.g., majority voting-like heuristics described in (Piskorski et al., 2008). To give a more precise example, in the context of extracting descriptive slots, among the phrases that apear as a filler of a given slot in the event templates extracted from all articles in the cluster, the most frequent one is selected.

Event classification is done using: (i) detecting keyword combinations, e.g., if a word in: *soldiers, troops, tanks, marines, etc.* occurs in the vicinity of a word in: *attacked, destroyed, raided, etc.*, then *Armed conflict* type is inferred, (ii) type-preference heuristics, e.g., if the text talks about violence, but simultaneously arrested people were detected using some pattern, then *Arrest* is preferred to *Violence*, and (iii) SVM-based word

ngram text classifier, which is applied, when the rule-based classification yields no result.

Our event types, e.g. *Armed Conflict, Terrorist Attack, Protest, Earthquake, etc.*, were chosen among those that have the strongest impact on the security of the society.

Finally, a keyword-based filter (semi-automatically created using bootstrapping lexical learning (Tanev and Zavarella, 2014)) is deployed to eliminate events that are vaguely related to some past security-related events, e.g., commemorations related to past natural disasters, political meetings with the purpose of resolving violence-related issues, fake threats of terrorist attacks.

Our event extraction system relies on lightweight linguistic processing vis-a-vis state-of-the-art systems that use more linguistic sophistication (Kilicoglu and Bergler, 2009; Chen et al., 2015) due to: (a) specifics of the environment our system used in, where the key feature is scalability, i.e., one has to be able to quickly extend the system to detect new event types and process news in many languages, and (b) the paramount importance of providing the analysts some sort of event-centric navigation structure to guide further reading and analysis, in whose context the high quality extraction of certain slots and extraction of very fine-grained information (e.g. guessing the most specific event location information versus guessing the administrative region in which an event happened) is of lower importance.

3 Evaluation

3.1 Test Data Set

For the purpose of evaluating the performance of the automatically extracted information we have first selected 15 event types, taken from the full list of 62 types that the system is designed to detect, reported in Annex (see Sec. 4.2). The chosen types are representative of 5 broader event categories: (a) Natural disasters: *Wildfire, Flood, Earthquake*, (b) Man-made disasters: *Maritime Accident, Explosion, Ordinary Man-Made Disaster*, (c) Violence: *Kidnapping/Hostage Taking, Shooting, Terrorist attack*, (d) Military-related: *Heavy Weapons Fire, Armed Conflict, Air/Missile Attack*, and (e) Socio-political: *Riot/Turmoil, Boycott/Strike, Public Demonstration*. Then, we have randomly collected 16 news clusters that the system had tagged with each target event type, from system data between 1/05/2016 and 31/12/2016, for a total of 240 clusters.

For each event news cluster, the annotators were given the title and first two sentences of each of the 15 (max) latest articles, including duplicates. The rationale of this setting is that we intended to 'simulate' the limited amount of data an analyst is usually able to process in order to pick up the main facts of the event reported in an article set.

For each news cluster the annotators were then tasked to provide: (a) a ranked list of up to three event types, where higher rank is given to more specific event types applicable (e.g., riot vs. disorder) and to the main event reported in the cluster vis-a-vis background events mentioned in the cluster[1], (b) a non-ranked list of locations, each represented by an ID, where in case of two or more locations being in 'administrative' inclusion relation only the most specific one is retained, (c) for each event role descriptor slot a non-ranked list of all names and descriptions found in the text, and (d) for each event role amount slot a single integer or a span of integers reflecting the minimum and maximum values reported.

Gold standard was annotated by 4 annotators. We analyzed inter-annotator agreement (IAA) for the event type classification task on a sample of 120 clusters, by considering only the first type in the ranked lists, obtaining a Fleiss Kappa score of 0.7 (Fleiss, 1971).

3.2 Evaluation metrics

For the purpose of evaluating the performance of event extraction methods the research community has been predominantly using mention-based metrics and standards such as ACE (Doddington et al., 2004), where, e.g., the scores for extracted slot fillers are summed up over their mentions in text. However, motivated by the specific environment in which our event extraction system is used, we propose partly novel evaluation metrics that try to quantify from a user perspective the most relevant semantic dimensions of event information aggregated from multi-document sets. As an example, evaluating geo-coding as the task of locating events both on a geographical reference system and an administrative unit hierarchy (rather than as a standard entity recognition task (Mandl et al., 2009)) allows to estimate its usefulness for spatial analysis of aggregated event data. For an analyst responsible for studying events that happened in a particular administrative region (e.g., country, state) an incorrect extraction of the place, although within the boundaries of the region assigned to him, still does provide some value, which should be awarded with a non-zero score.

We first introduce the metrics for the evaluation of event type and location extraction. Let $C = \{c_1, \ldots, c_n\}$ denote the set of input clusters of articles. Let also t_c (l_c) denote the event type (location) for cluster c returned by the system. Further, let T_c^G denote an ordered list of event types in the gold truth for cluster c, and let L_c^G denote an unordered list of event locations l_c^G for c in the gold truth[2].

For the evaluation of event type classification we use an adapted version of the Mean Reciprocal Rank (MRR) (Craswell, 2009) defined as follows:

$$MRR = \frac{1}{|C|} \sum_{c \in C}^{|C|} score(t_c)$$

where $score(t_c) = 1/rank(t_c)$ with $rank(t_c)$ denoting the rank of t_c in T_c^G, or $score(t_c) = 0$ if $t_c \notin T_c^G$. In our context the reciprocal rank of a system response for cluster c is the multiplicative inverse of the rank thereof in the gold truth.

For the evaluation of the event location extraction we define two basic metrics: Geographical Closeness (GC) and Administrative Closeness (AC) which are maximized over the gold truth locations. The GC metric is defined as follows:

$$GC(c) = \max_{l_c^G \in L_c^G} \frac{1}{\ln(dist(l_c, l_c^G) + e)}$$

where $dist(a, b)$ denotes the physical distance (in km.), between a and b, which is computed using the GEONAMES gazetteer[3];

The AC metric is a modification of WUP, the semantic metric presented in (Wu and Palmer, 1994), whose main aim is to reflect how close the system location response is to the corresponding gold truth location in the administrative hier-

---

[1]For 56 clusters the annotator estimated that no type from the list in Annex (see Sec. 4.2) could be inferred as main event of the cluster, which we marked with a fictitious NA event type tag; however in 27 cases secondary gold truth event(s) matched system response, producing a non-zero score.

[2]While the system returns the most relevant location of the event in c, semantically the event could sensibly be distributed over multiple locations.

[3]http://www.geonames.org

archy of geographical references. Let T_{GEO} denote the administrative hierarchy in the GeoNames gazetteer[4] and let $LCS(x, y)$ denote the lowest common subsumer for nodes x and y in T_{GEO}. AC is then defined as follows:

$$AC(c) = \max_{l_c^G \in L_c^G} \frac{2 \cdot \omega(LCS(l_c, l_c^G))^2}{\omega(l_c)^2 + \omega(l_c^G) \cdot \omega(l_c)}$$

where $\omega(v) = \sum_{i=0}^{depth(v)} \delta/2^i$ is a weighted depth of a node v in T_{GEO}, with δ empirically set to 10. The main intuition behind AC is to apply a higher penalty to system errors: (a) closer to the root of T_{GEO} (e.g., guessing wrong country is worse than guessing wrong city within a province), and (b) resulting from providing over-specific, false information vis-a-vis system responses being not as specific, but still encompassing, gold truth location (e.g. guessing only the region of a gold truth town).

We also compute Location Accuracy (LC) as a weighted harmonic mean of GC and AC, maximized over the gold truth locations:

$$LC_\beta = \max_{l_c^G \in L_c^G} \frac{2 \cdot \beta \cdot GC(c) \cdot AC(c)}{GC(c) + AC(c)}$$

where β was set to 1 in the evaluation.

For event slot descriptors we first distinguish two cases: definite description phrases are normalized and possibly merged to the morphological base forms of their noun/adjective components (e.g. 'three Iraqi militants' and 'Iraqi militants' are merged into 'Iraqi militant', while all upper case phrases (supposedly person names) are kept as such. In the former case, if $descr_c$ is a system output descriptor for a certain role of event in cluster c and $descr_c^G$ is a gold standard descriptor for the same role, the match between $descr_c$ and $descr_c^G$ is computed as:

$$\max_{m \in descr_c^N \wedge n \in descr_c^{GN}} WUP(m, n)$$

where $descr_c^N$ and $descr_c^{GN}$ are the sets of all N-grams of $descr_c$ and $descr_c^G$, resp., and $WUP(m, n)$ is a WordNet-based semantic relatedness measure (Wu and Palmer, 1994). In the latter case, matches are computed as:

$$\max_{m \in descr_c^N \wedge n \in descr_c^{GN}} StringSim(m, n)$$

where $StringSim(m, n)$ is modification of the Jaro metric boosting agreeing initial characters (Winkler, 1999).

In both cases, in order to penalize cases of role filler inversion, we score as 0 the matches of a system output role descriptor if it is lower than the max similarity with any of the other event role fillers in gold standard. Given the scores above, standard Precision, Recall and F1 measure are computed.

Finally, we record the root Mean Squared Error (MSE) of system output victim count values against gold standard, over all applicable roles[5].

3.3 Results

The evaluation results for the extraction of the event type and location are provided in Table 1. The overall results are good vis-a-vis the state-of-the-art results reported elswhere. A rudimentary error analysis of event type extraction revealed that somewhat worse results for *Violence*, *Socio-political* and *Military* categories were caused by the semantic 'proximity' of the event types contained in each of these categories. In particular, based on the low performance of extraction of *Explosion* events they were not included in the event corpus. The overall 0.4 score for GC corresponds to an average geographical error of around 9.2km from the gold standard location point, while the 0.49 for AC translates to a level of granularity between country and region levels.

The evaluation results for the extraction of the 'descriptor' and numerical slots are provided in Table 2, mF and MF columns for each role description task represent resp. the micro/macro average F1-measure. Extraction of numerical slots is quite accurate, except than for the *Dead* role, as dead counts are more likely to occur as cumulative figures in highly deadly events such as military conflicts; the systems often fails to separate them from real-time victim count updates.

---

[4]We distinguish between four levels: country, region, province and populated place.

[5]Gold truth count could sensibly be represented as an interval of max and min values, when the annotator can not pick up a unique figure among the ones mentioned in text; in those case error is computed wrt the interval boundary closest to system response

	All	Natural disaster	Man-made disaster	Violence	Military	Socio-political
MRR	0.71	0.84	0.8	0.64	0.67	0.62
GC	0.4	0.32	0.44	0.4	0.41	0.42
AC	0.49	0.45	0.56	0.11	0.53	0.41
LC	0.4	0.34	0.46	0.4	0.41	0.39

Table 1: Evaluation results for event type and location extraction for the different event type subsets.

SLOT	MF1	mF1	MSE
dead	0.46	0.62	14.6
injured	0.26	0.48	4.54
arrested	0.02	0.25	1.07
kidnapped	0.15	0.66	0.44
displaced	0.03	0.34	5.39
perpetrator	0.19	0.22	NA
weapon	0.23	0.53	NA

Table 2: Evaluation of descriptive/numerical slots.

4 Corpus release

4.1 Data sets

The current version of the corpus contains two sets: (a) moderated events (MOD) resulting from manual curation of the automated extractions in 6 languages by one trained human expert responsible for providing 'cleaned' data to the end-users, and (b) automatically extracted events (AUTO) from English news. The quantitative data on the MOD set containing 17536 event templates is given in Table 3. The (MOD) set was created during the period of 1/02/2009 to 18/08/2015. The breakdown of the events w.r.t. to languages covered is as follows: English (45.3%), Spanish (16.3%), Italian (12.0%), French (11,2%), Portuguese (7,7%) and Russian (7,5%).

The AUTO set contains ca. 600K events extracted from online news in English for the period 1/1/2009 to 1/4//2017. We have selected ca. 330K of the most 'reliable' event templates therefrom, i.e, whose extraction appears to be more accurate vis-a-vis other event types. The preliminary quantitative data on the corpus[6] is given in Table 4.

----

[6]The figures are subject to change since we are currently

TYPE	NUM	TYPE	NUM	TYPE	NUM
Arrest	2753	Terrorist attack	497	Maritime accid.	178
Disorder	2109	Earth quake	411	Stabbing	174
Man-made dis.	1971	Kidnapping	305	Physical attack	171
Trial	1903	Explosion	283	Hostage release	169
NONE	1510	Bombing	265	Hum. crisis	161
Armed conflict	1214	Air attack	253	Assassination	137
Medical	1117	Flood	223	Tropical storm	103
Shooting	906	Storm	185	OTHER	538

Table 3: Quantitative data on the MOD event set. The *OTHER* category includes all less frequent event types; *NONE* stands for events which include information on dead/injured, but whose type does not match any predefined event types

TYPE	NUM	TYPE	NUM	TYPE	NUM
Arrest	91	Armed confl.	18	Earthquake	6
Disorder/Protest	59	Flood	11	Air attack	5
Man-made dis.	42	Storm	11	Marritime accid.	3
Shooting	42	Kidnapping	8	Heavy weapon	2
Terrorist attack	36	Wildfire	7	fire	

Table 4: Quantitative data on the AUTO set (numbers of events are provided in thousands).

4.2 Format and Access

The current version of the corpus accompanied with additional information (including, i.a., list of event types and corresponding slots, instructions on how to access the underlying news stories from which the events were extracted, etc.) can be accessed at: `http://labs.emm4u.eu/events.html`

The corpus is available in two formats: (a) comma separated values (csv) and (b) JSON. The former contains only the following (reduced) data: unique event id; type of the event; event type category[7]; the date when it was detected; the title of the centroid article in the cluster; and the identified place name (including latitude/longitude and computed administrative path, where the first element therein provides most fine-grained information). The unique event id can be used to publicly access the articles in the cluster from which the event was extracted. The JSON format contains the full template structure including the descriptive slots: who was killed/injured; the perpetrators; the weapons used; any other descriptors that were identified for that particular event type.

It is envisaged to further extend the corpus through the provision of: (a) annotated data for new languages, (b) a new attribute reflecting extraction reliability (c) cross-language event links (Ji, 2010; Piskorski et al., 2011), and (d) additional access methods (e.g., KML).

References

Douglas Appelt. 1999. Introduction to Information Extraction. *AI Communications* 12:161–172.

Naveen Ashish, Doug Appelt, Dayne Freitag, and Dmitry Zelenko. 2006. *Proceedings of the Workshop on Event Extraction and Synthesis*. Held in conjunction with the AAAI 2006.

----

considering adding events of other types to the corpus. Updated information will be provided on the web page of the project (see Section 4.2).

[7]Currently there are six event type categories: *Natural Disaster, Man-mad Disaster, Civic-Political Action, Crime or Violence, Military Action* and *Other*

Martin Atkinson, Jakub Piskorski, Roman Yangarber, and Erik van der Goot. 2011. Multilingual Real-Time Event Extraction for Border Security Intelligence Gathering. In Uffe Kock Wiil, editor, *Open Source Intelligence and Counter-terrorism.* Springer, LNCS, Vol. 2.

Martin Atkinson and Erik Van Der Goot. 2009. Near Real Time Information Mining in Multilingual News. In *Proceedings of the 18th International World Wide Web Conference (WWW'2009).* pages 1153–1154.

Yubo Chen, Liheng Xu, Kang Liu, Daojian Zeng, and Jun Zhao. 2015. Event extraction via dynamic multi-pooling convolutional neural networks. In *Proceedings of the 53rd Annual Meeting of the Association for Computational Linguistics and the 7th International Joint Conference on Natural Language Processing.* pages 167–176.

Nick Craswell. 2009. Mean Reciprocal Rank. In Ling Liu and M. Tamer zsu, editors, *Encyclopedia of Database Systems,* Springer US, page 1703.

Agata Cybulska and Piek Vossen. 2014. Using a Sledgehammer to Crack a Nut? Lexical Diversity and Event Coreference Resolution. In Nicoletta Calzolari (Conference Chair), Khalid Choukri, Thierry Declerck, Hrafn Loftsson, Bente Maegaard, Joseph Mariani, Asuncion Moreno, Jan Odijk, and Stelios Piperidis, editors, *Proceedings of the Ninth International Conference on Language Resources and Evaluation (LREC'14).* European Language Resources Association (ELRA), Reykjavik, Iceland.

Vera Danilova and Svetlana Popova. 2014. Sociopolitical event extraction using a rule-based approach. In *OTM Confederated International Conferences "On the Move to Meaningful Internet Systems".* Springer, pages 537–546.

George R Doddington, Alexis Mitchell, Mark A Przybocki, Lance A Ramshaw, Stephanie Strassel, and Ralph M Weischedel. 2004. The Automatic Content Extraction (ACE) Program-Tasks, Data, and Evaluation. In *LREC 2004: : 4th International Conference on Language Resources and Evaluation.* volume 2, page 1.

Joseph L. Fleiss. 1971. Measuring nominal scale agreement among many raters. *Psychological Bulletin* 76(5):378–382.

Jianbo Gao, Kalev H Leetaru, Jing Hu, Claudio Cioffi-Revilla, and Philip Schrodt. 2013. Massive media event data analysis to assess world-wide political conflict and instability. In *International Conference on Social Computing, Behavioral-Cultural Modeling, and Prediction.* Springer, pages 284–292.

Ralph Grishman, Silja Huttunen, and Roman Yangarber. 2002. Real-time Event Extraction for Infectious Disease Outbreaks. In *Proceedings of HLT 2002.*

Yu Hong, Tongtao Zhang, Tim O'Gorman, Sharone Horowit-Hendler, Heng Ji, and Martha Palmer. 2016. Building a Cross-document Event-Event Relation Corpus. In *Proceedings of the 10th Linguistic Annotation Workshop held in conjunction with ACL 2016, LAW@ACL 2016, August 11, 2016, Berlin, Germany.*

Heng Ji. 2010. Challenges from Information Extraction to Information Fusion. In *Proceedings of the 23rd International Conference on Computational Linguistics: Posters.* Association for Computational Linguistics, Stroudsburg, PA, USA, COLING '10, pages 507–515.

Heng Ji, Ralph Grishman, Zheng Chen, and Prashant Gupta. 2009. Cross-document Event Extraction and Tracking: Task, Evaluation, Techniques and Challenges. In Galia Angelova, Kalina Bontcheva, Ruslan Mitkov, Nicolas Nicolov, and Nikolai Nikolov, editors, *RANLP.* RANLP 2009 Organising Committee / ACL, pages 166–172.

Halil Kilicoglu and Sabine Bergler. 2009. Syntactic dependency based heuristics for biological event extraction. In *Proceedings of the Workshop on Current Trends in Biomedical Natural Language Processing: Shared Task.* Association for Computational Linguistics, pages 119–127.

Gary King and Will Lowe. 2003. An Automated Information Extraction Tool For International Conflict Data with Performance as Good as Human Coders. *International Organization* 57:617–642.

Kalev Leetaru and Philip A Schrodt. 2013. Gdelt: Global data on events, location, and tone, 1979–2012. In *ISA Annual Convention.* Citeseer, volume 2.

Thomas Mandl, Paula Carvalho, Giorgio Di Nunzio, Fredric Gey, Ray Larson, Diana Santos, and Christa Womser-Hacker. 2009. GeoCLEF 2008: the CLEF 2008 cross-language geographic information retrieval track overview. *Evaluating Systems for Multilingual and Multimodal Information Access* pages 808–821.

Kiem-Hieu Nguyen, Xavier Tannier, Olivier Ferret, and Romaric Besancon. 2016. A Dataset for Open Event Extraction in English. In Nicoletta Calzolari (Conference Chair), Khalid Choukri, Thierry Declerck, Sara Goggi, Marko Grobelnik, Bente Maegaard, Joseph Mariani, Helene Mazo, Asuncion Moreno, Jan Odijk, and Stelios Piperidis, editors, *Proceedings of the Tenth International Conference on Language Resources and Evaluation (LREC 2016).* European Language Resources Association (ELRA), Paris, France.

Jakub Piskorski, Jenya Belayeva, and Martin Atkinson. 2011. Exploring the Usefulness of Cross-lingual Information Fusion for Refining Real-time News Event Extraction: A Preliminary Study.

Jakub Piskorski, Hristo Tanev, Martin Atkinson, and Erik Van Der Goot. 2008. Cluster-Centric Approach to News Event Extraction. In *Proceedings of the 2008 Conference on New Trends in Multimedia and Network Information Systems*. IOS Press, Amsterdam, The Netherlands, The Netherlands, pages 276–290.

Jakub Piskorski and Roman Yangarber. 2013. Information extraction: Past, present and future. In Thierry Poibeau, Horacio Saggion, Jakub Piskorski, and Roman Yangarber, editors, *Multi-source, Multilingual Information Extraction and Summarization*, Springer Berlin Heidelberg, Theory and Applications of Natural Language Processing, pages 23–49.

Horst Pöttker. 2003. News and its communicative quality: The inverted pyramidWhen and why did it appear? *Journalism Studies* 4(4):501–511.

Ellen Riloff. 1996. Automatically Generating Extraction Patterns from Untagged Text. In *Proceedings of the Thirteenth National Conference on Artificial Intelligence - Volume 2*. AAAI Press, AAAI'96, pages 1044–1049.

Alan Ritter, Evan Wright, William Casey, and Tom Mitchell. 2015. Weakly supervised extraction of computer security events from twitter. In *Proceedings of the 24th International Conference on World Wide Web*. ACM, pages 896–905.

Roser Saurí and James Pustejovsky. 2009. FactBank: a corpus annotated with event factuality. *Language resources and evaluation* 43(3):227.

Hristo Tanev, Jakub Piskorski, and Martin Atkinson. 2008. Real-Time News Event Extraction for Global Crisis Monitoring. In *Proceedings of NLDB 2008.*. pages 207–218.

Hristo Tanev and Vanni Zavarella. 2014. Multilingual Lexicalisation and Population of Event Ontologies: A Case Study for Social Media. In *Towards the Multilingual Semantic Web*, Springer, pages 259–274.

Hristo Tanev, Vanni Zavarella, Jens P. Linge, Mijail A. Kabadjov, Jakub Piskorski, Martin Atkinson, and Ralf Steinberger. 2009. Exploiting Machine Learning Techniques to Build an Event Extraction System for Portuguese and Spanish. *Linguamática* 1(2):55–66.

Michael D Ward, Andreas Beger, Josh Cutler, Matt Dickenson, Cassy Dorff, and Ben Radford. 2013. Comparing GDELT and ICEWS event data. *Analysis* 21:267–297.

William E. Winkler. 1999. The State of Record Linkage and Current Research Problems. Technical Report Statistical Research Report Series RR99/04.

Zhibiao Wu and Martha Palmer. 1994. Verbs Semantics and Lexical Selection. In *Proceedings of the 32Nd Annual Meeting on Association for Computational Linguistics*. Association for Computational Linguistics, Stroudsburg, PA, USA, ACL '94, pages 133–138.

Roman Yangarber, Peter Von Etter, and Ralf Steinberger. 2008. Content Collection and Analysis in the Domain of Epidemiology. In *Proceedings of DrMED 2008: International Workshop on Describing Medical Web Resources at MIE 2008: the 21st International Congress of the European Federation for Medical Informatics 2008*. Goeteborg, Sweden.

Roman Yangarber, Ralph Grishman, Pasi Tapanainen, and Silja Huttunen. 2000. Unsupervised Discovery of Scenario-level Patterns for Information Extraction. In *Proceedings of the Sixth Conference on Applied Natural Language Processing*. Association for Computational Linguistics, Stroudsburg, PA, USA, ANLC '00, pages 282–289.

Inducing Event Types and Roles in Reverse:
Using Function to Discover Theme

Natalie Ahn
University of California, Berkeley
`natalieahn@berkeley.edu`

Abstract

With growing interest in automated event extraction, there is an increasing need to overcome the labor costs of hand-written event templates, entity lists, and annotated corpora. In the last few years, more inductive approaches have emerged, seeking to discover unknown event types and roles in raw text. The main recent efforts use probabilistic generative models, as in topic modeling, which are formally concise but do not always yield stable or easily interpretable results. We argue that event schema induction can benefit from greater structure in the process and in linguistic features that distinguish words' functions and themes. To maximize our use of limited data, we reverse the typical schema induction steps and introduce new similarity measures, building an intuitive process for inducing the structure of unknown events.

1 Introduction

Automated event extraction is mainly used in a few areas of high interest and resource investment, especially conflict and biomedical research. Yet there is growing interest in applying event extraction to new languages and substantive domains. Identifying meaningful representations of who did what to whom can enable us not only to study how known topics are described in pre-categorized texts, but to use unlabeled records to discover what has happened in the world that we don't yet know how to label, or disagree about how to define.

Event extraction is a complex task, combining multiple subtasks that continue to be studied in their own right. To determine that an election occurred and who voted, won, or lost, we must identify segments of text that mention the topic of electing public officials, and determine which entities are attributed certain roles. Finding that a document is about elections is not enough to determine who attained power and which citizens they represent. Finding only that someone won a vote, without thematic context, is not enough to know whether they won political power, a corporate board decision, or figurative social approval.

There is growing interest in finding new ways to induce event frames and patterns linking entities to event roles. This paper builds on that emerging body of work, while introducing new ideas about event narratives and their components. Our contributions involve reversing the typical schema induction process and combining multiple measures of word similarity, to dissect words' functional relatedness and incorporate hierarchical information from public WordNet and Wikipedia resources.

This paper proceeds as follows. Section 2 discusses prior work and defines the terms we use. Section 3 explains our methodology, including our re-ordered process and steps for inducing event roles and event types. Section 4 presents evaluations using the MUC-4 data set, with comparison to other work, and Section 5 offers discussion.

2 Related Work

Early automation of event extraction relied on rule-based pattern matching, using hand-written templates (Chinchor et al., 1993; Schrodt et al., 1994). Modern efforts have focused on supervised machine learning, using annotated corpora for training data, again with pre-defined event types and roles (Miyao et al., 2008; Bjorne and Salakoski, 2011; Bunescu and Mooney, 2004).

Semi-supervised approaches have been used to identify relations between pairs of entities, using seed pairs with known relations (Brin, 1998; Culotta and Sorensen, 2004; Mintz et al., 2009).

Proceedings of the Events and Stories in the News Workshop, pages 66–76,
Vancouver, Canada, August 4, 2017. ©2017 Association for Computational Linguistics

Open IE systems (Banko et al., 2007; Angeli et al., 2015) extract general relational patterns between entity pairs, based on domain-independent patterns or heuristics. Similar efforts have emerged to extract more complex event frames by bootstrapping from seed event patterns (Huang and Riloff, 2012; Surdeanu et al., 2006; Yangarber et al., 2000; Patwardhan and Riloff, 2007).

There has been growing work over the past decade on purely unsupervised role induction. Most of these efforts begin with a set of documents known to cover a type of event or domain, then cluster verb arguments to determine each verb's role slots within that domain (Filatova et al., 2006; Sekine, 2006). These approaches typically learn verb-specific roles, rather than multi-verb event schemas. Other recent work models multiple verb roles in combination, in various forms of subject-verb-object relational triples (O'Connor et al., 2013; Balasubramanian et al., 2013).

In the last few years, several important efforts have broken new ground with more comprehensive event schema induction. These efforts discover new event types in unfiltered text, and identify verb argument positions associated with overall event roles. Chambers and Jurafsky (2011) used a pipeline approach, first discovering related event patterns, then clustering arguments into event slots. For the first step, they tested both LDA and agglomerative clustering, based on event terms' co-occurrence. They used the MUC-4 data set, but relied on an additional external corpus for role induction, due to data limitations when clustering roles separately in each event category.

Chambers (2013), Cheung et al (2013), Nguyen et al (2015), and Sha et al (2016) all use probabilistic generative models that jointly model the assignment of predicates to event schemas and arguments to event roles. Chambers uses an entity-driven model, linking coreferring arguments to the same event role. Cheung et al focus on event clauses and model transitions between them, using a pair of HMMs. Nguyen et al (2015) add phrase modifiers to argument similarity scores, and Sha et al (2016) add a normalized cut approach to maximize intra-class similarity within slots.

2.1 Problem Setup and Terminology

Our goal is to learn a set of meaningful events and participant roles from a body of text. For instance, given a collection of news reports, we may want to identify that some of them are about elections, others are about crime, etc. We also want to learn that an election involves voters, candidates, polling sites, and the office to be won.

As we identify meaningful roles, we also want to learn how to extract particular instances, by identifying textual positions that refer to each role. The subjects of the verbs *vote* and *elect* are likely to be voters, while the direct object of *elect* or the subject of *campaign* is likely to be a candidate.

We use the term "event type" to refer to a thematic event category (e.g. *election*), which may be described using a variety of related verbs. We use "role" to refer to the semantic role of an event participant (e.g. *candidate*), and "event schema" to refer to the set of an event type's roles. We use "entity" to refer to a specific actor or object, which might be described by multiple coreferences.

To distinguish specific words, we use "predicate" to refer to a verbal or nominal event predicate (e.g. *campaign*), and "argument" to refer to a syntactic argument of a predicate; "argument term" refers to the argument's head word. We use "argument position" to refer to the combination of a predicate and a dependency relation in which an argument might appear (e.g. *elect:dobj*). We cluster these positions into "slots" which map to event roles. Figure 1 shows an example.

Event type: *election*	
Schema slots: {*voter, candidate, ...*}	
Slot positions: *voter*:{*elect:subj, vote:subj*}	
candidate:{*elect:dobj, win:subj*}	
Mention 1	Mention 2
predicate: *elect*	predicates: *vote, win*
position: arg term:	position: arg term:
elect:subj *Berliners*	*vote:subj* *Canadians*
elect:dobj *Merkel*	*win:subj* *Trudeau*

Figure 1: Example of an event schema.

3 Process Overview

The traditional event extraction process generally involves two parts: 1) identifying segments of text with action terms or phrases that relate to a particular event type, and 2) identifying entities in relevant argument positions that fill the event type's roles. The first task represents a text classification or topic identification problem at the level of the document. The second task (semantic role labeling) is more difficult, since it involves complex word-level assignments and relationships, requiring a lot of data and features to capture all possible patterns that link an argument to its correct role.

If we attempt to learn semantic roles only after separating documents by event type, we have much less data to work with in identifying event-specific roles. To overcome this limitation, Chambers and Jurafsky (2011) augmented their role induction stage with a larger external corpus, but our goal is to induce roles using only the documents contained in the MUC-4 dataset. Many event types share similar roles, and some argument positions will signal the same role in multiple event types (e.g. *kill:dobj*, signaling the victim of a bombing, murder, or other attack).

We can make much greater use of limited data by learning general semantic roles from the whole corpus. Learning general roles first also helps us identify event types, by segmenting the text into narrative sequences with coherent argument roles, then identifying trigger words that represent these event narratives. Finally, we construct event schemas by refining the general roles based on argument frequencies in specific event contexts.

3.1 Inducing General Argument Roles

We begin with dependency parsing and coreference resolution, using the Stanford CoreNLP toolkit (Manning et al., 2014), then identify all predicates' arguments as candidates for semantic roles. Predicates are any verb or any noun under the WordNet synset for "event"; arguments are any of their syntactic dependents. We collect arguments by their argument position, defined as the argument's predicate head paired with its dependency relation, e.g. *kill:dobj*. All arguments with the dependency relation *dobj* to the verb *kill* are assigned to the same slot. Similar to Chambers and Jurafsky (2011) and Cheung et al (2013), we separate slots by high-level entity type: 1) Person or Organization, 2) Location, 3) Physical Object, or 4) Other. The position *take:dobj:[person]* is clustered separately from *take:dobj:[object]*.

We cluster argument positions using two similarity scores: one for the functional position itself (i.e. the predicate dependency relation), and one for the argument terms that appear in that position throughout the text. We begin with Chambers and Jurafsky's (2011) measures of argument similarity: the cosine similarity between vectors of argument terms, and the cosine similarity between vec-

tors of other positions that share coreferring arguments. To build on Chambers and Jurafsky's work and show a meaningful comparison, we use their method for combining these two scores, taking the maximum if either score is above 0.7 (which they optimized on the MUC-4 training set) and backing off to the average between the two otherwise. We also add noun phrase modifiers to the argument term vector, following Nguyen et al (2015).

3.1.1 Adding Argument Hypernyms

Our contributions to this stage of the process are to add two major sources of information about argument positions, that shed greater light on the similarity between their semantic roles. First, we add argument hypernyms. Many entity terms appear infrequently in the corpus, such as names of specific people, locations, or precise objects. Yet categorical groupings that fall between the word itself and its high level entity type may be important.

For instance, the two positions *attack:iobj-on:[object]* and *attack:iobj-with:[object]* have the same high-level entity type. But the first is more likely to contain buildings, while the second is more likely to contain weapons. Even some person types share more hypernyms than others, such as the terms "attacker" and "kidnapper," which share the hypernym "wrongdoer". Using the full hypernym chain enables us to avoid making arbitrary decisions about how much granularity to use in subdividing entity types. Figure 2 shows an example of top hypernym counts from the data set:

$pos_1 = kill{:}dobj$	$pos_2 = die{:}subj$
$H_{pos_1}=\{person{:}\ 387,$	$H_{pos_2}=\{person{:}\ 70,$
$group{:}\ 155,$	$group{:}\ 35,$
$worker{:}\ 50,$	$unit{:}\ 11,$
$leader{:}\ 45...\}$	$worker{:}\ 10...\}$

Figure 2: Top hypernyms in two similar positions.

To label argument hypernyms, we look up the argument head word in WordNet. If more than one synset is given, we select the synset whose other lemmas have the most similar word embeddings to the target word, using Word2Vec cosine similarity. This is a simple approach to select one synset for all mentions of the same term throughout the corpus, rather than performing word sense disambiguation on each mention, since existing methods for WSD still rarely beat selecting the first WordNet synset for all mentions (Raganato et al., 2017).

If a term does not appear in WordNet, we look it up in Wikipedia. We use Wikipedia's API to query for a page with a title exactly matching the argument phrase or head word, and if not found, use the search query for a page with a partially matching title. For each page returned, we retrieve the description, label, alias, and page categories, and look up the head word of the first noun phrase in each, until we find a match in WordNet. To make sure we should use the synset, we again compare the word embeddings of the synset's lemmas and the target term in our corpus. We keep the synset from Wikipedia if its lemmas have a higher average Word2Vec similarity to the target term than the average for all other nouns in the corpus.

This process works well at finding person and place names that don't appear in WordNet. It works less well for common nouns, which don't usually have their own Wikipedia page, but those terms are overwhelmingly found in WordNet already. In the MUC-4 training set, we found about 95% of noun phrase head words in WordNet. Our Wikipedia search found a suitable synset that met the word embedding check for close to 30% of remaining noun phrases, which slightly improved our evaluation scores over using WordNet alone.

We then construct a vector of hypernym counts H_{pos_i} for each argument position pos_i, as in Figure 2 above. For all arguments in pos_i throughout the corpus, we take their assigned WordNet synsets and count all hypernyms in their full hypernym chains, except the three most general categories of "entity", "physical entity", or "abstraction". We take the cosine similarity between these hypernym vectors and multiply it by the Chambers and Jurafsky (2011) similarity score for argument terms and coreferring positions.

$$hyp\_sim(pos_i, pos_j) = cosine(H_{pos_i}, H_{pos_j})$$
$$arg\_sim(pos_i, pos_j) = CJ\_sim(pos_i, pos_j)$$
$$\times hyp\_sim(pos_i, pos_j)$$

3.1.2 Adding Predicate Functionality

Second, we add a new measure of functional similarity between two predicate dependency relations (i.e. the syntactic base of the argument position, as opposed to the terms that fill the position). Again, an argument position is defined by a predicate and a dependency relation, e.g. *kill:dobj*. There are two parts to our functional similarity measure: the similarity between the predicates themselves, and whether the positions share the same dependency relation to their respective predicates.

Consider a victim-type role, which might appear in the positions *kill:dobj, murder:dobj,* or *die:subj*. The verbs *kill* and *murder* are functionally similar; they both have human subjects and direct objects (and often instruments after "with"). But *die*, while thematically related, is functionally different: it is intransitive and has no direct object. The *victim* role appears in the same dependency relation (*dobj*) to *kill* and *murder*, but in a different relation (*subj*) to *die*. If two positions represent the same semantic role, they should either fill the same dependency relation to functionally similar predicates, or have different relations to predicates that tend to have different argument structures.

For each predicate, we assemble a count vector of all of its arguments' dependency relations in the corpus, and take the cosine similarity between two predicates' dependency relation count vectors. We multiply this dependent similarity score by the cosine similarity of the predicates' word embeddings, to confirm that the two verbs are used in similar ways throughout the corpus.

Then for each pair of argument positions pos_i = $pred_i:dep_i$ and $pos_j = pred_j:dep_j$, we look at whether they have the same *dep*. If they do, we use the functional similarity score for their two predicates $pred\_sim(pred_i, pred_j)$ as the similarity score for the two argument positions. If the positions have different *deps*, we use $1 - pred\_sim(pred_i, pred_j)$, so that positions with different *deps* will only be merged if they're dependent on functionally different predicates.

We're more confident that this is a meaningful comparison of positions with the same *dep* than with different *deps*. So far, we would give *kill:dobj* and *die:subj* the same similarity score as any other non-matching dependents of *kill* and *die*. Instead, we'd like to infer which non-matching dependents of two functionally different predicates might fill similar roles. To do so, we weight the second case by the cosine similarity of the two positions' hypernym vectors. (This means we use hypernym similarity twice for positions with different *deps*, effectively squaring it in our final slot similarity score, which we consider reasonable given the greater uncertainty that they fill the same role.)

$$funct\_sim(pos_i, pos_j) =$$
$$\begin{cases} pred\_sim(pred_i, pred_j) & \text{if } dep_i = dep_j \\ (1 - pred\_sim(pred_i, pred_j)) & \text{if } dep_i \neq dep_j \\ \quad \times hyp\_sim(pos_i, pos_j) \end{cases}$$

3.1.3 Clustering Combined Scores

For two positions' overall similarity, we multiply the argument similarity and functional similarity scores, to ensure we merge positions that are related on both dimensions. We use agglomerative clustering with average linkage scores, and apply constraints against merging two positions that meet any of the following conditions. Versions of the first two were also used by Sha et al (2016) and Chambers and Jurafsky (2011), respectively:

1. *Sentence co-occurrence*: The positions appear in the same sentence for more than a minimal percentage of occurrences.

2. *Functional incompatibility*: The positions share the same predicate but different base dependency relations (e.g. *subj* vs. *dobj* or *dobj* vs. *iobj*). These pairs already have a functional similarity score of 0, but we allow indirect objects to merge if they have different prepositions, since *iobj-at* and *iobj-in* may both refer to a verb's location.

3. *Non-overlapping hypernyms*: The positions have a hypernym similarity score equal to 0, which only applies to functional positions with the high-level entity type "Other".

These constraints prevent highly dissimilar argument positions from being merged even as average similarities between clusters grow. We merge up to a maximum distance close to 1 (0.999), to merge as many compatible slots as possible. The resulting clusters have reasonable sizes (the largest usually had about 50 argument positions).

3.2 Segmenting Event Narratives

To leverage information from our first step to identify thematic event types, we add an intermediate step: chunking the text into potential event narratives. This relates to Cheung et al's (2013) modeling of event frame transitions between clauses.

The motivation for segmenting narrative sequences is to help us determine which verbs might be part of the same event descriptions, to cluster event triggers in our final stage. Other papers have clustered event predicates based on nearness in the text, using different sentence windows (Chambers and Jurafsky, 2011; Jiang et al., 2014). Chunking event narratives allows us to relate predicates in nearby sentences, when the text between them appears to be part of a continuous event report, without selecting an arbitrary window of how many words or sentences apart they can be.

Cheung et al used a stickiness parameter to encourage neighboring clauses to remain in the same event frame. We approach event segmentation from the other direction, assuming that neighboring text is part of the same event until it no longer can be, because it contains elements that have internally incoherent semantic roles. We segment by paragraph, since the MUC-4 corpus contains news reports, which have short paragraphs of one or two sentences usually referring to the same event.

Consider the following two segments, each of which contain the same number of sentences, predicates and arguments:

1. "***Insurgents*** *attacked a* ***village***.
   Four people *were killed.*"

2. "***Insurgents*** *attacked a* ***village***.
   An airport *was bombed.*"

In the first example, the insurgents are the only perpetrators, the village is the physical target of *attacked* and the four people the victims of *killed*. In the second example, the village is again the target of *attacked*, but there is a second physical target – the airport – of *bombed*. This suggests that the second example might contain two different events.

Our narrative segmentation is simple. If two neighboring paragraphs have non-coreferring arguments (i.e. different entities) in the same general semantic role, we assume that they are part of different event narratives, and split the document between those paragraphs. We consider the resulting sequences likely to be coherent narratives with internally consistent themes, and use them to cluster thematically related event predicates next.

3.3 Inducing Trigger Verbs for Event Types

In supervised or rule-based document classification, a common approach to identifying events is to search for "trigger" words, i.e. action terms that are highly representative of a specific type of event. For instance, verbs like *choose* or *win* might signal their arguments' roles in an election context, but those same verbs appear in other thematic contexts as well. The verbs *vote* or *elect*, or the nominal predicate *election*, are better indications that a document is actually about an election. Trigger words are often hand selected, which does not enable the discovery of new event types.

When inducing event types, other researchers have sought to assign all predicates in a corpus to event clusters, often using probabilistic distributions to allow more general verbs to appear in more than one event type. However, very general terms can still have much in common with thematically specific terms, so that including all of them can result in loosely associated clusters that may shift considerably with different algorithm parameters. Cheung et al (2013) included a "background" frame with a binary switching variable in their event sequences, so that some clauses may contain terms used in any context.

We focus instead on identifying only a limited number of highly eventful verbs that are likely to represent a particular type of event. We inspected mentions of events in the corpus, comparing more event-specific terms like "election" to more thematically general verbs like "take" or "see". We observed that event trigger words tend to appear in prominent syntactic positions like the root of a sentence, in both verb and nominal form (e.g. "attacked" and later "the attack"), and to often have theme-specific objects, while general verbs have a wider variety of argument terms.

Based on this review, we chose two criteria for triggers that also roughly parallel our approach to semantic roles, combining aspects of functional positions and argument terms. We did not test other ideas, so there may be room to add other features related to event-specific verbs in the future. Our criteria for event triggers are as follows:

1. *Major functional positions*: We count the number of times that a form of the verb appears in the following positions: a) in a sentence's "root" dependency relation; b) as an object of a reporting verb in the position *report:iobj-that*; c) in nominal form with definite article as the subject of another verb; and d) in nominal form with definite article as the direct object of an auxiliary or control verb. We use lists of reporting verbs, auxiliary verbs, and control verbs from Wiktionary (a Wikimedia dictionary resource) to identify these major action positions, and exclude the enabling terms from being event triggers themselves, as well as the Wiktionary category for copulative verbs and WordNet synonyms of "occur" and "happen".

2. *Argument concentration*: We calculate a verb's argument concentration using a type

of ratio used in economics for industry firms. For each verb, we count how many of its arguments contain one of the verb's top 50% most frequent argument terms, and divide by the verb's total arguments. This gives us the percentage of the verb's arguments that are covered by its most repeated argument terms.

We apply these criteria to verb infinitives, including all mentions of the verb in conjugated or nominal form. For each verb in the corpus that appears in at least three of the major functional positions, we multiple the log number of mentions in major positions with the argument concentration ratio to get our potential event trigger score. We select all predicates with a score above a threshold (0.2, chosen by inspection to ensure enough meaningful candidate terms in the training set).

We cluster these trigger words to get event types, based on their proximity in the text and similarity of arguments. As discussed in section 3.2, we use the narrative sequences from the previous stage to identify term co-occurrence. For each pair of trigger verbs, we calculate how many times they appear in the same narrative sequence, as a percentage of their total mentions in the corpus. We multiple this co-occurrence score by the percentage overlap in the two verbs' argument term count vectors, and by the cosine similarity of the triggers' word embedding vectors.

As in the first stage, incorporating multiple criteria enables us to focus on words that perform prominent eventful functions in the text, in similar ways and in meaningful proximity to each other. We again cluster using average linkage scores, applying constraints so that two predicates will not be merged if they have no co-occurring mentions and no overlapping argument terms.

3.4 Event Role Extraction

After inducing general roles and event triggers, we are ready to extract specific mentions of events. We classify a narrative sequence as a mention of a specific event type if it contains at least one of the event type's trigger words. For event schema slots, we look for argument positions from the general roles that appear in event-specific narratives, and calculate the probability of argument terms falling into each slot within each event context. This allows us to refine the general roles into thematically relevant versions for each event type, without having to recluster argument positions within a much more limited set of event-related documents.

Our extraction rules follow those used by Chambers and Jurafsky (2011). First, if an argument in an event narrative has a predicate and dependency relation assigned to an event slot, and has the correct high-level entity type for that slot, we assign it to the corresponding event role. If an argument's functional position was not assigned to any learned slot, we see if the argument term has a high probability of falling into one of the learned slots in the given event context, and assign the argument to the corresponding role if it does.

Our argument hypernym vectors enable us to add a similar rule for the probability of certain hypernyms appearing in specific event slots. If an argument has a hypernym with a high probability of appearing in a learned slot, we assign the argument to the corresponding role. For instance, if we come across the name of a rebel group we haven't seen before, but Wikipedia identifies it as an insurgent group, we can assign it to the same slot that other insurgent groups were clustered into, when the group is mentioned in an event context in which insurgents usually fill one particular role.

We get our best results if we only cluster argument positions that appear in the corpus at least 10 times, because less frequent positions are unlikely to have enough data to end up in the right cluster. This restriction also makes the time complexity and memory usage more manageable, given that we're calculating multiple pairwise similarity scores between argument positions. Then during extraction, for arguments in rare unclustered positions, we use the term or hypernym slot probabilities to assign them to their most likely event role.

4 Evaluation

We used the same information extraction task and sought to match our evaluation settings to those used in the other event schema induction papers. The evaluation data set is from the Fourth Message Understanding Conference (MUC-4) (Sundheim, 1992), which contains 1300 documents for training, plus 200 documents for development and 200 documents for testing.

The documents contain English newswire articles about conflict events in Latin America, annotated with four types of events: Attack, Bombing, Kidnapping, and Arson. As in the other papers, we tested entity extraction for the four main template roles: *perpetrator* (combining both individuals and organizations), *human target* (i.e. victim), *physical target*, and *instrument*, and ignored entries marked "optional". For the final tests, we induced event schemas from all 1700 documents in training, development, and test sets, and report scores for the 200 documents in the test set.

4.1 Experiments: General Role Extraction

To evaluate our first stage, we present results for the best mapping of our general roles to the four MUC-4 template roles, combining like roles (e.g. all *perpetrator* roles) across the four event types. To isolate the analysis of our new predicate structure and hypernym similarity measurements, we use this stage to compare our contributions to previous measures of argument similarity. We apply our general roles to test documents labeled with at least one of the four MUC-4 event templates, and show our results alongside Chambers' (2013) and Cheung et al's (2013) scores assuming perfect document classification. Since we induced corpus-wide roles using only the documents in the MUC-4 data set, the most relevant comparison is among the versions of our own implementation, in which we've sought to replicate argument similarity metrics used by others, then added our own.

Evaluation: General Roles, Gold Documents

Comparison scores (as reported)			
Role	P	R	F1
Chambers 2013	41	44	43
Cheung et al 2013	49	43	46
Component measures (our implementation)			
Arg terms+corefs (C&J 2011)	26	41	32
w/ mods (Nguyen et al 2015)	38	31	34
+ hypernym similarity	47	30	37
+ pred-dep functional sim	51	39	45
+ hyper sim + pred-dep sim	**53**	**42**	**47**

Table 1: MUC-4 role extraction, mapping general slots to documents with at least one labeled event.

Our first stage performs well, applying general learned roles to gold documents. Adding each of our contributions individually improved upon the scores we obtained using others' argument term similarity scores alone. Adding both of our contributions of hypernyms and argument position functional similarity performed best overall.

Again, we were able to do so using only the documents in the MUC-4 dataset, because we reversed the order of the process and only induced general semantic roles at this stage. One concern might be that our general roles could be overly broad when induced from corpora with more varied topics, since the MUC-4 data is overwhelmingly dominated by conflict events that share the same set of roles. We discuss the need for more varied evaluation datasets in the final section.

4.2 Full Process Evaluation: Event Roles

For our second stage, we used our induced trigger words to assign narrative sequences to MUC-4 event types, then extracted entities in event slots as described in 3.4. To evaluate the full process, we need to map our event-specific slots to MUC-4 template roles. Since we now have both event types and component slots, there are two ways to do the mapping: 1) map any learned slot to any template role (called "slot-only mapping"), or 2) map learned schemas to MUC-4 templates, then only map slots from one schema to roles in its matching template (called "template mapping"). Most of the recent papers reported slot-only mapping scores for the MUC-4 dataset, while fewer reported stricter template mapping scores as well. However, as Chambers (2013) discussed, the latter is the more comprehensive (and ideal) method for evaluating induced event schemas as a whole.

We first report slot-only mapping scores in comparison to the scores from the previous papers, in Table 2. We then discuss the greater difficulty but more precise evaluation using template mapping, in Table 3, along with possible ways to improve.

Evaluation: Learned Events, Slot Mapping

	P	R	F1
C&J 2011	**48**	25	33
Chambers 2013	41	41	41
Cheung et al 2013	32	37	34
Nguyen et al 2015	36	54	43
Sha et al 2016	39	**70**	**50**
Our results, all template roles	33	39	36

Table 2: MUC-4 role extraction on narratives with event triggers, mapping slots to any template role.

The results in Table 2 are comparable to some of the earlier work on this task, but do not reach the level achieved by the most recent efforts. We believe there is room for improvement in our document classification stage, since we only induced event trigger words. We explored more complex approaches to clustering all event predicates while allowing some to appear in multiple events. However, the more promising options became too complicated to fully develop in this paper. We opted instead for a focused approach to event triggers that highlights our intuition about functional relationships between eventful words.

For slot-only mapping, we still restricted candidate slots to the four schemas that mapped to the MUC-4 templates. Since the slots in each of our schemas are derived from the same general semantic roles, the difference between the two mappings is that the stricter template mapping tests whether we were able to correctly distinguish an entity as the perpetrator of a bombing, rather than the perpetrator of another form of attack. In other words, for schema slots that share a general role structure, the stricter template mapping places greater emphasis on our ability to distinguish between specific event types in document classification.

The relatively homogenous nature of the MUC-4 corpus makes it easier to identify documents that contain any of its main event types, but more difficult to distinguish between them. Bombings, kidnappings, arson, and (other) attacks often use similar argument terms. For the stricter template mapping evaluation, we found that we needed to stop clustering event trigger words at a slightly smaller maximum distance score (0.99 rather than 0.999, chosen on the training set), to keep some trigger words for each MUC-4 event type in separate clusters. This resulted in very few triggers for each schema, but reasonable template mapping scores for at least some events, both shown in Table 3.

Evaluation: Strict Template Mapping

	Arson	Bomb	Attack	Kidnap
triggers	*burn*	*explode, damage*	*attack, kill*	*kidnap, release*
F1	40	36	25	29

Table 3: Event trigger words and MUC-4 role extraction F1 scores, mapping slots to roles separately for each mapped schema-template pair.

The difference in performance across event types seems to relate to the number of triggers needed to capture each event concept. (Note that schema slots still use more predicates, the trigger words only classify the event narratives.) If we stop merging even sooner and retain a schema with only the trigger word "kidnap", the F1 score for Kidnapping goes up to 40, but the score for Attack (the largest category in the dataset) goes down. Chambers and Jurafsky (2011) achieved their best results when mapping several schemas to the Attack template, including subtypes for shootings, murders, and coups. Our trigger learning approach does not enable us to learn a larger cluster of Attack trigger words without merging in the trigger words for the other MUC-4 event types as well.

This suggests that a challenge for correct one-to-one mapping of event schemas to gold templates is achieving the right level of aggregation for all event types in a given corpus. Whether to label very fine-grained events like shootings and murders, or higher-level categories like attacks, crimes, or conflicts, is a subjective judgment often driven by the substantive motivation of the research. To induce event types that can be mapped to labeled events with the right level of granularity between related concepts, we may need to learn hierarchies of actions or events. Emerging efforts to identify event-event relations and event coreference offer promising avenues (Hong et al., 2016).

We might also do better at distinguishing similar event types if we combine our structural and functional contributions with a more probabilistic approach to schema induction. By breaking apart the process as we've done, we've been able to explore and test various new components, that could be incorporated into more concise models for better overall task performance in the future.

5 Discussion

In this paper, we have offered a novel approach to event schema induction, reversing the typical pipeline process to maximize the use of limited training data, and inducing general semantic roles that help distinguish coherent event narratives. Our approach differs from the dominant use of generative probabilistic models that jointly model event schemas and role slots. In keeping the steps separate, while leveraging rich information throughout, we've constructed a process that can be manipulated intuitively at different stages, incorporating structure and distinguishing word features related to function and theme.

While joint models may be mathematically cleaner, our process yields meaningful components along the way, that might be useful to researchers in their own right. These include the mapping of event-specific roles to common general semantic roles, the segmentation of coherent event narratives, and the induction of prominent eventful trigger words. Separating out the steps in a pipeline process also allows us to explore different types of intuition at each stage, since event topics are qualitatively different types of concepts from semantic roles.

In general, we've sought to induce event components intuitively, and to aid those tasks by incorporating knowledge from public, general-domain resources. WordNet and Wikipedia don't contain event frames, but they add general information about word functions and themes beyond what can be observed in relatively small corpora. We include word embeddings to confirm the relevance of certain elements to our corpus, in order to construct domain-specific event schemas when the only domain resource is raw text. WordNet and Wikipedia are available in multiple languages and are easy to use, reducing the burden on other researchers seeking to apply similar methods. In the future, we would also be interested in inductive approaches to learning word taxonomies, to ensure that the hierarchical structures used to induce semantic roles accurately reflect the senses and relationships of words as used in the relevant domain.

As a final note about data, we sought to make our evaluation directly comparable to previous work, and the MUC-4 dataset has been the standard for evaluating event extraction in the past. But the dataset is now over two decades old, and we struggled with some of its shortcomings. It was designed to evaluate rule-based pattern matching and supervised extraction algorithms, and there are coding nuances that may not be inferable from the raw text alone. In addition to the narrow focus on four somewhat overlapping types of violent attacks, our inspection of incorrect extractions in the training set revealed some entities that are clearly attack perpetrators or targets, but are not labeled as such in the key. We are encouraged by current efforts to develop new annotated corpora that might be more useful for evaluating the emerging research on inductive event extraction, and that cover a wider variety of real-world events.

Acknowledgments

Many thanks to the reviewers for thoughtful feedback, to David Bamman and Christopher Hench for helpful draft comments and discussion, to Brendan O'Connor for general advice, and to Sarah Anzia for encouragement and support.

References

Gabor Angeli, Melvin Jose Johnson Premkumar, and Christopher D. Manning. 2015. Leveraging linguistic structure for open domain information extraction. In *Proceedings of the 53rd Annual Meeting of the Association for Computational Linguistics and the 7th International Joint Conference on Natural Language Processing.* pages 344–354. https://doi.org/10.3115/v1/P15-1034.

Niranjan Balasubramanian, Stephen Soderland, Mausam, and Oren Etzioni. 2013. Generating coherent event schemas at scale. In *Proceedings of the 2013 Conference on Empirical Methods in Natural Language Processing.* volume 1721–1731. http://aclweb.org/anthology/D13-1178.

Michele Banko, Michael J Cafarella, Stephen Soderland, Matt Broadhead, and Oren Etzioni. 2007. Open information extraction from the web. In *Proceedings of the International Joint Conferences on Artificial Intelligence (IJCAI).* pages 2670–2676. https://doi.org/10.978.157735/2983.

Jari Bjorne and Tapio Salakoski. 2011. Generalizing biomedical event extraction. In *Proceedings of BioNLP Shared Task 2011 Workshop of the Association for Computational Linguistics (ACL).* pages 183–191. http://aclweb.org/anthology/W11-1828.

Sergei Brin. 1998. Extracting patterns and relations from the world wide web. In *Proceedings of the International Workshop on the World Wide Web and Databases.* https://doi.org/10.1007/10704656_11.

Razvan Bunescu and Raymond J. Mooney. 2004. Collective information extraction with relational markov networks. In *Proceedings of the 42nd Annual Meeting of the Association for Computational Linguistics (ACL-04).* http://aclweb.org/anthology/P04-1056.

Nathanael Chambers. 2013. Event schema induction with a probabilistic entity-driven model. In *Proceedings of the 2013 Conference on Empirical Methods in Natural Language Processing.* pages 1797–1807. http://aclweb.org/anthology/D13-1185.

Nathanael Chambers and Dan Jurafsky. 2011. Template-based information extraction without the templates. In *Proceedings of the 49th Annual Meeting of the Association for Computational Linguistics: Human Language Technologies.* http://aclweb.org/anthology/P11-1098.

Jackie Chi Kit Cheung, Hoifung Poon, and Lucy Vanderwende. 2013. Probabilistic frame induction. In *Proceedings of the 2013 Conference of the North American Chapter of the Association for Computational Linguistics: Human Language Technologies.* pages 837–846. http://aclweb.org/anthology/N13-1104.

Nancy Chinchor, David D. Lewis, and Lynette Hirschman. 1993. Evaluating message understanding systems: an analysis of the third message understanding conference (muc-3). *Journal of Computational Linguistics* 19(3):409–449. http://aclweb.org/anthology/J93-3001.

Aron Culotta and Jeffrey Sorensen. 2004. Dependency tree kernels for relation extraction. In *Proceedings of the 42nd Annual Meeting of the Association for Computational Linguistics (ACL-04).* http://aclweb.org/anthology/P04-1054.

Elena Filatova, Vasileios Hatzivassiloglou, and Kathleen McKeown. 2006. Automatic creation of domain templates. In *Proceedings of the Conference on Computational Linguistics and the Association for Computational Linguistics (COLING/ACL).* pages 207–214. http://aclweb.org/anthology/P06-2027.

Yu Hong, Tongtao Zhang, Tim O'Gorman, Sharone Horowit-Hendler, Heng Ji, and Martha Palmer. 2016. Building a cross-document event-event relation corpus. In *Proceedings of the 10th Linguistic Annotation Workshop held in conjunction with ACL 2016 (LAW-X 2016).* pages 1–6. https://doi.org/10.18653/v1/W16-1701.

Ruihong Huang and Ellen Riloff. 2012. Bootstrapped training of event extraction classifiers. In *Proceedings of the 13th Conference of the European Chapter of the Association for Computational Linguistics.* pages 286–295. http://aclweb.org/anthology/E12-1029.

Tingsong Jiang, Lei Sha, and Zhifang Sui. 2014. Event schema induction based on relational co-occurrence over multiple documents. *Communications in Computer and Information Science, Third International Conference on Natural Language Processing and Chinese Computing (NLPCC)* https://doi.org/10.1007/978-3-662-45924-9_3.

Christopher D. Manning, Mihai Surdeanu, John Bauer, Jenny Finkel, Steven J. Bethard, and David McClosky. 2014. The stanford corenlp natural language processing toolkit. In *Proceedings of the 52nd Annual Meeting of the Association for Computational Linguistics: System Demonstrations.* pages 55–60. https://doi.org/10.3115/v1/P14-5010.

Mike Mintz, Steven Bills, Rion Snow, and Dan Jurafsky. 2009. Distant supervision for relation extraction without labeled data. In *Proceedings of the Joint Conference of the 47th Annual Meeting of the ACL and the 4th International Joint Conference on Natural Language Processing of the AFNLP.* pages 1003–1011. http://aclweb.org/anthology/P09-1113.

Yusuke Miyao, Rune Sætre, Kenji Sagae, Takuya Matsuzaki, and Jun'ichi Tsujii. 2008. Task-oriented evaluation of syntactic parsers and their representations. In *Proceedings of the Association for Computational Linguistics: Human*

Language Technologies (ACL-HLT). pages 46–54. http://aclweb.org/anthology/P08-1006.

Kiem-Hieu Nguyen, Xavier Tannier, Olivier Ferret, and Romaric Besancon. 2015. Generative event schema induction with entity disambiguation. In *Proceedings of the 53rd Annual Meeting of the Association for Computational Linguistics and the 7th International Joint Conference on Natural Language Processing*. pages 188–197. https://doi.org/10.3115/v1/P15-1019.

Brendan O'Connor, Brandon M. Stewart, and Noah A. Smith. 2013. Learning to extract international relations from political context. In *Proceedings of the 51st Annual Meeting of the Association for Computational Linguistics*. pages 1094–1104. http://aclweb.org/anthology/P13-1108.

Siddharth Patwardhan and Ellen Riloff. 2007. Effective information extraction with semantic affinity patterns and relevant regions. In *Proceedings of the 2007 Joint Conference on Empirical Methods in Natural Language Processing and Computational Natural Language Learning (EMNLP-CoNLL)*. http://aclweb.org/anthology/D07-1075.

Alessandro Raganato, Jose Camacho-Collados, and Roberto Navigli. 2017. Word sense disambiguation: A unified evaluation framework and empirical comparison. In *Proceedings of the 15th Conference of the European Chapter of the Association for Computational Linguistics*. pages 99–110. http://aclweb.org/anthology/E17-1010.

Philip A. Schrodt, Shannon G. Davis, and Judith L. Weddle. 1994. Political science: Keds - a program for the machine coding of event data. *Social Science Computer Review* 12(4). https://doi.org/10.1177/089443939401200408.

Satoshi Sekine. 2006. On-demand information extraction. In *In Proceedings of the Joint Conference of the International Committee on Computational Linguistics and the Association for Computational Linguistics (COLING/ACL)*. pages 731–738. http://aclweb.org/anthology/P06-2094.

Lei Sha, Sujian Li, Baobao Chang, and Zhifang Sui. 2016. Joint learning templates and slots for event schema induction. In *Proceedings of the 2016 Conference of the North American Chapter of the Association for Computational Linguistics: Human Language Technologies*. pages 428–434. https://doi.org/10.18653/v1/N16-1049.

Beth M. Sundheim. 1992. Overview of the fourth message understanding evaluation and conference. In *Proceedings of the Fourth Message Understanding Conference (MUC-4)*. http://aclweb.org/anthology/M92-1001.

Mihai Surdeanu, Jordi Turmo, and Alicia Ageno. 2006. A hybrid approach for the acquisition of information extraction patterns. In *Proceedings of the Workshop on Adaptive Text Extraction and Mining (ATEM 2006)*. http://aclweb.org/anthology/W06-2207.

Roman Yangarber, Ralph Grishman, Pasi Tapanainen, and Silja Huttunen. 2000. Automatic acquisition of domain knowledge for information extraction. In *Proceedings of the 18th Conference on Computational Linguistics (COLING)*. http://aclweb.org/anthology/C00-2136.

The Event StoryLine Corpus: A New Benchmark for Causal and Temporal Relation Extraction

Tommaso Caselli and **Piek Vossen**
Vrije Universiteit Amsterdam
De Boelelaan 1105 1081 HV Amsterdam (NL)
{t.caselli;p.t.j.m.vossen}@vu.nl

Abstract

This paper reports on the Event StoryLine Corpus (ESC) v0.9, a new benchmark dataset for the temporal and causal relation detection. By developing this dataset, we also introduce a new task, the StoryLine Extraction from news data, which aims at extracting and classifying events relevant for stories, from across news documents spread in time and clustered around a single seminal event or topic. In addition to describing the dataset, we also report on three baselines systems whose results show the complexity of the task and suggest directions for the development of more robust systems.

1 Introduction

Humans have an appetite for information to explain the things they observe. Our minds constantly mine the present for cues, merge this with information from the past, and derive models for reasoning and taking decisions. It is by means of such explanatory patterns, and by extension of *explanatory relations* among entities and events, that we understand the changing world.

The current stream of information poses a big challenge both to humans and systems to extract, organize, and represent events and their relations. News aggregation systems can easily monitor the burst and the development of a topic, or news story, but they fail in providing a content-based analysis. Given a topic or trending story, people still have to read the documents and reconstruct a unitary and coherent report mentally. Current NLP systems can identify complex information but they lack a method to connect it in a unitary and coherent message. Steps in this direction have been conducted but are very limited and do not cover the full story that is told by these documents (e.g. the textual entailment task, or script extraction).

Monitoring a news story from its beginning to end is a challenging task, which requires systems to be able to: 1) reconcile information from different sources distributed in time; 2) resolve deduplication of information; and 3) extract informative semantic structures.

It is surprising to observe how humans can perform these tasks with relative little effort. It has been suggested that this capacity is partly based on narrative strategies (Boyd, 2009; Gottschall, 2012). Such a structuring is possible thanks to a key component of narratives, the *plot structure* (Bal, 1997), which provides a chronological and logical ordering of events. This means that events are not simply ordered in time but they are selected and connected in such a way that their relations are meaningful, i.e., they give rise to a network of explanatory relations. Accessing and reconstructing plot structures for different topics would be beneficial for lots of Natural Language Understanding applications (question answering, summarization, co-reference resolution, event processing, and script extraction, among others).

One of the necessary step for a StoryLine Extraction task is to decide on a corpus to evaluate performance of systems. This paper presents such as resource: the Event StoryLine Corpus v0.9, specifically designed for the evaluation of systems aiming at reconstructing event-centric plot structures. The resource is still being extended with new annotated texts, but in the remainder of the paper we will refer to this first version. The corpus has been developed by applying annotation guidelines designed to mark-up the network of explanatory relations which can be realized between pairs of events in a document belonging to a specific topic. Furthermore, the guidelines

77

Proceedings of the Events and Stories in the News Workshop, pages 77–86,
Vancouver, Canada, August 4, 2017. ©2017 Association for Computational Linguistics

are compliant with other initiatives for event annotation: temporal processing (TimeML (Pustejovsky et al., 2003a) and Richer Event Description (RED) (O'Gorman et al., 2016)), event coreference (Event Coreference Bank+ (ECB+) (Cybulska and Vossen, 2014b)), and causal relations (Causal-TimeBank (Mirza and Tonelli, 2016), BECauSE (Dunietz et al., 2015), ROCStories (Mostafazadeh et al., 2016b) among others).

The remainder of the paper is structured as follows: Section 2 will explain the annotation scheme, describe the annotation layers of the Event StoryLines Corpus (ESC) v0.9, and report on agreement measures. Section 3 will describe experiments related to the development of baselines for the StoryLine Extraction task. In Section 4 a review of previous annotation initiatives is given, showing differences and commonalities between them and the ESC data. Finally, conclusions and future work are reported in Section 5. The annotated data, the evaluation scripts, and the baselines models are publicly available. [1]

2 The Event StoryLine Corpus v0.9

The primary goal of the ESC v0.9 dataset is to provide an intrinsic evaluation benchmark for the event-centric StoryLine Extraction task. The task can be best described as a combination of three basic subtasks:

- **Event Detection and Classification** Identify and classify events in each document which compose a topic, or a *seminal event*;

- **Temporal Anchoring of Events** Anchor each event mention to the temporal expression expressing the time of its happening, as well as to the Document Creation Time (DCT);

- **Explanatory Relation Identification and Classification** Select event pairs which are temporally and logically connected, and then, classify the storyline relation type.

A storyline relation can be best described as a loose causal and temporal relation between a pair of event mentions, where one event mention explains/justifies the occurrence of the other event mention in the pair (more details are reported in

Section 2.3). Relations can be classified either as `rising_action`, or `falling_action`.

An additional task is **Event Co-reference Resolution**, which aims at identifying co-referential chains of events mentions both at within- and cross-document levels. The availability of this information allows us to deduplicate information across event mentions by creating *event instances*, i.e. formal semantic representation in RDF compliant URIs that may integrate linguistic information with external resources, and thus, allow reasoning (Fokkens et al., 2013).[2] In the following sections, we will illustrate the components of the ESC Annotation Scheme and its annotation framework.

2.1 Basic Components: Events and Temporal Expressions

Events and temporal expressions are the basic components of the annotation scheme for the ESC v0.9 dataset.

The term "event" is used as a cover term to refer to any situations that can happen, occur, or hold. The use of the term event is a synonym to "eventuality" introduced by Bach (1986), covering both dynamic and static situations (i.e. events and states). The annotation of events in NLP is a topic that got a lot of interest and on which yet no consensus has been reached. In this work, we adopted a definition of events that is provided in the ECB+ Annotation Guidelines (Cybulska and Vossen, 2014a), which is compatible with definitions in ACE (Linguistic Data Consortium, 2005) and TimeML. In particular, an event is any punctual, durational, or stative situation which happens or holds, and which results from a combination of four components such as: 1) an **action** component referring to what happens or holds; 2) a **time** slot which is responsible for anchoring the action in time ; 3) a **location** component which links the action component to a place/location; and 4) a **participant** component, which illustrates the "who" or "what" is involved in the action component.

The annotation of the extent of events in ECB+ follows the solution adopted in TimeML. This means that for each event mention, regardless of its part-of-speech, only the lexical item which is the bearer of the action meaning is annotated. This normally corresponds to the head of the phrase

---

[1] https://github.com/cltl/
EventStoryLine.git

[2] http://groundedannotationframework.
org/files/2013/05/GAF_Poster.pdf

realizing the action component, i.e. *the minimal chunk*, as illustrated in the following example[3]. Annotated events are in bold.

1. This terrible **war** could have **ended** in a month

However, exceptions to this rule apply. Adopting an event-centric annotation framework, adherence to the text surface is not always maintained. For instance, cases of historically significant events which may be referred to with proper nouns, such as *World War II*, *the American Civil War*, are annotated with a unique action component tag. Similarly, as the annotation is also primarily focused towards event co-reference, pre-modifiers of events can be included in the action component tag any time they contribute to the identification of a unique event instance:

2. **6.1-magnitude quake** strikes Indonesia's Aceh.

Furthermore, ECB+ allows the annotation of present- and past-participles in modifier position as event mentions:

3. The **earthquake** [...] left hundred trapped in **collapsed** buildings.

Each action component is classified as belonging to one of seven possible classes. Five of them, *ACTION_OCCURRENCE*, *ACTION_ASPECTUAL*, *ACTION_REPORTING*, ACTION_STATE, and *ACTION_PERCEPTION*, mirror TimeML classes. The two additional classes , *ACTION_CAUSATIVE* and *ACTION_GENERIC*, have been introduced to annotate events expressing casual relations, and events which are not anchored to a specific time and location expressing generic actions (i.e. event mentions whose truthfulness is independent of the specific moment of utterance).

Temporal expression mark-up is inherited from TimeML following the *TIMEX3* annotation guidelines. We modified the original ECB+ annotation guidelines to be compatible with the *TIMEX3* TimeML ones by: 1) using the *TIMEX3* tag to annotate temporal expressions, 2) re-introducing the `type` attribute as part of the temporal expression tag; 3) re-introducing the attribute `value` for temporal expressions' normalization. We also allow

<hr>

[3]All examples are taken from the ECB+ Annotation Guidelines or the ECB+ annotated data

the creation of empty *TIMEX3* tag, i.e. non-text consuming temporal expression markables corresponding to implicit, i.e. not realized in the text, beginning and/or end points of temporal expressions denoting a duration. In addition to this, temporal expressions which have been included in action tags as part of the action component description must be annotated also as independent temporal expressions. This means that we allow multiple annotations on overlapping tokens over different text expressions. We made this choice because these temporal expressions in most cases also function as temporal anchor of the event component.

2.2 Temporal Anchoring of Events (TLINKs)

Temporal information plays an essential role for StoryLine Extraction. At the same time, the annotation of temporal relations is by no means a trivial task.

Two types of temporal relations can be identified: 1) ordering relations, which involve elements of the same ontological type, e.g. pairs of events or temporal expressions; and 2) anchoring relations, which involve cross-type element relations, e.g. pairs of event and related temporal expression. Although both types of temporal relations are useful, they have different informational status. Following Pustejovsky and Stubbs (2011), we assume that the informational level of a temporal relation can be expressed as a function of the information contained in each temporal link and their closure. Under this assumption, anchoring relations expressing when an event mention occurred or its duration, are more informative than ordering relations. The former allow us to put event mentions on a specific point (or interval) on an imaginary timeline and, as a consequence, also gives us the ordering relations between event mentions.

The ESC Annotation Scheme expresses temporal relations using the TimeML *TLINK* tag and restricts them to anchoring relations. *TLINKs* between an event mention and a temporal expression are systematically annotated when an anchoring relation is instantiated. Anchoring relations may hold between an event mention and a temporal expression at intra- and inter-sentential levels In addition to this, each event mention is also connected to the Document Creation Time (DCT) of each document.

Limiting the annotation to anchoring relations

is also a strategy to avoid the complexity of ordering relations between events. Most of the current solutions are not optimal, as they give the annotators too much freedom in the the selection of the event pairs (e.g. TimeML), or force the annotators to mark all possible relations (e.g. TimeBank-Dense (Cassidy et al., 2014)), or limit the annotations to the presence of explicit linguistic evidence (e.g. RED).

The temporal values in ESC are derived from the RED guidelines. We apply two sets of *TLINK* values according to the type of anchoring relation annotated: four values apply for relations between events and DCTs (namely `before`, `after`, `overlap`, and `contains`), while only one value (`contains`) applies to relations between events and temporal expressions. Annotators are also instructed on the directionality of the *TLINK*, which should always go from the temporal expression, or DCT, to the target event.

2.3 Explanatory Relation Annotation (PLOT_LINKs)

The annotation of explanatory relations between event pairs is encoded in the *PLOT_LINK* tag, following a previous proposal described in Caselli and Vossen (2016). *PLOT_LINK*s are specifically designed to capture the semantics of plot structures.

PLOT_LINK annotation is conducted in two steps: first, annotators have to identify all eligible relations between event pairs, and then they have to classify each relation as belonging to one of the two classes: `rising_action`, events which are circumstantial to, cause or enable another event, or `falling_action`, which explicitly mark speculations and consequences, i.e. events which are the (anticipated) outcome or the effect of another event.

*PLOT_LINK*s are related to causal and temporal relation annotation (Miltsakaki et al., 2004; Bethard et al., 2008; Mirza and Tonelli, 2014; Dunietz et al., 2015), but they differ in three ways: 1) they include the standard causal relations, i.e. *cause*, *enablement*, and *prevention*, but also additional event-event relations such as contingency, sub-event, entailment, and co-participation relations; 2) they are often not explicitly marked in the text through a relational structure; and 3) they are more specific than all events that stand in a temporal relation as they add explanatory information.

*PLOT_LINK*s can be positioned in between temporal and causal annotations by overcoming current shortcomings, such as creation of uninformative pairs of events, in the former case, and an extremely limited annotation in the latter, i.e. presence of an explicit causality trigger. Each pair of events in a *PLOT_LINK* relation is basically helping the reader (and the machine) to connect events in a meaningful way. In a nutshell, *PLOT_LINK*s aim at answering "why" something has happened. Given their event-centric nature, the answer to such a question must be another event mention explicitly stated in the document in analysis.

PLOT_LINK relations are asymmetrical and non-transitive. Non-transitivity is justified by considering the nature of this type of relations. They apply at a local level of analysis between pairs of events, and cannot be transferred to a global level, i.e. inherited by the full chain of event mentions which contribute to the identification of a story-line. Although subjected to the chronological order of events, this type of relations aims at making explicit the coherence, or logical connections, of the events in a (news) story.

When annotating *PLOT_LINK*s, the (broad) "causal" dimension of the relation is more prominent than the temporal aspect. We are not filling-up a timeline, where the axiom of the Internal Directionality of Time[4] (Bonomi and Zucchi, 2001) holds, but we are looking for explanations of "why" events happened, according to the information that we are given in the document of analysis. Thus, in example 4, the relation between the events "earthquake" and "trapped" is obtained by answering the question "why were people trapped?" and not by means of transitive relation between the pairs *earthquake* `rising_action` *collapsed* and *collapsed* `rising_action` *trapped*.

4. The **earthquake killed** 14 and **left** hundred **trapped** in **collapsed** buildings.
   earthquake `rising_action` killed
   earthquake `rising_action` trapped
   earthquake `rising_action` collapsed
   collapsed `rising_action` trapped

Annotators are free to identify the pairs of events which may stand in a *PLOT_LINK* rela-

---

[4]Internal Directionality of Time: if it is true of my current position in time, t, that the event **e** occurred in the past of t, then it is true of any future position t' that **e** is in the past of t

tion. We did not create a predefined set of pairs of events which may stand in a plot link, as in the TimeBank-Dense corpus, as this will require to create a really large graph between all events occurring both in the same sentence and across all sentences. However, we limited the annotation of *PLOT_LINK*s to events which correspond to one of the following three classes: *ACTION_OCCURRENCE, ACTION_PERCEPTION, ACTION_STATE*. We label those events as "semantically full" or "semantically loaded" events. Event mentions in these classes do have a content component describing a situation, rather than expressing meta-level information on the events.[5] The class of *ACTION_REPORTING* is excluded as well. In this case, the meaningful information is represented by the "content" of a speech event rather than by the lexical expression that introduces it. This choice guarantees that only meaningful events are part of a storyline.

Finally, *PLOT_LINK*s also allow the annotation of explicit causal relations between pairs of events. Two binary attributes, `cause` and `caused_by`, must be selected in presence of explicit causal relations. Explicit causal relations are introduced either by *ACTION_CAUSATIVE* events, or causal signals such as conjunctions (e.g. *because*), prepositions (e.g. *by, from, for*, among others), and other connectives. An additional attribute, `signal`, has been created to annotate the "markers" of the causal relation. At this stage of development, the attribute is filled only when *ACTION_CAUSATIVE* events are used to signal the presence of a casual relation:

5. A massive **quake struck** off Aceh in 2004 , **sparking** a **tsunami**.
   quake `rising_action` tsunami
   `signal`= sparking
   `cause` = YES

2.4 Event Co-reference

Currently, the annotation of co-referential chains among event mentions has been inherited from ECB+ The ECB+ guidelines consider two event mentions, either in the same document or across documents, as co-referential when they refer to the same event instance, i.e. if they describe the same action component, and 1.) share the same participants; 2) share the same temporal anchor; and 3) share the same location.

2.5 Data

The ESC v0.9 dataset is currently composed by 22 topics from the ECB+ corpus concerning calamity events, i.e. natural disasters, shootings, killings, accidents, and trials, among others.

The corpus contains 258 documents, and a total of 7,275 event mentions (191 of which being negated mentions).[6] A total of 1,297 temporal expressions are present, 248 of them corresponds to DCTs, of which 22 are realized by empty *TIMEX3* tags. In the remainder of the cases, 10 articles, it was not possible to recover a DCT, neither from the articles, nor by searching the Web.

Following the extended anchoring relation approach for *TLINK*s, we annotated a total of 6,904 relations between events and DCT and events and temporal expressions. The breakdown of the distribution of the values is reported in Table 1.

TLINK Value	DCT	TIMEX3
CONTAINS	522	2816
BEFORE	52	n.a.
AFTER	3283	n.a.
OVERLAP	160	n.a.

Table 1: *TLINK* value per DCT and temporal expression in the document.

As for the *PLOT_LINK*s, a total of 2,265 explanatory relations have been annotated, with an average of 8.7 relations per document. 1,147 relations have been classified as `rising_action`, while 1,118 as `falling_action`. By extending the manually annotated relations with within-document event co-reference chains, we reach a total of 5,519 *PLOT_LINK*s, almost three times the average relation per document, i.e. 21.39. This results in 2,653 `rising_action` and 2,844 `falling_action` relations, respectively. Finally, only 117 explicit causal relations have been identified.[7]

---

[5] We consider event mentions contributing to the assessment of the factuality profiling of an event mention, including cognitive events, events belonging to the class *ACTION_ASPECTUAL*, which functions as lexical morphosyntactic markers of the the internal temporal structure of a situation, and *ACTION_CAUSATIVE* as meta-level event mentions, and thus they are excluded.

[6] Event annotation is directly inherited from ECB+, where only sentences containing relevant mentions of the topic were annotated.

[7] Note that this can be extended further using the cross-document event coreference chains of ECB+

The annotation of the ESC v0.9 corpus has been conducted by 2 experts following a multi-step process and using the web-based tool CAT (Bartalesi Lenzi et al., 2012). In the first phase, both annotators went through a training phase to familiarize with the task, and were allowed to discuss and compare their annotations, especially for the *PLOT_LINK* task. This phase led to a revision of the annotation guidelines, by introducing more specific rules to select event pairs. In the second phase, the inter-annotator agreement was calculated on a subset of the ESC v0.9 dataset. In particular, given that the basic components, i.e. event mentions, temporal expressions, and event co-referential chains, are directly inherited from the ECB+ corpus, the agreement was calculated only for anchoring (i.e. *TLINK* tags) and explanatory relations (i.e. *PLOT_LINK* tags). Inter-annotator agreement has been computed using the Dice coefficient, both for relation detection and relation classification. Two different subsets of the ESC v0.9 corpus have been used for the two relations: one seminal event[8] for *TLINK*s and 4 seminal events[9] for *PLOT_LINK*s. We made this choice because of the different nature of the two types of relations. Results are reported in Table 2. The scores for *PLOT_LINK*s have been computed as an average over the 4 seminal events.

Relation Type	Identification	Classification
TLINK	0.767	0.744
PLOT_LINK	0.638	0.638

Table 2: Inter-annotator agreement: Dice coefficient at token level.

One of the most interesting observations on the *PLOT_LINK* analysis is that the agreement may vary according to the type of seminal event. For instance, the highest agreement has been observed for T19: a shooting accident :Dice 0.723 for relation identification, and 0.728 for relation classification. The lowest agreement was found for an escape from prison (T3): Dice 0.48 for relation identification, and 0.471 for relation classification. The results, although preliminary, suggest that different types of seminal events may be narrated in different ways following different story patterns (e.g. more or less linear stories).

3 Experiments: Baselines

In this section, we describe the experimental results for a number of StoryLine Extraction baseline systems on the ESC v0.9 dataset. The outcomes of these experiments will be useful to compare the performance of future (and more complex) systems, as well as to have a preliminary assessment of the complexity of the task.

The ESC v0.9 dataset has been divided into a development set, consisting of 6 seminal events[10] and a test set of 16 seminal events[11]. The test subset contains a total of 4,027 *PLOT_LINK*s when extended with within-document event co-reference chains. All experiments have been conducted considering gold data for event mention extent, temporal expression extent and values, and event co-reference.

Three baselines have been developed: 1) OP: selection of event pairs in relations that mimic the textual order of presentation; 2) PPMI1: selection of event pairs using Positive Pointwise Mutual Information (PPMI) obtained from a set of selected seed pairs and the manually annotated pairs from the development set; 3) PPMI-CONTAINS: selection of the event pairs using PPMI as in the PPMI1 model but restricting the sets of events to those which share the same temporal anchors, i.e. have a *TLINK* of type `contains`.

The seed pairs for the PPMI based models have been extracted from the SemEval 2012 Task-2: Measuring Degrees of Relational Similarity (Jurgens et al., 2012). In particular, we extracted words pairs from the test set Phase-1 Answers corresponding to class-8 (CAUSE-PURPOSE), retaining only word pairs in the categories Cause:Effect, Cause:Compensatory Action, Action/Activity, and Prevention, where both words express events. This initial set of seed elements has been further extended by looking for "cause", "enablement", and "entails" relations in SUMO (Niles and Pease, 2001, 2003) and in WordNet (Miller, 1995). This resulted in a list of 1,609 unique seed pairs. PPMI has been computed using the DISSECT Toolkit (Dinu et al., 2013), and pair frequencies have been extracted from Google bigrams(Brants and Franz, 2006). Rather than identifying a unique threshold for eligible pairs, we looked for a range of PPMI values.

---

[8]T37

[9]T3, T19, T37, T41

[10]T5, T7, T8, T32, T33, T35

[11]T1, T12, T13, T14, T16, T18, T19, T20, T22, T23, T24, T3, T30, T37, T4, T41

Baseline Model	PLOT_LINK Detection			PLOT_LINK Classification		
	P	R	F1	P	R	F1
OP	0.156	**0.988**	**0.265**	0.07	**0.97**	**0.14**
PPMI1	0.137	0.174	0.137	0.065	0.098	0.068
PPMI-CONTAINS	**0.227**	0.091	0.121	**0.114**	0.05	0.064

Table 3: Results of three baselines models on *PLOT_LINK* identification and classification .

This has been identified by normalizing the PPMI scores between 0 and 1, computing average and standard deviation. This allowed us to identify a minimum and a maximum normalized score[12] for PPMI, representing the boundaries of the range inside which event pairs in a *PLOT_LINK* relation can be identified and selected.

As for the extraction of the events in a *PLOT_LINK* relation from the test data, co-occurrence frequencies were computed per pairs of eligible event types (i.e. *ACTION_OCCURRENCE, ACTION_PERCEPTION, ACTION_STATE*) both at sentence and at document level. PPMI values were obtained by applying the same procedure used for the seed pairs. In the PPMI1 model, all event pairs whose score is within the range obtained from the seed pairs were selected. On the other hand, in the PPMI-CONTAINS model, the event pairs were further filtered by applying the temporal anchor constraints, i.e. they must both have a *TLINK* of type `contains` with the same temporal expression.

As for relation classification, i.e. the assignment of the values `rising_action` or `falling_action` to an event pair, we decided to always assign the `rising_action` value, i.e. the most frequent value from the manually annotated data. In addition to this, we also aimed at evaluating the impact of the order of presentation of the information in a document on *PLOT_LINK*s.

In Table 3, we report on the aggregated results, i.e. average score over the test data, of the three baselines. The relation detection subtask limits the evaluation to the correctness/validity of the event pairs identified by each model against the extended gold data. On the other hand, in the classification subtask, both the event pair and the relation value must be correct. This means that if the *PLOT_LINK* value is wrong but the event pair is correct, then the entire *PLOT_LINK* is considered

incorrect. Standard Precision (P), Recall (R), and F1-score (F1) apply for both subtasks.

The results, though preliminary, highlight the complexity of the task. Not surprisingly the best Recall value is obtained by the OP model. The creation of all possible pairs between eligible event types clearly gives rise to a lot of False Positive pairs (P=0.156), showing that even when only events in relevant sentences of specific topic are selected, there is still information which is not to be included in a storyline. For instance, there could be references to events which occurred in the past and which do not have any explanatory relations with the event mentions referring to the current topic, and presented to the reader for comparison or as additional background knowledge.

Different observations apply to the PPMI-based models. In PPMI1, we can observe a big drop in Recall (-0.841) and as well as in Precision, though lower (-0.019). On the other hand, temporal containment seems to facilitate the aggregation of the relevant pairs of a storyline, as shown by Precision (P=0.227). At this stage of the implementation, there is a lack of connection between events in different temporal anchors, thus limiting the connections between event pairs and having a negative impact on the Recall.

By observing the results on the classification task, it immediately appears that the textual order of presentation of the information badly correlates with *PLOT_LINK* values. The low results were in part expected given the distribution of the `rising_action` and `falling_action` relations in the test data. To better understand the results, we run an additional evaluation on the baselines by taking into account only same sentence pairs. In this case, we observed that all baselines increase the Precision (P=0.123 for OP, P=0.095 for PPM1, and P=0.151 for PPMI-CONTAINS) and downgrade the Recall scores. Given the evaluation framework for classification, this suggests that, at least when in the same sentence, there is a tendency to narrate the events following a logi-

---

[12] Average PPMI value=0.582; standard deviation=0.181; minimum PPMI value=0.4; maximum PPMI value=0.763

cal order, not only a temporal one. However, this does not hold anymore when cross-sentence relations are taken into account.

4   Related Work

Frameworks and models for understanding narratives have mainly focused on fictional texts (Lehnert, 1981; Goyal et al., 2010; Mani, 2012) Modern day news reports still reflect narrative structures but they have proven difficult for automatic tools (Rospocher et al., 2016). To the best of our knowledge, previous work on StoryLine Extraction is limited, if we exclude the contribution by Caselli and Vossen (2016). However, there are several related works in NLP dealing with related tasks. The extraction of *causal relations* is the nearest task. One of the most prominent work is represented by the Penn Discourse Treebank (PDTB) (Miltsakaki et al., 2004), where explicit and implicit causal relations are annotated between discourse units.

The Causal-TimeBank (Mirza and Tonelli, 2016) has introduced a TimeML-based annotation of causal relations between events on top of the TempEval-3 TimeBank data. Casual relations are annotated by means of a *CLINK* tag and only explicit causal relations are marked-up, i.e. the relation must be signaled by a linguistic markers (e.g. a preposition or a causal verb). This results in 318 *CLINK*s, 296 of which are in same-sentence. The RED guidelines (O'Gorman et al., 2016) combines event co-reference, temporal and causal relations. In particular, causal relations are expressed by means of `precondition` and `cause` values, allowing both same sentence and adjacent sentence relations, thus aiming at achieving a richer semantic representations of event relations. The BECauSe Corpus 2.0 (Dunietz et al., 2015) focuses on causal language, by representing what causal relationships are expressed in a text/document, rather than taking into account real world causality. Causal relations are annotated only in presence of a causal connective (i.e. a lexical item signaling the causal relation). The annotation scheme is very rich as it allows the mark-up of overlapping relations (e.g. temporal, correlation, hypothetical, among others) as well.

Another relevant work is the CaTeRs annotation scheme (Mostafazadeh et al., 2016b). In CaTeRs, causal relations between events are annotated from a "commonsense reasoning" perspective rather than starting from linguistic markers, inspired by the mental model theory of causality. The scheme identifies 9 classes of causal relations as well as 4 classes of temporal relations. The scheme has been applied over 320 stories from the ROCStories Corpus (Mostafazadeh et al., 2016a), which collects everyday stories (e.g. "got a phone call") composed by 5 sentences. The main goal of the annotation is to focus on those causal and temporal relations which may facilitate the learning of stereotypical narrative structures.

In this work, we have extended the set of event-event relations to be annotated using the notion of explanatory relation. In our work both implicit and explicit relations are annotated, allowing the annotation at both intra- and inter-sentential levels. In addition to this, the availability of within- and cross-document event co-reference chains allows the extension of the annotated data across documents, providing access to a larger, "global" level of analysis.

5   Conclusion and Future Works

This paper presents the Event StoryLine Corpus v0.9, the first benchmark corpus for a StoryLine Extraction task, i.e. temporally and logically connected sequences of events related to a specific topic from documents spread in time. We also presented three baseline systems with their performance on the data base. This task aims at moving away from current approaches on timeline and causal relation extraction. With respect to the former task, storylines aim at the chronologically ordering only of events that are relevant to a story, thus cleaning timeline structures. At the same time, storylines extend causal relation extraction by covering both explicit and implicit causal relations between events, both at a intra- and inter-sentential levels. This facilitates the learning of narrative models, i.e. explanatory patterns in news data, which can be used to identify both stereotypical and episodic narrations of seminal events, or topics, in news. One the innovative aspects is the connection with co-reference relations of events across documents, thus making the annotated data also useful for the development of cross-document summarization systems.

The corpus will be extended in the future by means of crowd-sourcing and by introducing annotations of climax events, i.e. the main events in the story. In parallel, we aim at developing more robust systems.

Acknowledgments

This work has been supported the NWO Spinoza Prize project "Understanding Language by Machines" (sub-track 3).

References

Emmon Bach. 1986. The algebra of events. *Linguistics and philosophy* 9(1):5–16.

Mieke Bal. 1997. *Narratology: Introduction to the theory of narrative*. University of Toronto Press.

Valentina Bartalesi Lenzi, Giovanni Moretti, and Rachele Sprugnoli. 2012. CAT: the CELCT Annotation Tool. In *In Proceedings of LREC 2012*. pages 333–338.

Steven Bethard, William J Corvey, Sara Klingenstein, and James H Martin. 2008. Building a corpus of temporal-causal structure. In *LREC*.

Andrea Bonomi and Alessandro Zucchi. 2001. *Tempo e linguaggio: introduzione alla semantica del tempo e dell'aspetto verbale*. Pearson Italia Spa.

Brian Boyd. 2009. *On the origin of stories*. Harvard University Press.

Thorsten Brants and Alex Franz. 2006. Web 1t 5-gram corpus version 1.1. *Google Inc* .

Tommaso Caselli and Piek Vossen. 2016. The storyline annotation and representation scheme (star): A proposal. In *Proceedings of the 2nd Workshop on Computing News Storylines (CNS 2016)*. Association for Computational Linguistics, Austin, Texas, pages 67–72. http://aclweb.org/anthology/W16-5708.

Taylor Cassidy, Bill McDowell, Nathanael Chambers, and Steven Bethard. 2014. An annotation framework for dense event ordering. In *Proceedings of the 52nd Annual Meeting of the Association for Computational Linguistics (Volume 2: Short Papers)*. Association for Computational Linguistics, Baltimore, Maryland, pages 501–506. http://www.aclweb.org/anthology/P14-2082.

Agata Cybulska and Piek Vossen. 2014a. Guidelines for ECB+ annotation of events and their coreference. Technical Report NWR-2014-1, VU University Amsterdam.

Agata Cybulska and Piek Vossen. 2014b. Using a sledgehammer to crack a nut? Lexical diversity and event coreference resolution. In *Proceedings of the 9th Language Resources and Evaluation Conference (LREC2014)*. Reykjavik, Iceland.

Georgiana Dinu, Nghia The Pham, and Marco Baroni. 2013. Dissect - distributional semantics composition toolkit. In *Proceedings of the 51st Annual Meeting of the Association for Computational Linguistics: System Demonstrations*. Association for Computational Linguistics, Sofia, Bulgaria, pages 31–36. http://www.aclweb.org/anthology/P13-4006.

Jesse Dunietz, Lori Levin, and Jaime Carbonell. 2015. Annotating causal language using corpus lexicography of constructions. In *Proceedings of The 9th Linguistic Annotation Workshop*. Association for Computational Linguistics, Denver, Colorado, USA, pages 188–196. http://www.aclweb.org/anthology/W15-1622.

Antske Fokkens, Marieke van Erp, Piek Vossen, Sara Tonelli, Willem Robert van Hage, Luciano Serafini, Rachele Sprugnoli, and Jesper Hoeksema. 2013. Gaf: A grounded annotation framework for events. In *Workshop on Events: Definition, Detection, Coreference, and Representation*. Association for Computational Linguistics, Atlanta, Georgia, pages 11–20. http://www.aclweb.org/anthology/W13-1202.

Jonathan Gottschall. 2012. *The storytelling animal: How stories make us human*. Houghton Mifflin Harcourt.

Amit Goyal, Ellen Riloff, and Hal Daume III. 2010. Automatically producing plot unit representations for narrative text. In *Proceedings of the 2010 Conference on Empirical Methods in Natural Language Processing*. Association for Computational Linguistics, Cambridge, MA, pages 77–86. http://www.aclweb.org/anthology/D10-1008.

David Jurgens, Saif Mohammad, Peter Turney, and Keith Holyoak. 2012. Semeval-2012 task 2: Measuring degrees of relational similarity. In **SEM 2012: The First Joint Conference on Lexical and Computational Semantics – Volume 1: Proceedings of the main conference and the shared task, and Volume 2: Proceedings of the Sixth International Workshop on Semantic Evaluation (SemEval 2012)*. Association for Computational Linguistics, Montréal, Canada, pages 356–364. http://www.aclweb.org/anthology/S12-1047.

Wendy G Lehnert. 1981. Plot units and narrative summarization. *Cognitive Science* 5(4):293–331.

Linguistic Data Consortium. 2005. ACE (Automatic Content Extraction) English annotation guidelines for entities.

Inderjeet Mani. 2012. Computational modeling of narrative. *Synthesis Lectures on Human Language Technologies* 5(3):1–142.

George A Miller. 1995. Wordnet: a lexical database for english. *Communications of the ACM* 38(11):39–41.

Eleni Miltsakaki, Rashmi Prasad, Aravind K Joshi, and Bonnie L Webber. 2004. The penn discourse treebank. In *LREC*.

Paramita Mirza and Sara Tonelli. 2014. An analysis of causality between events and its relation to temporal information. In *Proceedings of COLING 2014, the 25th International Conference on Computational Linguistics: Technical Papers*. Dublin City University and Association for Computational Linguistics, Dublin, Ireland, pages 2097–2106. http://www.aclweb.org/anthology/C14-1198.

Paramita Mirza and Sara Tonelli. 2016. Catena: Causal and temporal relation extraction from natural language texts. In *Proceedings of COLING 2016, the 26th International Conference on Computational Linguistics: Technical Papers*. The COLING 2016 Organizing Committee, Osaka, Japan, pages 64–75. http://aclweb.org/anthology/C16-1007.

Nasrin Mostafazadeh, Nathanael Chambers, Xiaodong He, Devi Parikh, Dhruv Batra, Lucy Vanderwende, Pushmeet Kohli, and James Allen. 2016a. A corpus and evaluation framework for deeper understanding of commonsense stories. *arXiv preprint arXiv:1604.01696* .

Nasrin Mostafazadeh, Alyson Grealish, Nathanael Chambers, James Allen, and Lucy Vanderwende. 2016b. Caters: Causal and temporal relation scheme for semantic annotation of event structures. In *Proceedings of the Fourth Workshop on Events*. Association for Computational Linguistics, San Diego, California, pages 51–61. http://www.aclweb.org/anthology/W16-1007.

Ian Niles and Adam Pease. 2001. Towards a standard upper ontology. In *Proceedings of the international conference on Formal Ontology in Information Systems-Volume 2001*. ACM, pages 2–9.

Ian Niles and Adam Pease. 2003. Mapping wordnet to the sumo ontology. In *Proceedings of the ieee international knowledge engineering conference*. pages 23–26.

Tim O'Gorman, Kristin Wright-Bettner, and Martha Palmer. 2016. Richer event description: Integrating event coreference with temporal, causal and bridging annotation. In *Proceedings of the 2nd Workshop on Computing News Storylines (CNS 2016)*. Association for Computational Linguistics, Austin, Texas, pages 47–56. http://aclweb.org/anthology/W16-5706.

James Pustejovsky, José Castao, Robert Ingria, Roser Saurì, Robert Gaizauskas, Andrea Setzer, and Graham Katz. 2003a. TimeML: Robust Specification of Event and Temporal Expressions in Text. In *Fifth International Workshop on Computational Semantics (IWCS-5)*.

James Pustejovsky and Amber Stubbs. 2011. Increasing informativeness in temporal annotation. In *Proceedings of the 5th Linguistic Annotation Workshop*. Association for Computational Linguistics, Portland, Oregon, USA, pages 152–160. http://www.aclweb.org/anthology/W11-0419.

Marco Rospocher, Marieke van Erp, Piek Vossen, Antske Fokkens, Itziar Aldabe, German Rigau, Aitor Soroa, Thomas Ploeger, and Tessel Bogaard. 2016. Building event-centric knowledge graphs from news. *Web Semantics: Science, Services and Agents on the World Wide Web* 37:132–151.

The Rich Event Ontology

Susan Windisch Brown,[1] Claire Bonial,[2] Leo Obrst,[3] and Martha Palmer[1]
[1] University of Colorado, Boulder, Colorado
[2] U.S. Army Research Lab, Adelphi, Maryland
[3] MITRE, McLean, Virginia

Susan.Brown@colorado.edu, Claire.N.Bonial.civ@mail.mil,
lobrst@mitre.org, Martha.Palmer@colorado.edu

Abstract

In this paper we describe a new lexical semantic resource, The Rich Event Ontology, which provides an independent conceptual backbone to unify existing semantic role labeling (SRL) schemas and augment them with event-to-event causal and temporal relations. By unifying the FrameNet, VerbNet, Automatic Content Extraction, and Rich Entities, Relations and Events resources, the ontology serves as a shared hub for the disparate annotation schemas and therefore enables the combination of SRL training data into a larger, more diverse corpus. By adding temporal and causal relational information not found in any of the independent resources, the ontology facilitates reasoning on and across documents, revealing relationships between events that come together in temporal and causal chains to build more complex scenarios. We envision the open resource serving as a valuable tool for both moving from the ontology to text to query for event types and scenarios of interest, and for moving from text to the ontology to access interpretations of events using the combined semantic information housed there.

1   Introduction

As NLP moves into tasks requiring deeper language understanding, inferencing, and reasoning, knowledge-based resources are being increasingly called on to support and supplement probabilistic and other data-driven methods (Hogenboom et al., 2011). Ontologies have been recognized as useful for tasks such as information extraction (IE) (Maedche et al., 2003; Wimalasuriyu et al., 2010), metaphor analysis (Brown, 2014) and automatic question answering (Lopez et al., 2011). By providing a formal specification of the shared concepts in a domain, an ontology allows users to identify entities and relations between them despite the myriad ways these can be expressed in language.

Existing general-purpose ontologies, such as the Descriptive Ontology for Linguistic and Cognitive Engineering, DOLCE (Masolo et al., 2003), the Suggested Upper Merged Ontology, SUMO (Pease, 2002), Cyc (Lenat, 1995), and the Basic Formal Ontology, BFO (Smith & Grenon, 2002) have either focused on providing only a very under-specified upper level ontology to which domain-specific ontologies can attach or have created much more fully developed object hierarchies than event hierarchies. SUMO has links to the well-known WordNet lexicon (Fellbaum, 1998), which is also the foundation for the BabelNet ontology (Navigli and Ponzetto, 2012). WordNet has well-developed subsumption relations in its noun lexicon. It's verb lexicon, however, has hypernym/meronym relations only four to five nodes deep. This situation translates to an ontology rich with object concepts and relations but a rather impoverished event network. In addition, none of

Proceedings of the Events and Stories in the News Workshop, pages 87–97,
Vancouver, Canada, August 4, 2017. ©2017 Association for Computational Linguistics

these ontologies have incorporated information from lexical resources that focus on events.

Most applications using ontologies have made heaviest use of these ontologies' object hierarchies, drawing on their often extensive representations of physical objects, people, and locations. Events, being more difficult to delineate and define, often have a sparser and more shallow class hierarchy in an ontology. Classes representing events, however, can provide the nexus for relating objects and properties and prove useful for many language understanding tasks. By explicitly representing events, we can deal directly not only with relations between events and objects, but between multiple events as well. One of the more difficult language understanding tasks is identifying temporal and causal relations between events. The ontology we describe here is intended to provide a rich structure of event concepts that connects varying levels of event specificity, relates events to their key objects and participants, and encodes the temporal and causal relationships between events.

We found that existing ontologies were not suitable for bridging the gap between spatio-temporal ontological approaches to representing events and the representations stemming from SRL resources. Our ontology provides this bridge by drawing heavily from the upper-level distinctions of DOLCE, but also linking to the widely used lexical resources FrameNet (FN) (Fillmore et al., 2002) and VerbNet (VN) (Kipper et al., 2008). Not only do these provide wide-coverage lexicons having to do with events, they also contribute annotated corpora and additional semantic and syntactic information that can be crucial to identifying events and their participants (see section 2.5). In addition, the ontology provides links to the annotations, event typing, and role specifications of both the Automatic Content Extraction (ACE) (Doddington et al., 2004) and the Rich Entities, Relations, and Events (ERE) (Song et al., 2015) Projects. Both are DARPA-funded resources that have figured prominently in the TAC-KBP (Text Analysis Conference – Knowledge Base Population) evaluations. The ontology thus allows one to draw on multiple linguistic resources and combine their annotations. This firstly ensures a larger, more diverse training corpus with the potential to detect a wide variety of events. Secondly, this allows the resources to be integrated in terms of common temporal and causal relationships be-tween annotated event types, making explicit higher-order relationships between events – information not found in any of the independent resources.

We have completed the early stages of ontology development and are now working toward a formal evaluation. To that end, we are integrating the ontology into an end-to-end IE pipeline in order to evaluate the ontology's ability to 1) increase the number and types of events recognized and classified in text, and 2) allow users to refine, expand or alter queries about events by making use of ontological relations. We report results on two sample use cases related to these goals.

In the remainder of the paper, we provide a description of the upper level of the ontology, some of the major mid-level classes, and the linked lexical resources. We then explain the modular structure of the ontology and its advantages. In section 3, we describe our progress towards evaluation by discussing our two use cases. Finally, we conclude with a description of our future work.

2   Ontology Description

Intended as a resource for a wide range of tasks, the Rich Event Ontology (REO) has been designed to encompass both meta-level concepts in its upper level and many general domains in its mid level. REO has been implemented in OWL, which allows for easy extension with more detailed, domain-specific ontologies. The main reference ontology now encompasses 161 classes and 553 axioms. Including the lexical resource ontologies and the linking models (described in detail in sections 2.5 and 2.6) in these counts brings the totals to 3,065 classes and 60,531 axioms, as well as 16,005 individuals representing the vocabulary (unique lemmas) of event denotations.[1]

This project's goal has been the development of a unified representation of events. To do this, however, we must be able to reference the participants of the events, necessitating a connection to a well-developed physical and abstract object ontology. Although this paper will include mentions of object classes, especially as they link to event classes as participants in those events, it will focus on the event portion of the ontology. In addition, we will focus on a description of the ontology's structure and content, rather than a description of

---

[1] For comparison: VN includes about 8,600 verb lemmas and FN includes about 13,000 lexical units.

our development methodology, which can be found in earlier work (Bonial et al., 2016).

2.1 Theoretical Framework & Approach

We attempt to describe those categories that underlie human language. DOLCE's basic assumptions reflect our own: "We do not commit to a strictly referentialist metaphysics related to the intrinsic nature of the world: rather, the categories we introduce here are thought of as cognitive artifacts ultimately depending on human perception, cultural imprints and social conventions" (Masolo et al., 2003, p. 8). Our upper level ontological distinctions align with DOLCE's largely spatiotemporal distinctions. However, given our practical NLP goals, our mid-level distinctions shift towards Davidsonian (Davidson, 1980) distinctions more aligned with SRL resources.

2.2 The Upper Ontology

The fundamental distinction at the top level of our ontology is between Endurant and Perdurant entities. Borrowing heavily from DOLCE, we define "Endurants" as *those entities that can be observed/perceived as a complete concept, no matter which given snapshot of time* and "Perdurants" as *those entities for which only a part exists if we look at them at any given snapshot in time. Variously called events, processes phenomena, or activities and states, perdurants have temporal parts or spatial parts and participants*. We continue to follow DOLCE's lead in dividing the PERDURANT class into the subclasses EVENTIVE PERDURANT and STATIVE PERDURANT. This dichotomy is based on the notions of homeomericity and cumulativity (Masolo et al., 2003). So, in this case, a stative would be distinguished from an eventive by way of possessing the property of cumulativity, i.e., a *sitting* occurrence type is a stative because the mereological sum of two sittings is still a sitting. This is somewhat similar to the "waterfall" analysis of Galton & Mizoguchi (2009), that more radically proposes a property of dissectivity for processes and matter, so that processes are similar to mass nouns in semantics. In the waterfall model, processes are dependent continuants, similar to objects, which are independent continuants. Unlike DOLCE and the waterfall model (see also Mizoguchi et al (2011), Galton (2012), Borgo & Mizoguchi (2014), Rovetto & Mizoguchi (2015), which more directly address notions of causality), however, we do not currently subdivide these cat-

egories into the aspectual classes of states, processes, achievements and accomplishments. Although these categories have a long history in linguistic and philosophical literature (Vendler, 1957; Moens and Steedman, 1988) and more recently in semantics, distinguishing kinds of states (Maienborn, 2011; Maienborn et al., 2011), these divisions are difficult to apply in a commonsense way to domains we consider coherent. For example, Vendlerian divisions would place a chatting eventuality in a fundamentally different section of the ontology from a telling eventuality. Instead, as we move into the middle level of the ontology, we shift to a neo-Davidsonian perspective, in which event participants become a greater focus. We expect that we will refine the underlying event formalization over time, as it becomes clearer how to reconcile our commonsense semantic application focus with more recent semantic and ontological analyses.

2.3 Mid-level Classes

The EVENTIVE PERDURANT class splits into many daughter classes, of which some of the most extensive are COGNITIVE EVENT, LIFE EVENT, INTENTIONALLY ACT, and MOTION. These are still very general concepts, and have no direct connections to the lexical resources and specific lexical items. For some of these classes, such as LIFE EVENT, the next level down introduces concepts with direct links to the lexical resources, such as the LIFE EVENT daughter class BIRTH linking to FN's BEING_BORN frame and VN's BIRTH class (among others).

For other classes, another sublevel with few direct lexical realizations seemed necessary. For example, INTENTIONALLY ACT includes the subclasses SOCIAL INTERACTION, INTENTIONALLY AFFECT, TRANSFER POSSESSION, and ORGANIZATIONAL EVENT. Each of these has multiple subclasses. To illustrate the level of class granularity, we present ORGANIZATIONAL EVENT in more detail (Figure 1).

Its daughter classes include START ORGANIZATION, END ORGANIZATION, MERGE ORGANIZATION, DECLARE BANKRUPTCY, START POSITION WITH AN ORGANIZATION, and END POSITION WITH AN ORGANIZATION. Most of these have no further subclasses, although START POSITION subdivides further into START LEADERSHIP POSITION, HIRING, and HIRING ON. END POSITION has similar subclasses. The decision to include the very specific classes

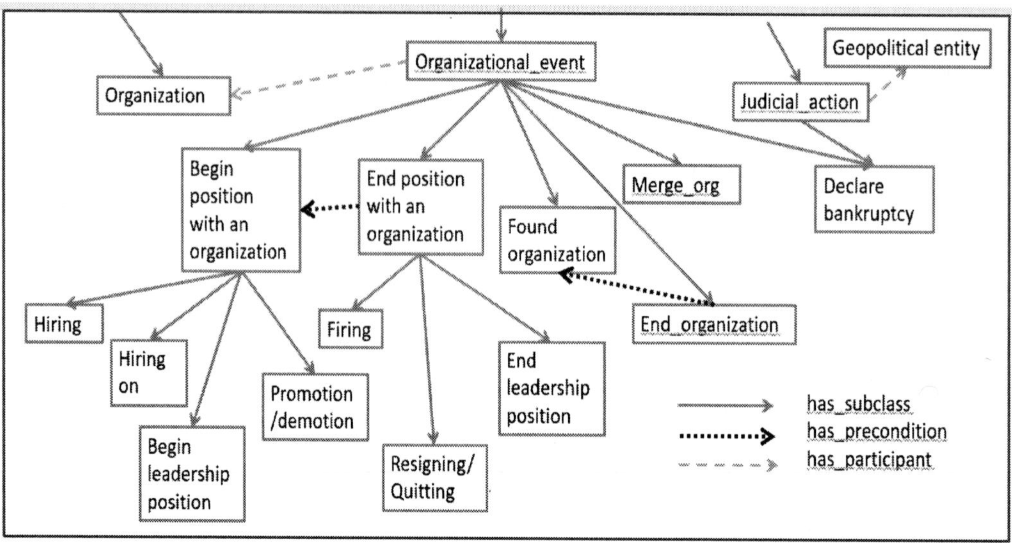

Figure 1: ORGANIZATIONAL EVENT section of the ontology.

concerning leadership positions resulted from the many lexical items, across languages, for events like 'crown', 'ordain', 'oust' and 'depose', and the frequency with which starting and ending leadership positions are discussed in print and oral corpora.

The decision to create the closely related classes HIRING and HIRING ON stems from a similar desire to take common human distinctions into account and to allow for the shift in role relations that usually accompany such shifts in perspective. The agent of a hiring event is the employer and the employee is a theme. However, the agent of a hiring-on event is the employee. Although *Company hiring Person* is arguably the same event as *Person hiring on with Company,* the shift in perspective is commonly lexicalized and therefore represented in the ontology. Such perspective-shifting classes are rare in the ontology and always share a common parent class, which ignores the perspective shift. They are important, however, in the TRANSFER POSSESSION domain, with such divisions as GIVE and GET. We highlight the perspective shift by having two relations between a class like TRANSFER and a class like GIVE: both TRANSFER *hasSubclass* GIVE and TRANSFER *hasPerspective* GIVE. For applications that need a more perspective-neutral classification, one can generalize to the parent class.

2.4 Relations between Classes

The main relation between classes (i.e., concepts) in the ontology is the subclass relation, which specifies that every subclass is a more specific type of the superclass. This entails that a subclass inherits all the domain and range restrictions of the parent class as well as other types of relations the parent class holds, such as *hasResult.*

The subclass relation, however, barely taps into the rich, complex relations between events or between events and objects. To capture some of that, we have included temporal and causal relations extended from the Richer Event Description (RED) project (Ikuta et al., 2014; O'Gorman et al., 2016). The RED project aims to annotate text with mentions of eventualities and entities, with the goal of representing the temporal and causal relationships between those eventualities in such a way that an accurate timeline of events could be automatically constructed. We have adapted and expanded their relations to our *hasPrecondition, hasCause, hasResult,* and *hasSubevent* relations.[2] Examples of these relations include:

1. END ORG *hasPrecondition* BEGIN ORG
2. KILLING *hasResult* DYING
3. TRIAL *hasSubevent* VERDICT

The *hasSubevent* relation is intended to capture events that are temporally contained within another event and considered a proper part of that event. For example, Verdict is not a type of Trial, so the *Subclass* relation is inappropriate. The *has-*

---

[2] In some cases the relations encode opposite perspectives on the same relation between classes (e.g., DEAD *hasCause* DYING and DYING *hasResult* DEAD), but those relations do not always coincide (e.g., (2) does not entail that DYING *hasCause* KILLING).

Subevent relation, however, indicates that a verdict happens within the greater context of a trial.

We have currently defined ten such cross-event relations. As part of the process of selecting and defining these relations, we created 49 instances of event-to-event relations in a small portion of the existing ontology. Future work will involve applying these relations to the rest of the reference ontology.

Other relations connect events with object classes (physical or abstract), such as the *hasLocation*, *hasAgent*, and *hasPatient* relations. As mentioned earlier, these relations are inherited by descendent classes. For example, DECLARE BANKRUPTCY is a subclass of both ORGANIZATIONAL PROCESS and JUDICIAL ACTION. ORGANIZATIONAL PROCESS *hasParticipant* some ORGANIZATION, and JUDICIAL ACTION *hasParticipant* some GOVERNMENTAL AUTHORITY. DECLARE BANKRUPTCY would thus inherit both ORGANIZATION and GOVERNMENTAL AUTHORITY as participants in the event.

The relations described in this section are being applied to the main, "reference" REO ontology. For an explanation of how the main ontology links to the lexical resources, see section 2.6.

2.5 Lexical Resource Ontologies and Their Linking Models

One of the primary goals of the ontology is to provide a means of combining the information in multiple lexical resources, despite differences in their categorization of lexical items. With our focus on event modeling, we have chosen to link to resources with rich event representations and broad coverage of English verbs and eventive nouns. We have represented the categorizations, lexical items, and participant roles included in each of these resources as separate OWL ontologies.

FrameNet: This resource, based on Fillmore's frame semantics (Fillmore, 1976; Fillmore & Baker, 2001), groups verbs, nouns and adjectives into "frames" based on words or "frame elements" that evoke the same semantic frame: a description of a type of event, relation, or entity and the participants in it. For example, the Apply_heat frame includes the frame elements Cook, Food, Heating_instrument, Temperature_setting, etc. The "net" of frames makes up a rather complex network, including simple *isA* inheritance relations as well as more complex relations such as *Precedes* and *PerspectiveOn*.

These relations highlight important aspects of many frames, for example, the Apply_heat frame is *UsedBy* the Cooking_creation frame, but often the frames involved are not anchored to the main *isA* hierarchy. In addition, the automatic reasoning capabilities of ontologies implemented in OWL are restricted to strictly logical relationships between classes. The complexity of FN precludes complete representation in OWL, as others have found (e.g., Scheffczyk et al., 2006). Therefore, we flattened the FN hierarchy, connecting every frame to a single parent node, FrameNetFrame, and relying on our main ontology to provide *isA* and event-event relations. This decision reduces the relational information from FN that is directly represented in our ontology, but users can of course trace the frames back to FN proper and access FN's full relational structure there.

VerbNet: This resource, based on Levin (1993), groups verbs into "classes" using their compatibility with certain syntactic alternations (e.g., *She rolled the ball down the hill* vs. *The ball rolled down the hill*). Although the groupings are primarily syntactic, the classes do share semantic features as well, since, as Levin posited, the syntactic behavior of a verb is largely determined by its meaning. Each class specifies its member verbs and their typical participants (i.e., semantic roles), lists the syntactic patterns they are all compatible with, and connects those patterns to semantic representations (Kipper et al., 2008).

By linking to VN, the ontology gains valuable syntactic information about how events are expressed in English. Generally, a VN class is linked in a one-to-one relation to one of the main ontology classes. A class's syntactic alternations, however, sometimes cut across semantic distinctions made by the main ontology. For example, events expressible with causative-inchoative alternations are grouped in the same VN class, but are divided in the main ontology (since the main ontology makes distinctions based on the number and types of event participants). For these VN classes, we link an ontology class to specific frames in a class, using VN thematic roles to distinguish the appropriate frames. These cases coincide with places where VN's semantic representation also differs for a particular frame, indicating that the reference ontology is consistent with VN semantic distinctions.

ERE/ACE: ERE is based on the ACE project's semantic role annotation schema. The goal of the

ERE/ACE projects is to mark up the events and the entities involved in them, and to mark coreference between these. This provides a somewhat shallow representation of the meaning of the text. The ERE/ACE schema can also serve as a lexicon imported into the ontology, with its event type designations serving as links to the lexical items marked up with that designation. ERE annotated eventualities are limited to certain types of special interest within the defense community, with top-level types referred to as *Life, Movement, Transaction, Business, Conflict, Manufacture, Contact, Personnel* and *Justice* events.

Both the FN and VN resource ontologies model lexical units and class members, respectively, as individuals that represent lemmas, which may be used as references for particular event concepts in REO. Because ERE and ACE are resources developed specifically for annotating data to be used as training data, they do not include pre-specified individuals or "triggers," of certain event types. Instead, these are always marked up in context. Thus, these resources provide a data-driven, ground-up perspective on event semantics that is very distinct from the other resources. The ACE and ERE models include as individuals English lemmas that have been annotated either in the freely available ACE 2005 Multilingual Training Corpus (Walker et al., 2005), or the as-of-yet unreleased ERE corpus, respectively.

2.6 Modular Architecture

The structure of the ontology is modeled after the architecture of the Ontologies of Linguistic Annotation (OLiA) (Chiarcos et al., 2016). OLiA serves as a reference hub for annotation terminology for largely (morpho-)syntactic information across a variety of languages. Similarly, REO can act as a bridge between semantic annotation resources. In this modular architecture (Figure 2), one reference ontology houses the schema-independent, primary event concepts and relations of REO. Each of the lexical resources currently included, FrameNet, VerbNet, ERE and ACE, are modeled as independent OWL ontologies, as described above. For each annotation resource model, a linking model defines the relationships between the concepts and

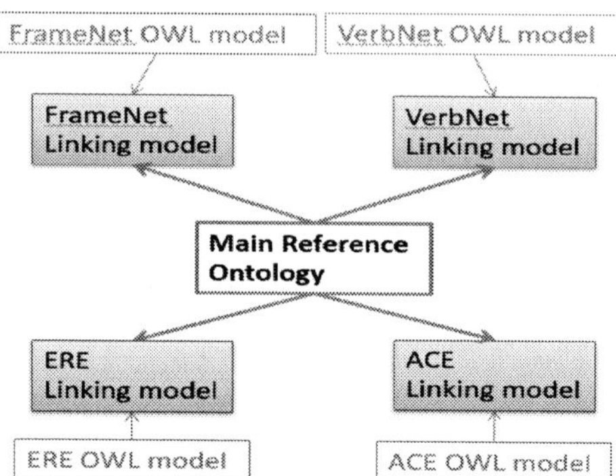

Figure 2: Modular architecture of the ontology

properties in the resource model and those of the reference model. Specifically, each linking model imports both the respective resource model and the reference ontology, and concepts in the reference ontology are linked to those of the resource model via the *hasReferenceGroup* relation. For example, the LEGAL ACTION event subclass DISCHARGE has the reference group Release-Parole from ERE and Releasing from FN (see Figure 3). Thus, all of the lexical units that are members of the Releasing Frame and all of the triggers annotated as Release-Parole form the group of references for a DISCHARGE event: *free, parole, release, let go, set free*, etc. Each of the linking models can be imported into a single ontology to query across all resources simultaneously. However, as Chiarcos et al. (2016) point out, maintaining independent ontologies in this modular structure allows one to integrate, or remove, terminology from different resources in a lossless and reversible way. Additionally, given the ongoing development of resources like FN, this structure also allows for independent lexical resource models to be updated without impacting the ontology as a whole. Finally, the modularity offers a certain level of customization for users. For example, if a user is looking for somewhat synonymous references to events, then it may be desirable to leave FN out of the final model, since FN frames include Frame Elements that may not be references to the event (e.g., *cop* in the Arrest frame).

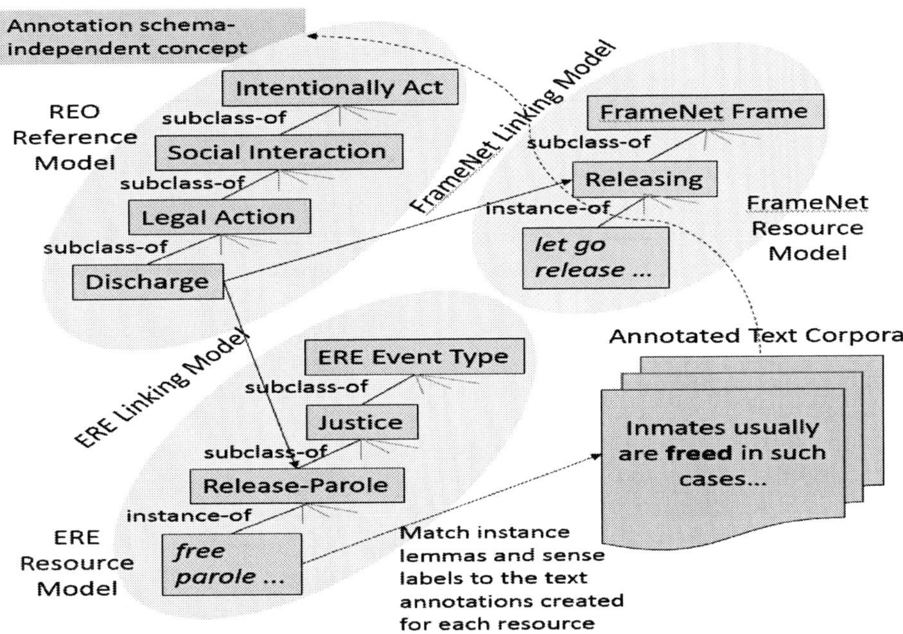

Figure 3: DISCHARGE, a daughter of LEGAL ACTION, *hasReferenceGroup* Releasing in FN and Release-Parole in ERE. The lexical items in these classes can be matched to sense-annotated lemmas found in the annotated corpora, and/or users can query the ontology for events to obtain a schema-neutral representation, including event-event relations, and access the combined semantic information from resources.

3 Use Cases of REO

We are working to integrate REO into an IE pipeline designed for intelligence analyst use. Within the pipeline we will evaluate the ontology's impact on two main areas. 1) Increasing the number and types of events recognized and classified in text. We will be incrementally examining the precision, recall and F-score of trigger identification and classification in systems that are trained on just ACE data, then ACE+ERE, ACE+ERE+FN, and finally all data sources: ACE+ERE+FN+VN. 2) Allowing users to refine, expand or alter queries about events by making use of ontological relations. We will be completing user studies for this evaluation and comparing efficiency in decision-making using the IE pipeline with and without the event ontology component. In the interm, we report results below on two sample use cases related to these goals.

3.1 Expanding Lexical Triggers for IE

The ontology can be leveraged to support event detection in IE systems by expanding the number and variety of lexemes recognized as potentially referring to a given event type. The aforementioned ACE program, and its inclusion in TAC, has established the ACE annotated data as a benchmark dataset for IE systems. As a result, many existing IE systems are tailored to, and can be limited to, the detection of events recognized and marked up in the ACE annotated data. To avoid the need for additional manually annotated data, the ontology and associated lexical resources can be used in backoff techniques to augment the trigger words associated with certain types of events, thus expanding the domain of application.

To explore the potential efficacy of the ontology in this application, we examined the reference groups associated with the LEGAL ACTION portion of the ontology. LEGAL ACTION is a type of SOCIAL INTERACTION, and is the parent class of several subclasses, including ARREST, SUE, and DECLARE BANKRUPTCY (which also inherits from ORGANIZATIONAL PROCESS). We first established a baseline of what a typical system, trained on

ACE, might recognize as triggers associated with the event concepts in this portion of the ontology. To do this, we examined what ACE types and subtypes are linked to the subclasses of LEGAL ACTION via the *hasReferenceGroup* relation. We then extracted all of the individuals that have been tagged as triggers for the *hasReferenceGroup* linked event types and subtypes. In total, we found 102 lexemes associated with the LEGAL ACTION subtypes in ACE. Presumably, systems trained on ACE data have the potential to recognize these lexemes as triggers of the LEGAL ACTION events.

To determine how the ontology may help to move beyond this baseline, we examined what other triggers might be found by using the ontology to access lexemes in the reference groups associated with LEGAL ACTION in ERE, FN and VN. This allowed us to extract groups of 204, 69 and 14 lexemes from ERE, FN and VN, respectively. Thus, we were able to expand the vocabulary of what lexemes may denote subtypes of LEGAL ACTION from 102 words to 389 words. This is summarized in Table 1.

Source	ACE	ACE + ERE	ACE + ERE + FN	ACE + ERE + FN + VN
Trigger Total	102	306	375	389
Ex's	*Arrest, fine, prosecute*	*Behind bars, get_life*	*Bust, put_away, guillotine*	*Book, collar, impeach*

Table 1: Expansion of event trigger vocabulary using the REO class LEGAL ACTION.

The variety of triggers found across the resources is quite remarkable: only 17 of the 389 lexemes are duplicated from one resource to another. We see the data-driven resources, ACE and ERE, capturing much more informal expressions, such as *share a needle*, referring to an execution event. In contrast, FN and VN capture more formal expressions like *mulct* and *amerce*, referring to fining events. Furthermore, few nodes in the ontology have reference groups in all four resources. For example, only FN distinguishes events at a level of specificity fine-grained enough to have a specific frame for Notification_of_charges, which is a reference group for the CHARGE events node of the ontology. We feel

that this highlights the potential for the ontology to overcome data sparsity by combining resources.

3.2 Querying: From Events to Scenarios

Although a mapping (similar to SemLink (Palmer, 2009)) of the resources included in the ontology may be able to achieve the vocabulary expansion described in the previous section, a unique contribution of the ontology is the causal and temporal event relations included. With the exception of limited relations in FN, the linked lexical resources do not provide information on such relations. The ontology has adapted the RED relations, as described in section 2.5, and therefore allows insights into how events are typically related, both causally and temporally. This can enable an understanding of how individual events fit into more complex real-world scenarios. What's more, users can take advantage of the temporal and causal relations in addition to subclass 'is-a' relations to expand, refine, or alter their queries.

One area of the ontology where these relations are particularly rich and informative is the domain of conflict. PROTEST, ATTACK, and RECIPROCAL CONFLICT are three daughters of the SOCIAL INTERACTION class CONFLICT. As in other areas of the ontology, we drew upon domain expertise in the development of this area. We reviewed social science literature to establish the basic sub-events and preconditions of PROTEST. Combining research on both the psychology of protest (Van Stekelenburg and Klandermans, 2013) and the theory of planned behavior generally (Ajzen, 1991), we established subevents and stages of protest scenarios: PROTEST has as a precondition MOBILIZATION, which in turn has TAKE SIDE as a precondition; TAKE SIDE has GROUP IDENTITY as a precondition, as well as the typical precondition GRIEVANCE; a communication event is a subevent of PROTEST. This excerpt of some of the relations to PROTEST captures social science theories suggesting that a protest is generally mobilized where there is a sense of a group identity and a grievance or trigger for intergroup conflict, and that protest by nature involves the communication of some claims calling for change. The event structure found in the ontology for PROTEST parallels the "stages" of protest outlined in Korolov et al. (2016), who find that trigger words associated with these stages can be used to predict social protest based on social media messaging.

REO users can take advantage of ontological relations in their queries. For example, a user interested in protest may start by querying for documents with PROTEST event trigger words (e.g., *boycott, burn, loot, march, occupation, take to the streets,* etc.), with accompanying SRL-annotated training data sentences, such as *"The events which unfolded over last week are still very unclear but peaceful protesters **took to the streets** in Tottenham Saturday to demand answers."* If users decided they were interested in a broader range of events, including both physical attacks and arguments, they could broaden the search space using the CONFLICT node of the ontology. If users were interested in querying for events that may be indicators of protest to come, they could query for the preconditions of protest, including TAKE SIDE with associated triggers *endorse, oppose, pro, side,* etc. Thus, the ontology links the annotated resources in a way that uniquely allows for users to search for events that are related to others in higher-order scenarios.

4 Future Work

The modular architecture of the ontology was designed to allow efficient linking to other lexical resources, including those from other languages. We intend to pursue such expansion, as well as expansion of the main ontology through alignment with or importation of other ontologies, such as the Emotion Ontology (Hastings et al., 2011).

Although we have emphasized the ontology's NLP applications, we have also begun testing the ontology's usefulness for activity recognition in video. We are currently exploring the use of REO for understanding how complex activities can be decomposed into simpler events, and how those events are broken down into semantic components in the linked resource VN. We hypothesize that activities that share similar event semantics will likely have some similar visual components. The potential to detect similar visual components may allow for generalizing from the recognition of one activity type (e.g., baseball pitch) to another that is semantically similar (e.g., throw discus). Thus, we hope to leverage information from the ontology instead of seeking out greater amounts of training data specific to fine-grained activity types.

We are also exploring new types of event-to-event relations that could enhance the inferencing power of the ontology. The logic requirements of OWL have prevented us from capturing relations that are not necessary but still highly probable. For example, a TRIAL event typically follows a CHARGE/INDICT event, but not always. We would like to explore ways to marry probabilistic methods with the ontology to allow for such commonsense (but not strictly logical) inferences.

5 Conclusion

The Rich Event Ontology is a freely available tool for semantic analysis of events, a key area in NLP tasks like question answering, information extraction, and knowledge representation. It provides an independent conceptual backbone that unifies valuable lexical resources and adds critical relational information in the form of event-to-event causal and temporal relations. Although this work is in the relatively early stages, we have shown how the ontology could be used to expand the number and variety of lexemes recognized as event denotations and to refine, expand or shift user queries using both subclass and temporal relations. We believe REO is unique among existing ontologies in combining in-depth representation of events with the ability to link valuable but disparate lexical resources and annotation schemes. REO is temporarily available by request, but we plan to migrate the ontology to an in-house server in the near future, where it will be freely available.

Acknowledgments

This project has deeply benefited from the expertise of the REO Advisory Board: Ann Bies, Diana McCarthy, Teruko Mitamura, James Pustejovsky, German Rigau, Roxane Segers, Clare Voss, Piek Vossen, Annie Zaenen, and additional members of the board. We sincerely thank them for their wise advice and the generous donation of their time.

In addition, we gratefully acknowledge the support of DARPA DEFT - FA-8750-13-2-0045 and DTRA HDTRA1 -16-1-0002/Project # 1553695, eTASC - Empirical Evidence for a Theoretical Approach to Semantic Components. Any opinions, findings, and conclusions or recommendations expressed in this material are those of the authors and do not necessarily reflect the views of DARPA or the US government.

Finally, we thank our anonymous reviewers for their constructive feedback.

References

Ajzen, I., 1991. The theory of planned behavior. *Organizational behavior and human decision processes*, 50(2): 179-211.

Bonial, Claire, Susan Windisch Brown and Martha Palmer. 2016. A lexically-Informed upper level event ontology. In *Proceedings of the LREC 2016 Workshop ISA-12 – 12th Joint ACL - ISO Workshop on Interoperable Semantic Annotation*, 28 May, Portorož, Slovenia.

Brown, Susan Windisch. 2014. From visual prototypes of action to metaphors: extending the imagact ontology of action to secondary meanings. In *Proceedings of the Tenth Joint ISO – ACL SIGSEM Workshop on Interoperable Semantic Annotation*, Reykjavik, May.

Chiarcos, C., C. Fäth, and M. Sukhareva. 2016. Developing and using the ontologies of linguistic annotation (2006-2016). In *Proceedings of the LREC 2016 Workshop "LDL 2016 – 5th Workshop on Linked Data in Linguistics: Managing, Building and Using Linked Language Resources"*.

Davidson, D. 1980. *Essays on Actions and Events*. Oxford: Clarendon Press.

Doddington, G. R., A. Mitchell, M. A. Przybocki, L. A. Ramshaw, S. Strassel and R. M. Weischedel. 2004. The Automatic Content Extraction (ACE) program-tasks, data, and evaluation. In *LREC* 2: 1.

Fellbaum, Christiane, ed. 1998. *WordNet: An Electronic Lexical Database*. MIT Press.

Fillmore, Charles J. 1976. Frame semantics and the nature of language*. *Annals of the New York Academy of Sciences*, 280(1): 20-32.

Fillmore, Charles J., and Collin F. Baker. 2001. Frame semantics for text understanding. In *Proceedings of WordNet and Other Lexical Resources Workshop, NAACL*.

Fillmore, Charles J., Christopher R. Johnson, and Miriam R. L. Petruck. 2002. Background to FrameNet. *International Journal of Lexicography*, 16(3): 235-250.

Galton, Antony, and Riichiro Mizoguchi. 2009. The water falls but the waterfall does not fall: New perspectives on objects, processes and events. *Applied Ontology* 4: 71–107.

Galton, A. 2012. The ontology of states, processes, and events. *InterOntology 2012*, 5: 35 - 45.

Hastings, J., W. Ceusters, B. Smith, and K. Mulligan. 2011. The emotion ontology: Enabling interdisciplinary research in the affective sciences. In *Modeling and Using Context*, pp. 119-123. Springer.

Hogenboom, F., F. Frasincar, U. Kaymak, and F. De Jong. 2011. An overview of event extraction from text. *Workshop on Detection, Representation, and Exploitation of Events in the Semantic Web (De-RiVE 2011)* at Tenth International Semantic Web Conference (ISWC 2011).

Ikuta, R., W. F. Styler IV, M. Hamang, T. O'Gorman, and M. Palmer. 2014. Challenges of adding causation to richer event descriptions. In *Proceeding of ACL 2014*.

Kipper, Karin, Anna Korhonen, Neville Ryant, and Martha Palmer. 2008. A large-scale classification of English verbs. *Language Resources and Evaluation Journal*, 42: 21– 40.

Korolov, R., D. Lu, J. Wang, G. Zhou, C. Bonial, C. Voss, L. Kaplan, W. Wallace, J. Han, and H. Ji. 2016. On predicting social unrest using social media. In *Advances in Social Networks Analysis and Mining (ASONAM), 2016 IEEE/ACM International Conference on* (pp. 89-95), August.

Lenat, D. B. 1995. Cyc: A large-scale investment in knowledge infrastructure, *CACM* 38(11): 33-38.

Levin, B. 1993. *English Verb Classes and Alternations: A Preliminary Investigation*. University of Chicago Press.

Lopez, Vanessa, Victoria Uren, Marta Sabou, and Enrico Motta. 2011. Is question answering fit for the semantic web?: A survey. Semantic Web, 2(2): 125-55.

Maedche, Alexander, Günter Neumann, and Steffen Staab. 2003. Bootstrapping an ontology-based information extraction system. In *Intelligent Exploration of the Web,* pp. 345-359. Physica-Verlag HD.

Maienborn, Claudia, Klaus von Heusinger, and Paul Portner, eds. 2011. Semantics: An International Handbook of Natural Language Meaning. Vol. 33. Walter de Gruyter.

Maienborn, Claudia. 2011. Event semantics. In *Semantics: An international handbook of natural language meaning*. Vol. 33. Maienborn, Claudia, Klaus von Heusinger, and Paul Portner, eds., pp. 802-829. Walter de Gruyter,

Masolo, C., S. Borgo, A. Gangemi, N. Guarino, A. Oltramari, and L. Schneider. 2003. DOLCE: a descriptive ontology for linguistic and cognitive engineering. WonderWeb Project, Deliverable D, 17.

Mizoguchi, R., K. Kozakil, H. Kou, Y. Yamagata, T. Imai, K. Waki and K. Ohe. 2011. River flow model of diseases. In *Proceedings of International Conference on Biomedical Ontology*, pp. 63–70.

Moens, Marc, and Marc Steedman. 1988. Temporal ontology and temporal reference. *Computational Linguistics,* 14: 15-28.

R. Navigli and S. Ponzetto. 2012. BabelNet: The automatic construction, evaluation and application of a wide-coverage multilingual semantic network. *Artificial Intelligence,* 193: 217-50.

Niles, I., and A. Pease. 2001. Towards a standard upper ontology. In *Proceedings of the 2nd International Conference on Formal Ontology in Information Systems (FOIS-2001),* Chris Welty and Barry Smith, eds. Ogunquit, Maine, October.

O'Gorman, Tim, Kristen Wright-Bettner, and Martha Palmer. 2016. Richer Event Description: Integrating Event Co-reference with temporal, causal and bridging annotation. In *Proceedings of 2nd Workshop on Computing News Storylines*, pp. 47-56.

Palmer, Martha. 2009. Semlink: Linking propbank, verbnet and framenet. In *Proceedings of the Generative Lexicon Conference (GenLex-09),* pp. 9-15. Pisa, Italy, September.

Pease, A., I. Niles, and J. Li. 2002. The suggested upper merged ontology: A large ontology for the semantic web and its applications. In *Working Notes of the AAAI-2002 Workshop on Ontologies and the Semantic Web* (Vol. 28), July.

Rovetto, R. J. and R. Mizoguchi. 2015. Causality and the ontology of disease. *Applied Ontology* 10: 79–105.

Scheffczyk, J., C. F. Baker, and S. Narayanan. 2006. Ontology-based reasoning about lexical resources. In *Proc. of OntoLex*, pp. 1-8.

Smith, B., and P. Grenon. 2002. Basic formal ontology. *Draft. Downloadable at http://ontology. buffalo. edu/bfo.*

Song, Z., A. Bies, S. Strassel, T. Riese, J. Mott, J. Ellis, ... and X. Ma. 2015. From light to rich ERE: Annotation of entities, relations, and events. In *Proceedings of the 3rd Workshop on EVENTS at the NAACL-HLT,* pp. 89-98, June.

Van Stekelenburg, J., and B. Klandermans. 2013. The social psychology of protest. *Current Sociology*, p.0011392113479314.

Vendler, Z. 1957. Verbs and times. *The Philosophical Review* 66(2): 143-60.

Walker, Christopher, et al. 2005. *ACE Multilingual Training Corpus* LDC2006T06. DVD. Philadelphia: Linguistic Data Consortium.

Wimalasuriya, Daya C., and Dejing Dou. 2010. Ontology-based information extraction: An introduction and survey of current approaches. *Journal of Information Science*, 36 (3): 306–323.

Integrating Decompositional Event Structures into Storylines

William Croft, Pavlína Pešková, Michael Regan
MSC 03 2130 Linguistics
1 University of New Mexico
Albuquerque NM 87131-0001, USA
`{wcroft,pavlinap,reganman}@unm.edu`

Abstract

Storyline research links together events in stories and specifies shared participants in those stories. In these analyses, an atomic event is assumed to be a single clause headed by a single verb. However, many analyses of verbal semantics assume a decompositional analysis of events expressed in single clauses. We present a formalization of a decompositional analysis of events in which each participant in a clausal event has their own temporally extended subevent, and the subevents are related through causal and other interactions. This decomposition allows us to represent storylines as an evolving set of interactions between participants over time.

1 Introduction

Stories are typically represented as a set of events and temporal relations among events (Caselli and Vossen, 2012). However, events are frequently given a decompositional analysis in linguistics, as surveyed in Levin and Rappaport Hovav (2005), and also in computational linguistics, for example Narayanan (1997). Many of the event decompositions in linguistics do not explicitly represent the temporal dimension, and distribute participants across different event components. Such representations do not lend themselves well to integration with storyline analysis.

The event decomposition proposed in Croft (2012) and applied to event annotation in Croft et al. (2016) is more suited to integration with storyline analysis. Croft's analysis of events explicitly represents time as a geometric dimension, as part of the representation of aspect—the structure of events as they unfold in successive phases over time. In addition to explicit representation of the temporal dimension, Croft introduces a second dimension, qualitative states, to model change over the course of the event. These two dimensions allow one to represent directly the pre-state and post-state of events (Im and Pustejovsky, 2010; Segers et al., 2015), as different states on the qualitative dimension, and as different points of time in the temporal dimension.

Croft's analysis also decomposes events into distinct subevents for each participant. The subevents represent directly the interactions of participants, instead of representing them indirectly and incompletely by semantic role labels. This decomposition allows for a smoother integration of complex event structure with story networks, albeit with a reinterpretation of the structure of stories.

The decompositional model of events allows us to consider an alternative model of the structure of stories. In this model, stories are made up of participant histories, that is, the participant's existence through time. A participant history is in turn made up of subevents, namely the states and processes that the participant has or undergoes during each interval of time. The participant histories are related to each other through participant interactions, that is, subevent relations within events, at certain times. This alternative decomposition of stories is also suggested by van Erp et al. (2014), who use a modified metro map visualization (Shahaf et al., 2012), with participants as "lines" and events as "stations". This alternative model can be more fully realized using a decompositional analysis of events in which each participant has its own subevent.

This alternative decomposition of stories is also more independent of the linguistic expression, in which events are realized as simple clauses with one or more argument phrases denoting partici-

98

Proceedings of the Events and Stories in the News Workshop, pages 98–109,
Vancouver, Canada, August 4, 2017. ©2017 Association for Computational Linguistics

pants, and interclausal syntax expresses temporal and other relations between events. Thus, it represents a story structure that must be derived indirectly from the linguistic expressions. In this paper we present a formalization of this alternative decomposition of stories and events, and show how this formalization can be used to construct a visualization of stories as an evolving network of interactions among participants over time.

2 Event Decomposition and Annotation

2.1 Subevents and Aspect

In Croft's decompositional analysis, each participant has its own subevent. Each subevent consists of a sequence of temporal phases, representing how the subevents unfold over time. A subevent is made up of phases that are defined on two dimensions, time and a dimension of qualitative states that can be used to define different types of states and processes. That is, instead of representing the qualitative states and changes of an event as an atomic predicate, a predicate is analyzed as a path through a one-dimensional quality space over time. Obviously, a one-dimensional representation of qualitative states/changes is a simplification, but it is an advance on analyses in which the qualitative event structure is left unanalyzed as the verbal "root" (Levin and Rappaport Hovav, 2005).

Subevents have an aspectual type. Semanticists have identified a number of different aspectual types, most of which can be analyzed as special cases of Vendler's categories of states, achievements, activities and accomplishments (Vendler, 1957; Croft et al., 2016). States lack change on the qualitative dimension. Some states are inherent properties of an individual (*She is French*), while others are reversible (*The window is open*) or irreversible (*The window is broken*), and still others exist only in a point of time (*The sun is at its zenith*).

Achievements represent a transition, construed as instantaneous, from one qualitative state to another. Directed achievements transition to a result state (*The window broke*), while semelfactives (called cyclic achievements by Croft) transition to the result state and back to the initial state (*The light flashed*). Accomplishments represent a gradual change on a qualitative dimension over time, attaining a natural endpoint. Incremental accomplishments represent a measurable, monotonic change (*She ran into the gym*), while

nonincremental accomplishments describe an activity that is not monotonic before achieving the result state (*He repaired the computer*). Activities represent change that does not have a natural endpoint. Directed activities represent a monotonic change (*The balloon rose*), while the change described by undirected activities is nonmonotonic (*The fans were dancing.*).

We argue that there is another Vendler-like category: processes that stop, returning to the base state. These events, which we call *endeavors*, are temporally bounded, but not by reaching a natural endpoint. They may be directed or undirected. Endeavors are not lexicalized as such in English, but certain subevents in complex events are endeavors. In Russian, there are lexicalized endeavors (Forsyth, 1970). Undirected endeavors are derived from undirected activities with the prefix *po-*, as in *On po-spal posle obeda* 'He had a sleep after dinner'. Directed endeavors are derived from directed activities with the prefixes *pri-, pod-*, and *nad-*, as in *On pri-otkryl dver'* 'He opened the door a little'.

Participant subevents cause other participant subevents; this is the domain of force dynamics (Talmy, 1988). Croft (2012) extends Talmy's notion of force dynamics to cover a wide range of asymmetric relations between participants. The commonest noncausal interaction is a spatial relationship between two entities, the figure and the ground, following Talmy (1983).

Many different event types are discussed in the linguistic semantic literature: caused motion, application, emission, change of state, and so on. Construction grammarians argue that these schematic event types represent the meanings of argument structure constructions (Goldberg, 1995, 2006).

2.2 Force Dynamics and Types of Qualitative Change

Croft et al. (2016) propose an analysis of the semantic types of argument structure constructions in terms of force-dynamic relations between participants, causal and noncausal, and the type of change that the theme participant undergoes. Among the most common types of force-dynamic relations are Force, the prototypical physical transmission of force relation; Constrain, Talmy's "causation of rest/stasis" (Talmy, 1988); and Path, the spatial figure-ground relation.

Croft et al. define four types of physical

changes, based in part on different types of incremental theme (Dowty, 1991; Hay et al., 1999). The simplest change subevent of the affected entity is a change of state of the entity, that is, a change in a scalar property of the entity as a whole (Hay et al., 1999).

Events involving change in a spatial figure-ground relation proceed in two different ways. Motion events of various kinds, such as *The boy ran across the road*, define a spatial path on the qualitative dimension that the figure traverses as a whole; for this reason Dowty (1991) calls the figure a "holistic theme".

Application, removal, combining and separating events, such as *The man picked pears from the tree*, define a mereological change in the location of figure on the qualitative dimension; this is Dowty's incremental theme proper. Covering and uncovering events, such as *I buttered the toast with hazelnut butter* and *They stripped the trees of bark*, differ from application and removal events in that the incremental change is conceptualized as happening to the ground object (toast, trees) rather than the figure.

Croft et al. define another type of theme change, which they call Design for creation of an object with a certain identity, for events of creation (*They built a shelter*), formation (*She carved a toy out of a stick*) and replication (*He scanned the article*).

We identify another type of physical change not described by Croft et al. (2016): internal change of a single participant, such as *The flag fluttered*. Internal events often also express a locative relation: *The flag fluttered (over the fort)*. Finally, simple static location is included as an internal event type, albeit static: *The flag is over the fort*.

The relations between subevents and properties of subevents summarized above cover a large range of the inventory of physical processes expressed by simple verbs in English. There are of course many other events involving mental processes and other interactions between humans and other entities (perception, cognition, emotion, intention, attention, etc.), and many other events involving social interactions, which remain to be analyzed in this decompositional framework.

2.3 Annotation and Visualization of Aspect and Force Dynamics of Events

We proposed an annotation scheme for annotating clauses with their aspectual type and force-dynamic type of change, based on the verb, tense-aspect construction, and argument structure construction (Croft et al., 2016). We retain this aspect annotation, with the addition of directed and undirected endeavors. The full list of aspectual types is found in Table 4 in the Supplementary Material, which also includes their formalization (see section 3). We are developing a revised annotation of aspectual types, a notoriously difficult area of linguistic semantics, that we believe will be simpler to use by annotators, yet still captures all of the distinctions in Table 4.[1]

The force dynamic annotation scheme in Croft et al. (2016) annotates only the type of change undergone by the theme participant in the clausal event. The revision and extension of the annotation scheme described above is found in Table 5 in the Supplementary Material. The theme change may be externally caused; annotation for external and internal cause can be found in Table 6 in the Supplementary Material.

A complete annotation of the structure of a clausal event consists of three annotations: the aspectual type (ideally, the fine-grained classification in Table 4); and for the force dynamics, the external/internal cause (Table 6) and the theme change type (Table 5).

We applied this annotation scheme, with the modifications described in this section, to clauses in three Pear Stories (Chafe, 1980). The Pear Stories are a set of oral narratives produced by speakers after viewing a short film which was designed to analyze patterns of verbalization. Since there is no language in the film, the narratives mostly encode physical events of the type already analyzed by Croft et al. We chose the Pear Stories since this allowed us to easily annotate most of the events in the narrative. We believe that the oral narratives share significant narrative structure with news stories. However, temporal ordering of events is much more regular in the Pear Stories.

Relations between clausal events in the Pear Stories were annotated using predicates from the temporal interval calculus (Allen, 1984; Mani and Pustejovsky, 2012). Temporal relations expressed by adverbial clauses and coordination are represented adequately for our purposes by the temporal interval calculus predicates. The temporal interval calculus predicates that expressed inter-

---

[1]The revised aspect annotation scheme, and annotation guidelines for aspectual and force dynamic annotation, will be found at http://www.unm.edu/~wcroft.

Event	FD 1	FD 2	Aspect	TR
And he comes down, . . from the ladder,	Self-volitional	Motion	Incremental Accomplishment	AFT
[1.1] and he's wearing an apron,	Volitional	Constrain	Undirected Activity	CONT
And he dumps them [.45] into some baskets . .	Volitional	Apply	Incremental Accomplishment	AFT

Table 1: Annotation of a passage from the Pear Stories

clausal relations occurring in the Pear Stories narratives that were annotated are Before (BEF), After (AFT), Meets (MEET), Equal (EQ), Overlap (OVER), and Contains (CONT). Coreference relations between participants across events were also annotated by using the same values for recurrent individuals in the constructional annotation (not shown in Table 1).

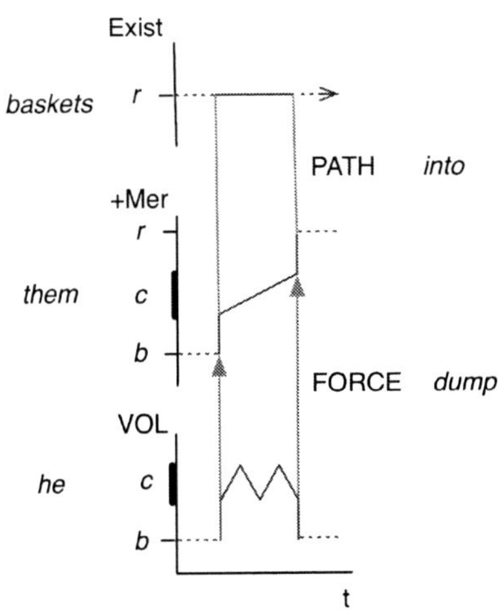

Figure 1: Graphic representation of decompositional event structure for *And he dumps them into some baskets*

A sample annotation is given in Table 1. From this annotation, we construct predicate calculus representations of the decompositional event structure based on the formalization in section 3. From the formal representation, we automatically generate a graphic representation of a clausal event. Figure 1 shows the graphic representation of the third sentence in Table 1. The graphic representation is a modified version of those found in Croft (2012). In particular, we add structure to the q dimension (the vertical dimension) for each participant, as described in section 3.

Adding the annotation of temporal relations between clausal events allows us to generate a visualization of the fragment of the story in Table 1; see Figure 4 and the discussion in section 4.

3   A Formalization of Event Structure

Here we formalize the idea that stories are made up of participant histories that interact over time. This view of story structure informs the formalization of the individual events in a story that express the participant interactions. Since event structure is complex, almost all of our attention here will be focused on the event structure formalization. The formalization expands the annotation to formulas that allow for inference about events and their participants, and allow for visualizations of the structure of events and the structure of stories.

3.1   Aspect and the Interval Calculus

Our formalization uses the interval calculus for both the temporal and qualitative dimensions (Allen, 1984; Mani and Pustejovsky, 2012), and the commonsense knowledge axioms of Gordon and Hobbs (2017).[2] Since event decomposition involves many composite entities, we use the notational simplification of $x=a+b$ to describe a composite entity x with exactly a and b component entities, that is, CompositeEntity(x) & Component-of(a, x) & Component-of(b, x) & $a \neq b$ & $((y \neq a$ & $y \neq b) \supset \neg$ Component-of$(y, x))$; likewise for composite entities with more than two component entities. The notation $x=a$ indicates equality, that is, there is exactly one component to the composite entity. However, we will use Equal(i, j) for interval equality following Allen (1984).

We begin with the formal analysis of subevents and their participants. Each participant is identified with its own subevent. A participant is modeled as a history, namely, the states and changes that a participant has, performs or undergoes over time. The identity of a participant as an individual is expressed by the unity of the participant history.

A subevent is a component of a participant history. The subevent consists of qualitative states and changes of the participant during a time interval of the participant history. We model the quali-

---

²We use the axioms that are presented at `http://www.isi.edu/~hobbs/csk.html`, which are basically identical to the axioms that will appear in Gordon and Hobbs (2017).

tative structure of a subevent by the qualitative dimension q orthogonal to the time dimension t.

Different verbs or predicates define different relevant qualitative states for each participant subevent. Hence each subevent has a distinct set of qualitative states. One can consider each predicate's set of qualitative states as an interval on the q dimension. Alternatively, each predicate can be thought of as representing a distinct qualitative dimension (see section 4). Where necessary, we will distinguish qualitative state dimensions for different predicates, for example for different subevents of a multiparticipant event, as $q_1, q_2 \ldots$

Following Allen (1984), we represent "points" in time as very small intervals. Specifically, we define a "point" interval as an interval that does not contain a smaller interval, that is, $\text{Pnt}(i) \equiv (\neg \exists j)\text{During}(j, i)$. Extended (Ext) intervals are not punctual. One reason for treating points as the smallest intervals is that an event that is construed as occurring in an "instant" (*The bridge collapsed*) may also be construed as occurring over an interval (*The bridge is collapsing*). We would represent these two construals as both occurring over intervals with different granularities (Hobbs, 1985a) such that for the coarser-grained temporal metric, there are no smaller intervals than the event interval, but for a finer-grained temporal metric, there are. (We have not yet modeled granularity shifts.)

3.2 The Structure of the Qualitative Dimension

We analyze the structure of the qualitative dimension q for each subevent also using the interval calculus, which can be generalized beyond time (Mani and Pustejovsky, 2012; Hobbs and Pan, 2004). Verbs and other predicates impose more specific structure on q.

We distinguish four types of qualitative dimensions that capture the potential variation of qualitative states defined by predicates over time. Inherent predicates cannot vary over time for a participant; for example one cannot start or stop being French. Hence only one point is defined on q, which we label r. Complementary predicates can vary between applying or not applying to a participant; for example a window can be either whole or broken. Only two points are defined on q, a "base state" b called a "rest state" in Croft (2012), and the "result state", also labeled r. Graded pred-

icates vary dynamically in their states beyond the base state b; for example, one can either dance or not dance, but dancing involves various changes on a dimension of bodily movements. Graded predicates involve the base state b and a continuous interval c for the process. Finally, telic predicates such as entering a room have a base state b (not being in the room), the central interval of dynamically varying states c (the entering movement), and a result state r (being in the room).

The types of predicates are defined in Table 3 in the Supplementary Material. The structure of a telic predicate is illustrated in Figure 2.

3.3 Phases and Subevents

A phase is defined as a function from an interval i on t to an interval j on the q dimension (see Table 3). Phases can be distinguished by properties of the domain and/or range. A state is a phase whose range is a point (that is, the smallest interval) on q. A process is a phase whose domain and range are extended on t and q respectively. Processes may be monotonic ($\text{Mon}(p)$) or nonmonotonic.

A transition (Trans) is a phase derived from two phases that meet: it is made up of the finish "point" of the first phase and the start "point" of the second phase. This is our solution to the "divided instant" problem described by Mani and Pustejovsky (2012, pg. 60); our solution is similar to that of Hobbs and Pan (2004) (however they distinguish instants from intervals). We divide the "instant" of transition of two phases that meet into the finish point of the first phase and the start point of the second phase. The transition phase is a composite phase made up of those two point phases.

In order to define transitions, we first define start and finish "points" of a temporal interval. We then define start and finish phases of a larger phase, namely the phases whose domains are the start and finish points of the larger phase. A transition phase

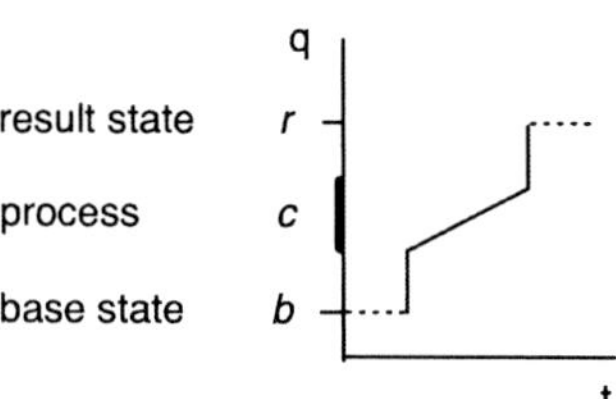

Figure 2: The structure of a telic predicate on the q dimension

102

is then defined as a composite phase made up of the finish of the first phase and start of the second phase. A transition phase is not a point interval, but it is the smallest extended interval: that is, there is no interval between the finish point of the first phase and the start point of the second phase, since the two phases meet.

Finally, for convenience we define specific phases in terms of the interval on q that serves as their range; these are b', c' and r' in Table 3 in the Supplementary Material. Because of the nature of b, c, r, it follows that $\text{State}(b', i, b, q)$, $\text{Process}(c', i, c, q)$ and $\text{State}(r', i, r, q)$.

A subevent has an aspectual type. Aspectual types are composite entities composed of one or more phases. The four types of states differ with respect to their domains (time intervals) on t, defined on the interval calculus. Unbounded events, that is noninherent states and activities, presuppose that there was a transition from the base state to the asserted phase; the presupposed phase is represented by an existentially quantified predicate. Formalizations of all aspectual types can be found in Table 4 in the Supplementary Material.

3.4 Events as Force Dynamic Chains of Subevents

Events expressed by single clauses are informally analyzed as interactions between participants for multiparticipant events. For example, in *The rock broke the window*, the rock acted on the window. We analyze these force-dynamic relations as relations between subevents that are components of the participant's history. In our example, the rock's contact subevent caused the window's change of state subevent (the specific qualitative state being contributed by the semantics of the verb *break*). The rock's contact subevent is a component of the rock's history, and likewise the window's change of state event is a component of the window's history.

The unity of an event expressed by a single clause (verb and argument structure construction) is defined by the fact that all subevents of an event are simultaneous, what Croft (2012) calls the temporal unity of events; and by the presence of force dynamic relations between the subevents.

We model the type of incremental change that a participant undergoes, described in section 2, as a property of that participant's subevent, or more precisely the qualitative dimension of that subevent. The types of change described in section 2 are Property change (Prop), Motion (Mot), Mereological change (Mer), Design change (Des), and Internal change (Int). Mereological change falls into four subtypes. Apply represents incremental change of the spatial figure with respect to the ground object, for example paint being gradually applied to a wall. Apply and Remove are inverses, represented by +Mer and -Mer. Cover represents a construal by which the incremental change happens to the spatial ground, for example the wall being gradually covered by the paint. Cover and Uncover are also inverses.

We also provide an analysis of the qualities of subevents of the agent and instrument, not discussed by Croft et al. (2016). Agents interact in physical processes using their body. Most of the time what the agent does is volitional, that is, a process involving mental as well as physical aspects of a person. For now, we model volitionality as the type of action that an agent engages in, that is, the agent's subevent has the property Vol. Instruments interact solely physically, of course, ultimately through some sort of contact. We model the interaction of instruments by attributing the property Contact to the instrument's subevent.

The aspectual annotation of the overall event describes the aspectual type of the theme participant. For this reason, the formalization of the aspectual annotation of the overall event is distinct from the representation of the aspectual type of each subevent. The formalization of the force dynamic annotation that includes the theme participant specifies which participant is the theme. The combination of the aspectual annotation predicate and the force dynamic annotation predicate(s) specifies the aspectual type of the theme participant subevent. The physical force and mental "force" applied by an instrument is dynamic but nonmonotonic. The aspectual type of an agent or instrument subevent varies depending on the aspectual type of the theme: an undirected activity if the overall event is unbounded, an undirected endeavor if the event is bounded and durative, or a semelfactive if the event is punctual.

Formalization of all of the force dynamic types analyzed so far, including external/internal cause, is found in Table 7 in the Supplementary Material.

Aspectual Types/Image Schemas *all below* $\supset$ AspTyp(x,i,j,q)	
Inherent state	Inhst$(x,i,r,q) \equiv$ Inherent(r,q) & Equal(i,t)
Inherent state phase	InhStPh$(b,i,j,q) \equiv$ Phase(b,i,j,q) & $(\exists p,l,m)$[Inhst(p,l,m,q) & During(i,l) & Maps(p,i,j)]
Incremental accomplishment	IncrAcc$(x,i,j,q) \equiv$ Telic(b,c,r,q) & $x=p_1+c'+p_2$ & Mon(c') & $(\exists b',r')$[Trans(p_1,b',c') & Trans(p_2,c',r')]
Undirected endeavor	UndEnd$(x,i,j,q) \equiv$ Graded(b,c,q) & $x=p_1+c'+p_2$ & $\neg$ Mon(c') & $(\exists b')$[Trans(p_1,b',c') & Trans(p_2,c',b')]
Force Dynamic Image Schemas	
Volitional	Volitional$(e,x,y,i) \equiv$ Component-of(f,x) & Component-of(g,y) & Subevent(f,i,j,q_1) & Subevent(g,i,k,q_2) & Force(f,g) & Vol(q_1)
Apply	Apply$(e,x,y,i) \equiv$ Theme-of(e,x) & Component-of(g,y) & Component-of(h,z) & Subevent(g,i,j,q_1) & InhStPh(h,i,k,q_2) & Path(g,h) & +Mer(q_1) & Exist(q_2)
Aspectual Type of Theme Participant	
Incremental Accomplishment	IncrementalAccomplishment$(e,i) \equiv$ Theme-of(x,e) & Component-of(g,x) & IncrAcc(g,i,j,q)
Predicate Calculus Representation of Example Sentence	
He dumped them into some baskets.	Dump$(Farmer, Pears, Baskets) \equiv$ Component-of$(f, Farmer)$ & Component-of$(g, Pears)$ Component-of$(h, Baskets)$ & UndEnd(f,i,j,q_1) & IncrAcc(g,i,k,q_2) & InhStPh(h,i,l,q_3) & Vol(q_1) & +Mer(q_2) & Exist(q_3) & Force(f,g) & Path(g,h)

Table 2: Formalization of aspectual and force dynamic image schemas for example sentence.

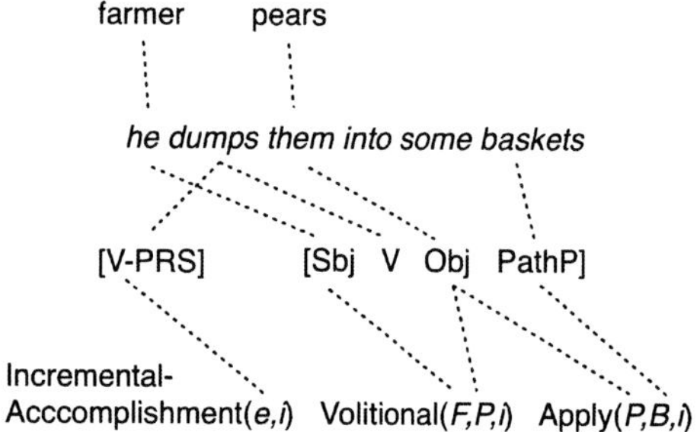

Figure 3: Linking constructions to the semantic representation

3.5 Deriving the Graphic Representation of the Event Structure of a Sentence

To illustrate the formalization of the aspectual and force-dynamic decomposition of events, we briefly go through the derivation of the semantic representation of the sentence represented graphically in Figure 1. The first step is extracting the argument structure construction and tense-aspect construction forms from the sentence (not modeled here). The associated meaning is represented by the aspectual and force dynamic annotations, with the arguments of the semantic annotations bound to the participants in the construction; see Figure 3.

The force dynamic annotation, in two parts, can be expanded with the representations in Table 2. A Volitional external cause involves the farmer's volitional subevent in a force relation with the pears' subevent. The pears' subevent involves mereolog-ically moving the pears with respect to the baskets' subevent. The baskets' subevent is simply the phase of the inherent state of existing as an entity with which the pears enter a spatial relationship; this is represented by the inherent state phase formalization in Table 2.

The incremental accomplishment aspectual type is associated with the theme argument, as noted above. The formalization of incremental accomplishments in Table 2 indicates that the q dimension of an incremental accomplishment defines base, center and result intervals. The subevent spans the transition from the base state to the central process and from the central process to the result state, that is, the subevent is bounded; it is also monotonic (see Figure 1).

The agent subevent is specified as an undirected endeavor, since the overall event is temporally bounded. As such, the q dimension defines base and center intervals only. The subevent spans the transition from the base state to the central process and back to the base state.

The predicate calculus representation allows the decompositional event structures and the relations between clausal events to be used for inference using commonsense reasoning axiomatizations such as those in Allen (1984), Hobbs (2005) and Gordon and Hobbs (2017). The predicate calculus representations also specify the structures of the events and their participants to the degree that visualizations can be constructed. These are described in the next section.

4 Visualization

We are also developing a visualization to capture the evolving interactions of participants over time. The basic idea is a modified metro map (Shahaf et al., 2012), in which the lines represent participant histories and the nodes represent interactions among participants, that is, clausal events. Figure 4 presents a visualization of the events, participants and interactions in the passage in Table 1 above.

Clausal events are related to other clausal events through temporal relations and relations of shared participants, as in van Erp et al. (2014). As with other storyline visualizations, temporally sequenced events—Before, After, and Meets in the interval logic—can be arranged horizontally, with sequenced events sharing participants aligned horizontally. Temporally overlapping events—Equal, Overlap, During and Contain—can be arranged vertically. Events whose temporal location is constrained but not totally specified would be situated relative to those events to which they hold temporal relations.

Of course, such metro maps get very tangled very quickly, since coherent narratives normally express many interwoven events with many different combinations of many different participants. Algorithms such as that of Liu et al. (2013) will, we hope, generate visually presentable metro maps of more complex participant interactions over time.

The primary innovation in the visualization is that the interactions between participants in a single clausal event are made explicit, as in Croft (2012) and Croft et al. (2016). That is, the nodes in the metro map visualization are elaborated as interactions between the participants. The roles of participants within a clausal event are kept separate because each participant has its own subevent. The qualitative states and changes of each participant are also explicitly represented. The visualization therefore describes not only the interactions that each participant engages in over the time of the story, but also exactly what they do or what happens to them.

Precise representation of participants and their states in events requires addressing certain issues. A group of participants may act as a unit in some events but separately in other events:

41 [.6] they g [.25] gather all the pears

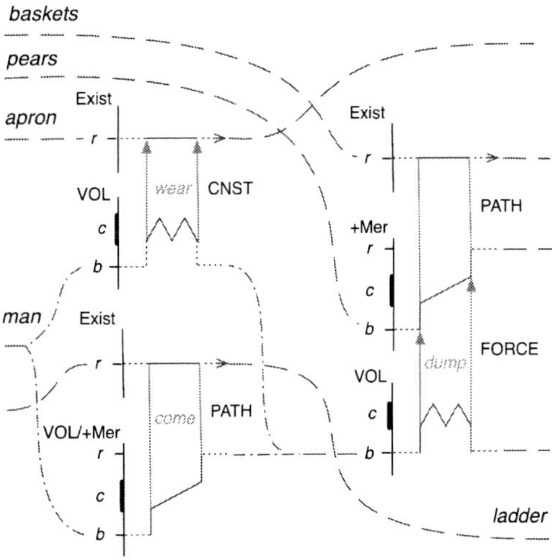

Figure 4: Event Decomposition and Interactions of Participants

42 and put them in the basket,

43 a–nd one of the guys, helps him

44 brush off the dust,

45 [.9] and another guy picks up the rock,

In this case, we must allow the history for the group of three boys to split in order to represent the interaction of individual boys from the group with other entities (the cyclist and the rock).

In other cases, the same participant is playing different roles in two different events at the same time:

140 then he . . takes a pear,

141 after carefully watching the man in the tree.

142 Who's still picking.

The man in the tree is functioning as the target of the watching event in 141 at the same time that he is the agent of the picking event in 142.

Ideally, there would be a n-dimensional representation with all the distinct relevant qualitative dimensions to describe the states of a participant during any given time interval. Of course, this is not easily visualized. In order to represent the distinct qualitative states of the man in the overlapping events, we allow a "virtual split" of the line representing the man's history, representing the different qualitative states of being watched and picking. Such virtual splits will be visualized in a distinct way from actual splits as found in passage 41-45 above. In Figure 4, we represent the virtual split of the man by dot-dashed lines.

5   Conclusion and Future Prospects

The participant-oriented description of storylines presented here allows for the representation of the qualitative state(s) that each participant is in at any temporal interval in the participant's history, and hence the storyline.

At this point, we have not represented the qualitative states of participants between events. However, some general patterns can easily be implemented. The identification of the theme participant indicates which participant undergoes and change, and the resulting state for that participant, if there is one, can be assumed to hold, other things being equal. Even for the case of events without a result state for the participant, the event can be assumed to persist. The subevents of agent and instrument participants will end at the end of the event; they will return to the base state.

In some cases, grammatical elements provide information that allows one to infer qualitative states between events. For example, in line 142, *Who's still picking,* the aspectual adverb *still* indicates that the picking activity described there is a continuation of the same picking activity reported earlier in the narrative. As we model additional tense-aspect constructions, including aspectual adverbs, we will be able to represent the persistence or not of subevents past the reported event.

However, in many cases, the persistence (or lack thereof) of qualitative states can only be inferred using world knowledge. These inferences can be done using the formalization in section 3, combined with representations of relevant common-sense knowledge.

The representation we have developed applies only to events presented as having actually happened in the narrative. Many events in narratives, including news stories, are unrealized in various ways at the point that they are introduced: they may represent planned events, desired events, or events reported with a degree of uncertainty. Even so, they can often be sequenced relative to realized events: planned events follow the current realized event, negated events are "simultaneous" with the actual state of affairs (which is the opposite of the negated event in relevant respects), and so on.

We have not included unrealized events in our annotation and representation. We are developing a model of non-real events using mental spaces (Fauconnier, 1985, 1997) or worlds (McCawley, 1993) in which the non-real events hold in their own mental space/world, and can be related to real events in different ways. Mental spaces would be represented by using the Holds predicate (Allen, 1984; Hobbs, 1985b), with a world argument w added, relativized to an agent holding the belief or intending a plan etc.: Holds(e,a,w). The relationship between mental spaces and their basis in reality will be modeled following Clark (1996). Other predicates represent relations between mental spaces or between agents and their mental spaces, building on Fauconnier (1985, 1997) and McCawley (1993).

Acknowledgments

The research was supported in part by grant HDTRA1-15-1-0063 by the Defense Threat Reduction Agency to the first author.

References

James Allen. 1984. Towards a general theory of action and time. *Artificial Intelligence* 23:123–154.

Tommaso Caselli and Piek Vossen. 2012. The Storyline Annotation and Representation Scheme (StaR): a proposal. In *Proceedings of the 2nd Workshop on Computing News Storylines*, Stroudsburg, Penn: Association for Computational Linguistics, pages 67–72.

Wallace Chafe, editor. 1980. *The pear stories.* New York: Ablex.

Herbert H. Clark. 1996. *Using language.* Cambridge: Cambridge University Press.

William Croft. 2012. *Verbs: aspect and causal structure.* Oxford University Press.

William Croft, Pavlína Pešková, and Michael Regan. 2016. Annotation of causal and aspectual structure of events in RED: a preliminary report. In *4th Events Workshop, 15th Annual Conference of the North American Chapter of the Association of Computational Linguistics: Human Language Technologies (NAAACL-HLT 2016)*, Stroudsburg, Penn: Association for Computational Linguistics, pages 8–17.

David Dowty. 1991. Thematic proto-roles and argument selection. *Language* 67:547–619.

Gilles Fauconnier. 1985. *Mental Spaces*. Cambridge, Mass: MIT Press.

Gilles Fauconnier. 1997. *Mappings in thought and language*. Cambridge: Cambridge University Press.

James Forsyth. 1970. *A grammar of aspect: usage and meaning in the Russian verb*. Cambridge: Cambridge University Press.

Adele E. Goldberg. 1995. *Constructions: A Construction Grammar Approach to Argument Structure*. Chicago: University of Chicago Pres.

Adele E. Goldberg. 2006. *Constructions at Work: The Nature of Generalization in Language*. Oxford: Oxford University Press.

Andrew S. Gordon and Jerry R. Hobbs. 2017. *A Formal Theory of Commonsense Psychology: How People Think People Think*. Cambridge University Press, to appear.

Jennifer Hay, Christopher Kennedy, and Beth Levin. 1999. Scalar structure underlies telicity in "degree achievements". In Tanya Matthews and Devon Strolovitch, editors, *Proceedings of SALT*, Ithaca: Cornell University Press, volume 9, pages 127–144.

Jerry R. Hobbs. 1985a. Granularity. In *Proceedings of the Ninth International Joint Conference on Artificial Intelligence, Volume 1*, San Francisco, Calif.: Morgan Kaugmann, pages 432–435.

Jerry R. Hobbs. 1985b. Ontological promiscuity. In *Proceedings of the 12th Annual Meeting of the Association for Computational Linguistics*, Stroudsburg, Penn: Association for Computational Linguistics.

Jerry R. Hobbs. 2005. Toward a useful concept of causality for lexical semantics. *Journal of Semantics* 22:181–209.

Jerry R. Hobbs and Feng Pan. 2004. An ontology of time for the semantic web. *ACM Transactions on Asian Language Information Processing* 3(1):66–85.

Syeohun Im and James Pustejovsky. 2010. Annotating lexically entailed subevents for textual inference tasks. In *Proceedings of the 23rd International Florida Artificial Intelligence Research Society Conference (FLAIRS-23)*, Daytona Beach, Florida, pages 204–209.

Beth Levin and Malka Rappaport Hovav. 2005. *Argument realization*. Cambridge: Cambridge University Press.

Shixia Liu, Yingcai Wu, Enxun Wei, Mengchen Liu, and Yang Liu. 2013. Storyflow: tracking the evolution of stories. *IEEE Transactions on Visualization and Computer Graphics* 19(12):2436–2445.

Inderjeet Mani and James Pustejovsky. 2012. *Interpreting motion: grounded representations for spatial language*. Oxford: Oxford University Press.

James D. McCawley. 1993. *Everything that linguists have always wanted to know about logic (but were ashamed to ask)*. Chicago: University of Chicago Press, 2 edition.

Srini Narayanan. 1997. *Knowledge-based action representations for metaphor and aspect (KARMA)*. Ph.D. thesis, Department of Computer Science, University of California at Berkeley.

Roxane Segers, Piet Vossen, Marco Rospocher, Luciano Serafini, Egoitz Laparra, and German Rigau. 2015. ESO: a frame-based ontology for events and implied situations. In *Proceedings of the MAPLEX-2015 Workshop*.

Dafna Shahaf, Carlos Guestrin, and Eric Horvitz. 2012. Trains of thought: generating information maps. In *Proceedings of the 21st International Conference on World Wide Web*, New York: Association of Computing Machinery, pages 899–908.

Leonard Talmy. 1983. How language structures space. In Herbert L. Pick (Jr.) and Linda P. Acredolo, editors, *Spatial orientation: theory, research and application*, New York: Plenum Press, pages 225–282.

Leonard Talmy. 1988. Force dynamics in language and cognition. *Cognitive Science* 2:49–100.

Marieke van Erp, Gleb Satyukov, Piek Vossen, and Marit Nijssen. 2014. Discovering and visualizing stories in the news. In *Proceedings of the 9th Language Resources and Evaluation Conference (LREC2014)*, European Language Resources Association, pages 3277–3282.

Zeno Vendler. 1957. Verbs and times. *The Philosophical Review* 66:143–60.

A Supplementary Material: Annotation and Formalization of Aspect and Force Dynamic Structure of Events

Structure of q:	Phases:
Inherent$(r, q) \equiv$ Pnt(r) & Equal(r, q)	Phase$(p, i, j, q) \equiv$ Function(p, i, j) & Interval-on(i, t) & Interval-on(j, q)
Complementary$(b, r, q) \equiv q{=}b{+}r$ & Pnt(b) & Pnt(r) & Meets(b, r)	b': Phase(b', i, b, q) & (Complementary(b, r, q) $\vee$ Graded(b, c, q) $\vee$ Telic$(b, c, r, q))$
Graded$(b, c, q) \equiv q{=}b{+}c$ & Pnt(b) & Ext(c) & Meets(b, c)	c': Phase(c', i, c, q) & (Graded(b, c, q) $\vee$ Telic$(b, c, r, q))$
Telic$(b, c, r, q) \equiv q{=}b{+}c{+}r$ & Pnt(b) & Ext(c) & Pnt(r) & Meets(b, c) & Meets(b, r)	r': Phase(r', i, r, q) & (Inherent(r, q) $\vee$ Complementary(b, r, q) $\vee$ Telic$(b, c, r, q))$
Transitions:	
Start point: Spt$(x, i) \equiv$ Starts(x, i) & Pnt(x)	*Finish point*: Fpt$(x, i) \equiv$ Finishes(x, i) & Pnt(x)
Start phase: Sph$(s, p) \equiv$ Phase(s, i, j, q) & Phase(p, k, l, q) & Spt(i, k) & Maps(p, i, j)	*Finish phase*: Fph$(f, p) \equiv$ Phase(f, i, j, q) & Phase(p, k, l, q) & Fpt(i, k) & Maps(p, i, j)
Transition phase: Trans$(p, p_1, p_2) \equiv$ Phase(p, i, j, q) & Phase(p_1, k, l, q) & Phase(p_2, m, n, q) & Meets(k, m) & Fph(f, p_1) & Sph(s, p_2) & $p{=}f{+}s$	

Table 3: Structure of q dimensions and types of phases. These axioms and definitions underlie the phasal geometrical model of aspect.

Aspectual types/image schemas	
Inherent States	
Full state	Inhst$(x, i, r, q) \equiv$ Inherent(r, q) & Equal(i, t)
Phase of state	InhStPhase$(b, i, k, q) \equiv$ Phase(b, i, k, q) & $(\exists p, l, m)($Inhst(p, l, m, q) & During(i, l) & Maps$(p, i, k))$
Noninherent States	
Reversible	RevSt$(x, i, r, q) \equiv$ Complementary(b, r, q) & Ext(i) & $(\exists p, b')$Trans(p, b', x)
Irreversible	IrrSt$(x, i, r, q) \equiv$ Complementary(b, r, q) & Finishes(i, t) & $(\exists p, b')$Trans(p, b', x)
Point	PntSt$(x, i, r, q) \equiv$ Complementary(b, r, q) & Pnt(i) & $(\exists p, b')$Trans(p, b', x)
Achievements	
Directed	DirAch$(x, i, j, q) \equiv$ Complementary(b, r, q) & $(\exists b', r')$Trans(x, b', r')
Cyclic	CycAch$(x, i, j, q) \equiv$ Complementary(b, r, q) & $x = p_1 + p_2$ & $(\exists b', r')($Trans(p_1, b', r') & Trans$(p_2, r', b'))$ & OverlapPnt(p_1, p_2)
Activities	
Undirected	UndAct$(x, i, c, q) \equiv$ Graded(b, c, q) & $\neg$ Mon(x) & $(\exists p, b')$Trans(p, b', x)
Directed	DirAct$(x, i, c, q) \equiv$ Graded(b, c, q) & Mon(x) & $(\exists p, b')$Trans(p, b', x)
Accomplishments	
Incremental	IncrAcc$(x, i, j, q) \equiv$ Telic(b, c, r, q) & $x = p_1 + c' + p_2$ & Mon(c') & $(\exists b', r')($Trans(p_1, b', c') & Trans$(p_2, c', r'))$
Nonincremental	NonincrAcc$(x, i, j, q) \equiv$ Telic(b, c, r, q) & $x = p_1 + c' + p_2$ & $\neg$ Mon(c') & $(\exists b', r')($Trans(p_1, b', c') & Trans$(p_2, n, c', r'))$
Endeavors	
Undirected	UndEnd$(x, i, j, q) \equiv$ Graded(b, c, q) & $x = p_1 + c' + p_2$ & $\neg$ Mon(c') & $(\exists b')($Trans(p_1, b', c') & Trans$(p_2, c', b'))$
Directed	DirEnd$(x, i, j, q) \equiv$ Graded(b, c, q) & $x = p_1 + c' + p_2$ & Mon(c') & $(\exists b')($Trans(p_1, b', c') & Trans$(p_2, c', b'))$

Table 4: Definitions of aspectual contours as composites of phases. The terms in the left hand column make up the annotation of the aspectual type of the overall event. The aspectual type of the overall event is identical to the aspectual type of the subevent of the theme participant; see Table 7. This mapping is done by rules of the type illustrated in the formalization of the example sentence in Table 2.

	Direct	Inverse
	Force (*contact, force exertion*)	Resist (*maintain*)
Theme	**Direct**	**Reverse**
Property	Change of State	
Path	Motion (*directed motion, manner of motion*)	
Mereological	Apply (*application, combining*)	Remove (*removal, separation*)
	Cover (*covering, filling*)	Uncover (*uncovering, emptying*)
Design	Create	
	Form	
Existence	Internal	
	Location	Dynamic Texture

Table 5: Force-dynamic image schemas for annotation: theme change type. The terms in the second and third columns make up the annotation.

External Cause		Example
Autonomous	no external cause	*Paint spilled onto the floor.*
Self-Volitional	no external cause; theme argument brings about action volitionality	*Wanda ran out of the room.*
Physical	external physical cause	*The baseball shattered the window.*
Volitional	external volitional cause; no distinct instrument	*I painted the wall.*
Instrumental	external volitional cause with distinct instrument	*I painted the wall with a roller.*

Table 6: External/Internal cause. The terms in the first column make up the annotation.

Initial part of causal chain	
Volitional	$\text{Volitional}(x, y, i) \equiv \text{Component-of}(f, x)$ & $\text{Component-of}(g, y)$ & $\text{Subevent}(f, i, j, q_1)$ & $\text{Subevent}(g, i, k, q_2)$ & $\text{Force}(f, g)$ & $\text{Vol}(q_1)$
Physical	$\text{Physical}(x, y, i) \equiv \text{Component-of}(f, x)$ & $\text{Component-of}(g, y)$ & $\text{Subevent}(f, i, j, q_1)$ & $\text{Subevent}(g, i, k, q_2)$ & $\text{Force}(f, g)$ & $\text{Cont}(q_1)$
Instrument	$\text{Instrument}(x, y, z, i) \equiv \text{Component-of}(f, x)$ & $\text{Component-of}(g, y)$ & $\text{Component-of}(h, z)$ & $\text{Subevent}(f, i, j, q_1)$ & $\text{Subevent}(g, i, k, q_2)$ & $\text{Subevent}(h, i, l, q_3)$ & $\text{Force}(f, h)$ & $\text{Vol}(q_1)$ & $\text{Force}(h, g)$ & $\text{Cont}(q_3)$
Self-volitional	$\text{Self-Volitional}(x, i) \equiv \text{Component-of}(f, x)$ & $\text{Subevent}(f, i, j, q)$ & $\text{Vol}(q)$
Central part of causal chain	
COS	$\text{COS}(x, i) \equiv \text{Theme-of}(e, x)$ & $\text{Component-of}(f, x)$ & $\text{Subevent}(f, i, j, q)$ & $\text{Prop}(q)$
Motion	$\text{Motion}(x, y, i) \equiv \text{Theme-of}(e, x)$ & $\text{Component-of}(f, x)$ & $\text{Component-of}(g, y)$ & $\text{Subevent}(f, i, j, q_1)$ & $\text{InhStPh}(g, i, k, q_2)$ & $\text{Path}(f, g)$ & $\text{Mot}(q_1)$
Apply	$\text{Apply}(x, y, i) \equiv \text{Theme-of}(e, x)$ & $\text{Component-of}(f, x)$ & $\text{Component-of}(g, y)$ & $\text{Subevent}(f, i, j, q_1)$ & $\text{InhStPh}(g, i, k, q_2)$ & $\text{Path}(f, g)$ & $+\text{Mer}(q_1)$ & $\text{Exist}(q_2)$
Remove	$\text{Remove}(x, y, i) \equiv \text{Theme-of}(e, x)$ & $\text{Component-of}(f, x)$ & $\text{Component-of}(g, y)$ & $\text{Subevent}(f, i, j, q_1)$ & $\text{InhStPh}(g, i, k, q_2)$ & $\text{Path}(f, g)$ & $-\text{Mer}(q_1)$ & $\text{Exist}(q_2)$
Cover	$\text{Cover}(x, y, i) \equiv \text{Theme-of}(e, y)$ & $\text{Component-of}(f, x)$ & $\text{Component-of}(g, y)$ & $\text{Subevent}(f, i, j, q_1)$ & $\text{Subevent}(g, i, k, q_2)$ & $\text{Path}(f, g)$ & $+\text{Mer}(q_2)$ & $\text{Int}(q_1)$
Uncover	$\text{Uncover}(x, y, i) \equiv \text{Theme-of}(e, y)$ & $\text{Component-of}(f, x)$ & $\text{Component-of}(g, y)$ & $\text{Subevent}(f, i, j, q_1)$ & $\text{Subevent}(g, i, k, q_2)$ & $\text{Path}(f, g)$ & $-\text{Mer}(q_2)$ & $\text{Int}(q_1)$
Create	$\text{Create}(x, i) \equiv \text{Theme-of}(e, x)$ & $\text{Component-of}(f, x)$ & $\text{Subevent}(g, i, j, q)$ & $\text{Des}(q)$
Form	$\text{Form}(x, y, i) \equiv \text{Theme-of}(e, y)$ & $\text{Component-of}(f, x)$ & $\text{Component-of}(g, y)$ & $\text{Subevent}(f, i, j, q_1)$ & $\text{Subevent}(g, i, k, q_2)$ & $\text{Transform}(f, g)$ & $\text{Des}(q_2)$ & $\text{Int}(q_1)$
Internal	$\text{Internal}(x, i) \equiv \text{Theme-of}(e, x)$ & $\text{Component-of}(f, x)$ & $\text{Subevent}(f, i, j, q)$ & $\text{Int}(q)$
Location	$\text{Location}(x, y, i) \equiv \text{Theme-of}(e, x)$ & $\text{Component-of}(f, x)$ & $\text{Component-of}(g, y)$ & $\text{Subevent}(f, i, j, q_1)$ & $\text{InhStPh}(g, i, k, q_2)$ & $\text{Path}(f, g)$ & $\text{Int}(q_1)$ & $\text{Exist}(q_2)$
Dynamic Texture	$\text{DynamicTexture}(x, y, i) \equiv \text{Theme-of}(e, y)$ & $\text{Component-of}(f, x)$ & $\text{Component-of}(g, y)$ & $\text{Subevent}(f, i, j, q_1)$ & $\text{Subevent}(g, i, k, q_2)$ & $\text{Path}(f, g)$ & $\text{Int}(q_2)$ & $\text{Int}(q_1)$

Table 7: Formal definitions of event types. The terms in the first column correspond to the force dynamic annotations in Tables 5 and 6. The aspectual type of the Theme-of argument is the aspectual type of the entire event. The the aspectual types of subevents are determined by the overall aspectual type of the event, based on rules not included here for reasons of space.